Brian Barton, the son of a Methodist minister, was born in Dunkineely, Co. Donegal, and educated at Methodist College, Belfast, Queen's University, and the University of Ulster. He tutors in history with the Open University, and has authored or edited twelve books on Irish history and politics. These include, *Secret Court Martial Records of the 1916 Easter Rising*, and *The Easter Rising* (co-author with Michael Foy). He also contributed chapters on Northern Ireland to *A New History of Ireland*, Vol.8. A revised and up-dated edition of his book *The Blitz: Belfast in the War Years* is being published by Ulster Historical Foundation in 2011.

GW00726746

St Peter's Parish Church, Anrim Road, Belfast, in the early 1900s

A History of
St Peter's
Parish Church

Antrim Road, Belfast

1900–2009

BRIAN BARTON

The Select Vestry of St Peter's Parish Church
and
Ulster Historical Foundation

FRONT COVER: Contemporary photograph of St Peter's Parish Church,
taken by Stephen Hamill.

BACK COVER: St Peter's in the late 1930s, sketched by Richard M. Close,
the architect responsible for the western extension.

First published 2009
by the Select Vestry of St Peter's Parish Church, Antrim Road, Belfast
and Ulster Historical Foundation,
49 Malone Road, Belfast BT9 6RY
www.ancestryireland.com
www.booksireland.org.uk

© Brian Barton and the Select Vestry
of St Peter's Parish Church, Antrim Road, Belfast

ISBN: 978-1-903688-45-8

Printed by Athenaeum Press
Design and typesetting FPM Publishing

CONTENTS

St Peter's Church as it looked after the landscaping had been completed in 2008

Acknowledgements

The writing of this update of Rev Dr R.S. Breene's *Golden Jubilee Book of St Peter's Church, Belfast, 1900–1950* has been a considerable time in gestation. On 5th January 1989, the minutes of the Parish's Select Vestry record its intention to bring this earlier history up to date. The decision was taken then: to gather together the Parish records and put the archives held by the church in order; contact the Library of the Representative Church Body in Dublin to establish what material was held there and also at the Public Record Office in Belfast; and to appeal to members of the congregation for any relevant memorabilia which they might have. Again, on 10th January 1994, the Vestry discussed the issue, and considered whether the third Rector of St Peter's, Canon W.E. Harris, might be prepared to work on the project. But the key decision was taken by Vestry members on 11th May 1998 when, as part of the centenary celebrations to be held in the year 2000, it was agreed that Dr Breene's history should be brought up to date. It was a propitious time for such an initiative – not only because of the centenary itself, but also because plans were already being prepared for the construction of a new Parochial Hall and for the land-scaping of the church's entire property; this was the most ambitious project ever undertaken by the Parish – apart from the actual building of the church and its sub-sequent extension in 1933. In addition, the Rev Charles J. McCollum, the fifth Rector at St Peter's, was due to retire in December 2008, and he was keenly com-mitted to the preparation and production of a new history of St Peter's.

In writing this history I wish to record my profound sense of gratitude to the Rev C.J. McCollum, who made available the records held by the church and provided detailed, written information on points too numerous to list, and to the Rector's Secretary, Mrs Anne Cromie. I wish especially to thank those members of the con-gregation of St Peter's who most generously provided visual material and written rec-ollections, both of which were indispensable in writing the text and in helping to illustrate it. Particular mention should be made of the numerous photographs of the church and its environs provided by Stanley McDowell, Noel Beattie and Stephen Hamill, and of the information provided by Tony Swan. In addition, Oonagh Haldane proofread, most meticulously, the entire text as also did Stanley McDowell.

I am also deeply indebted to the staff at the library of the Representative Church Body, Dublin, for their assistance. In addition, the insights provided by Mrs Diana Atkinson regarding the interpretation of the stained glass windows in St Peter's were illuminating and very deeply appreciated, as was her subsequent reading of the relevant sections of the text. Finally, I must record my feelings of gratitude to my wife, Valerie, for her encouragement and support during the years spent working on this history, and for her very careful reading and critical appraisal of the entire text.

BRIAN BARTON
OCTOBER 2009

I

St Peter's: The Setting

Arriving by tram (at the terminus in Salisbury Avenue, travelling out from the City centre) in the early summer of 1906, William J. Livingstone, a local journalist who visited St Peter's, commented: 'Ah, there it is down in that field on my right, a small piece of church, as if it had tumbled off the cart before it reached its proper destination and had been allowed to lie there'. At the time, the building was of course much smaller than it is now. But from the vantage point of its porch it was then, as it still is, dominated by the Cave Hill and by Belfast Castle, perched over 400 feet above. Rising to 1,182 feet in height, the Cave Hill is the dominant feature of the landscape and setting of the entire city. It comprises white limestone which first emerged from the sea some sixty million years ago; this is capped by black basalt, originally hundreds of feet in depth – the consequence of massive subterranean volcanic eruptions. On a clear day, the panoramic view from its south facing slopes is spectacular; it stretches from Carrickfergus Castle in the north as far as Slieve Croob in the Mournes to the south, and includes Scrabo and Stormont. From this lookout, an alert observer in the 8–9th centuries might have witnessed the marauding Viking fleets coming up the Lough for plunder prior to Brian Boru's decisive victory over them at Clontarf in 1014. In 1690, a glimpse might have been caught of William III, 'attended by one troop of horse', travelling along the northern shore of the Lough into Belfast – roughly along the line of the present Shore Road. Clergymen whose names are still familiar might also occasionally have been seen. One such young 'solitary horseman' who might have been observed riding to and from the town of Belfast, in 1695–96, was Jonathan Swift, who had recently been appointed to the Prebend of Kilroot; amongst those with whom he called was William Waring, a tanner in Waring Street (from whom the street takes its name) – mainly to see the craftsman's daughter, Jayne, for whom he had a strong, but unrequited, affection. It is said that the configuration of the Cave Hill – in appearance like a sleeping giant – provided the inspiration for *Gulliver's Travels*. From its slopes John Wesley might also have been seen; several times he rode along the shore between Carrick and Belfast, on one occasion 'soaked to the skin with chilly rain'. He visited the Poor House (Clifton House) in 1778 and, in 1789, preached at the 1st Presbyterian Church in Rosemary Street, which had opened six years before.

The Cave Hill has itself been occupied for as long as humans have lived in Ireland. The presence of flints in its limestone was what first attracted them; over millennia the agricultural and other activities practised by settlers have cleared away most of the extensive native woodlands which once covered all but the highest ground. Archaeological finds of jewellery, spear and arrow heads, and the remains of settlements, all indicate that it was occupied in the Stone Age (4,500–2,500 BC) and Bronze Age (2,500–500 BC). Its five caves were utilised in the Iron Age, and recall the days when primitive man with his poor weapons sought security in such recesses from the attacks of animals. The existence of raths or ringforts (for example, near the Hightown Road), and of crannogs (there is one at Hazelwood Park, Belfast Zoo), provide evidence of human occupation during the early Christian period (500–1,200 AD). In 1893–4, Francis Joseph Bigger described MacArt's Fort, the best known of remains such as these, as the 'pride and glory of our landscape'. In 1795, before going into exile, Wolfe Tone had met local United Irishmen there. He wrote in his autobiography: 'I remember particularly two days that we passed on Cave Hill. On the first, Russell, Neilson, Simms, McCracken and one or two more of us on the summit of MacArt's Fort, took a solemn obligation never to desist in our efforts till we had subverted the authority of England over the country, and asserted her independence'. The other occasion, he recalled, was spent 'pitched in the Deer Park' on the Donegall estate. On 13th June 1795, he sailed for Wilmington, Delaware, in the recently liberated United States of America, on the *Cincinnatus*, embarking at the Pool of Garmoyle which was, as he said, 'almost under the shadow of Ben Madigan'.

By the early nineteenth century a different, though short lived, tradition had become established amongst Belfast's inhabitants – that of celebrating the Easter Monday holiday with a great fete of sports, drinking, gambling, and courting, high up in the Cave Hill; the open space beneath the first cave appears to have been the location most favoured by the revellers. Buttermilk Lane was the route taken to the Cave Hill, via Skegoneill. But, by the 1840s, this annual ritual was already beginning to fade away owing to a combination of changing social attitudes and the emergence of alternative attractions – to go to Bangor by railway or steamer, or Belfast Museum, or Dargan's Island (later Queen's Island) in Belfast Lough which was by then laid out as a pleasure park. Meanwhile, more commercial usages were being found for the area. In 1840, the Belfast and Cave Hill Railway was opened; its purpose was to transport quarried limestone from the Cave Hill to the docks along the later aptly named, Limestone Road.

Ownership of the lands adjacent to the Cave Hill has been keenly contested down the centuries. Though originally in the hands of the native Irish, between the twelfth and fourteenth centuries the Anglo-Normans became firmly established, constructing a castle near the ford of Belfast in the thirteenth century – now the site of the BHS store, Castle Place – and another at Carrickfergus, begun in *c.* 1172, captured by King John on 17th July 1210, and still standing. But their domination was shattered by the slaying of 'the Brown Earl', the Earl of Ulster, William de Burgh, whilst on his way to divine service in Carrickfergus, on Sunday, 6th June 1333. The incident possibly occurred near Skegoneill – the name may mean 'the Earl's Hawthorn'. With his death, Norman prosperity in Ulster came to an end. But it had other, less direct, repercussions; his widow fled to England, with their infant daughter who was later to marry the Duke of Clarence, son of Edward III. Thus, through her, the Earldom of Ulster became a Crown possession in name and successive English monarchs, the Earls of Ulster. To this day the title is a regal one attached to the Crown of England.

After William de Burgh's death, the O'Neills, a native Irish family, enjoyed a period of ascendancy until the early seventeenth century when Arthur Chichester, the founder of the Donegall family, swept them aside. Arthur Chichester (1563–1625) was an Elizabethan adventurer, the younger son of a minor Devon landowner, who first came to Ireland as a professional soldier during the 'Nine Years War', 1593–1603. This conflict was caused by the rebellion of Hugh O'Neill, the 2nd Earl of Tyrone; its suppression and the resulting 'Flight of the Earls' enabled England to achieve complete control of Ireland. Chichester's pacification of northeast Ulster was thorough and ruthless; he himself boasted: 'I spare neither house or creature'. He became Governor of Carrickfergus and, as reward for his military services, was granted the Norman built Belfast Castle on 5th November 1603; he encouraged English and Scots settlers to come to the town, and in due course both it and the Castle were strengthened. The townlands of Ballyoghagan, Ballylistytollard, Ballyrenenytollard, Skegoniell and the castle at Greencastle formed part of the estate he was granted then; this includes the area now covered by St Peter's Parish. He was later gifted the surrounding lands in Antrim and Down, and Inishowen in Co. Donegal. In 1613 he became a baron and was awarded the title of Lord Belfast. His imposing tomb at St Nicholas's Church, Carrickfergus, disguises his lifelong struggle with debt – accumulated through his public service, and in his attempt to develop his hastily acquired Irish estates. His heirs were awarded the title Earl of Donegall in 1647 and, by the late eighteenth century, the family had become the largest landowners in Ireland.

The Donegalls had immense influence on the growth and development of Belfast, especially during the late eighteenth century, and controlled its corporation and political representation until the 1830s. Two legislative measures, passed at Westminster, had the effect of lessening their powers – the 1832 Reform Act which widened the parliamentary franchise, and the 1840 Municipal Corporations Act which resulted in an elected Town Council. Belfast was one of the few provincial towns anywhere in the British Isles, and the only one in Ireland, to be entirely owned by one family. Until the middle of the nineteenth century it lay entirely within the Donegall estate in Co. Antrim. And even then when its boundary was extended on the Co. Down side of the Lagan to include Ballymacarrett, the Donegalls owned extensive holdings there too; these included Ballynafeigh, which contained Ormeau.

In 1708, though, the Donegalls had been struck by tragedy. A fire destroyed their residence at Belfast Castle, and three of the daughters of the 3rd Earl and the Dowager Countess of Donegall (Lady Jane, Lady Frances and Lady Henrietta Chichester) were amongst those who perished in the flames – the town's inadequate water supply was partially to blame. As 'Joymount', the family home at Carrickfergus, had meanwhile fallen into disrepair, they moved to England. Arthur, the 4th Earl, was feeble minded. But his son, Arthur Chichester (1737–1799), the

5th Earl who became the 1st Marquis of Donegall in 1791, built an elaborate Palladian mansion designed by Capability Brown at Fisherwick Park, Staffordshire. Though an absentee landlord, he retained a strong interest in Belfast – expending money on its public buildings such as the Exchange and Assembly Rooms erected in 1769, and St Anne's Church built in 1776 (the land for the church was his gift to 'the Parish of Belfast, otherwise Shankill, in the diocese of Connor'); contributing £60,000 to help complete the Lagan Canal; and gifting land for a Poor House (Clifton House), the White Linen Hall, and a number of churches and other buildings. In addition, he controlled the development of Georgian Belfast through the stipulations contained in the leases he granted; amongst other provisions, these obliged tenants to build houses of uniform height and of good materials.

Arthur Chichester's second son became Lord Templemore (with estates which included Ballymacarrett; Templemore Avenue perpetuates his name). But he was succeeded by his eldest son, the imprudent George Augustus, 2nd Marquis of Donegall (1769–1844), who was born in London and spent his childhood both there, at the family's town residence in St James's Square, and at Fisherwick Park. He was a hopelessly undisciplined spendthrift. Largely due to gaming and gambling he had already built up debts totalling £250,000 by the time he succeeded to his father's title in 1799, and had twice been incarcerated in a debtors' prison. In 1802 he was persuaded to retire to Belfast, with his wife, Anna, and their children; he was the first Chichester to live in the town for almost one hundred years. Though he had at first intended his exile to be merely temporary, he remained in Belfast as he and his family could live there more cheaply, and he could more easily evade his numerous creditors. Initially he lived in a townhouse on the corner of Donegall Place and Donegall Square but, in 1807, moved to Ormeau – to a modest country-style dwelling known as 'Ormeau Cottage'. He also built a smaller house at Doagh, Co. Antrim, which served as a hunting lodge.

Meanwhile, George Augustus perpetuated his father's practice of providing land for public purposes. In 1810, for example, he provided land for the Academical Institution ('Inst'), which was to meet the needs of the 'middle and lower classes' (its construction was partly a response to Belfast Academy, then in Donegall Street, later known as Belfast Royal Academy, which was built by the Presbyterians in 1786 for 'the sons of gentlemen'). He made sites available for the Fever Hospital in 1815, the Commercial Buildings in 1819, and the gasworks in 1822. He was a popular figure both because of his gentle disposition and because he patronised Belfast's lighter social amenities as well as the more serious good causes. He helped make its first public baths fashionable (opened at Peter's Hill in 1805), regularly attended the theatre, and encouraged the formation of the town's first rowing and cricket clubs.

Despite his considerable income, George Augustus's financial position continued to deteriorate and eventually reached crisis point; in consequence, as a gentlemanly necessity, he was compelled to come to an arrangement whereby his debts would be settled by his estates. Between 1822–32, he sought to raise £200,000 by granting tenants perpetually renewable leases at their existing rents – in return for immediate cash payments. In the end he succeeded in acquiring some £330,000. But, as a consequence, the greater part of his estate was, in effect, signed off – some 70,000 acres in Co. Antrim, and a similar area in Co. Donegal. Crucially, almost all the ground of Belfast – both as it then was and as it was to become – was granted away during these years. As a result, the Donegall family's control over its future growth, planning, architecture and general appearance was removed.

Only after George Augustus died in 1844 did it become evident that the proceeds of this sale of leases had not after all been channelled into paying off his debts, but had been used for other purposes. A proportion of the money raised was used to educate and provide livings for his six sons, but most was secretly appropriated to finance his continuing extravagance. Some of it was used to indulge his interest in hunting and horseracing. The largest single item of his extraordinary expenditure that we know of was on the building of yet another Donegall family home. This one – named 'Ormeau House' ('Ormeau' meaning 'little elm tree') – was built on the then southern outskirts of Belfast in mock Tudor style, had a ground area of some 20,000 square feet, and was designed by William Morrison, a distinguished young Irish architect. Its construction began in 1822 on a site near the main present day entrance to Ormeau Park on the Ravenhill Road. However, it was occupied only very briefly because George Hamilton, the 3rd Marquis of Donegall (1797–1883) who inherited in 1844, made his career in the army and at court, and only occasionally visited Belfast. For about ten years it was occupied by his agent, Thomas Verner, and in the 1860s fell into ruin before eventually being demolished and razed to the ground.

When George Augustus died in 1844 he left debts which amounted to a staggering £300,000. At this time many Irish landowners were going bankrupt – not because of extravagance, but because the devastation wreaked by the potato famine was resulting in tenants being unable to pay their rents. In order to replace these landlords with others who were financially capable of improving their property, the British Government introduced new legislation at Westminster in 1849. Under its terms a body (usually known as the Encumbered Estates Court) was appointed with powers to take over indebted estates, and to sell as much of the property as was needed to pay off outstanding debts, so providing their new owners with a clear title, guaranteed by parliament. The 3rd Marquis, George Hamilton, had no choice but to dispose of the bulk of the Donegalls' property through this Encumbered Estates Court; his estate was one of the first and largest which it dealt with. Since most of his tenants – all but 100 of the 800 in Belfast – already had perpetually renewable leases at very low rents, much land had to be sold off before the £300,000 was raised and the slate wiped clean of debt. As a result, practically the whole town – even as greatly enlarged by another boundary extension in 1853 – was bought out either by its tenants or by wealthy speculators. After two and a half centuries, this marks the end of its ownership by the Donegall family.

Only two substantial areas still remained in Donegall hands by the mid 1850s – Ormeau demesne and their deerpark on the slopes of the Cave Hill. In 1862, the 3rd Marquis decided to abandon Ormeau, and several years later, in 1869, Belfast town council leased 150 acres of the estate there. Of these, one hundred acres was utilised to provide Belfast's first public park – Ormeau Park (Botanic Gardens was not acquired until 1895). Some of the remainder was sold off for building purposes (present day Park Road, and North and South Parade). What was left was initially rented out and used for grazing, but it was eventually transformed into Ormeau Golf Course. Nowhere in this entire area is there a stone or a trace of the Donegalls' original 'Ormeau House', though it does live on in some of the local place names – Donegall Pass, My Lady's Road, etc. These still bear witness to a family who, despite its failings in business, had a flair for spectacular building. The 3rd Marquis also shared this family flair – or weakness. The present Belfast Castle, finished by 1870, is his memorial. Oddly, it was only after he had sold off his estates in the Belfast area that he became interested in living there. Having already decided to relinquish Ormeau, the site he chose for a new residence was located in the family deerpark, on what were then the bare slopes of the Cave Hill. There he was responsible for the construction of Belfast Castle (and a gatehouse – later cut off by the growth of suburban housing). It was built in the Scottish baronial style between 1867–70 to the designs of W.H. Lynn, a junior partner in the Belfast firm of Lanyon and Lynn. It blends harmoniously with the rugged character of the mountain scenery behind and, indeed, some of the stone used had been extracted from the demesne.

The Donegalls might be said to have established Belfast, and they certainly contributed greatly to its ordered development to the 1820s. But they played little part in its subsequent dramatic transformation into a great industrial city, except perhaps in one crucial respect – by disappearing from the scene at the 'right' time. The family's financial difficulties were Belfast's opportunity. Whilst it had still owned its vast estates, its refusal to confer long leases had been a major constraint on the growth of the town. However, the indebtedness of George Augustus, the 3rd Marquis and the resulting dispersal of his property, removed this stranglehold once and for all. The pace of Belfast's growth during the nineteenth century was sensational. And indeed, the construction of St Peter's in 1900 was in itself one of its consequences.

In 1660, Belfast was a village, comprising 6 streets and 150 houses. By 1700, it had a population of 2,000, which had increased to 20,000 by 1800 (with roughly 3,200 houses). This had already risen to 48,000 by 1831 and, by 1901, it had reached an incredible 349,000. In fact, during the second half of the nineteenth century, it grew more rapidly than any other city in the British Isles, becoming the 12th largest in the United Kingdom. In 1800, Dublin's population had been roughly 180,000, and it was the undisputed 'second city of the empire'. By 1850 this had grown to 258,000 but, by 1891, the number had dropped back to 245,000. Though the population of greater Dublin was roughly 347,000 by the end of the century, its industries were in relative decline. Thus, Belfast had rapidly emerged as the biggest and most dynamic urban centre in Ireland; on 8th November 1888, it had officially conferred on it the status of 'city'.

The root cause of Belfast's growth was its phenomenal industrial expansion. By the early 1800s, a foundation had already been laid. It had a small cotton industry, centred around Smithfield where there were streams to provide power for spinning. The Donegalls had established a corn mill in the Millfield–Smithfield area, there were breweries and tanneries, there was a small shipbuilding works on Donegall Quay (William Richie's – it was the embryo of one of the North's greatest industries), and a nucleus of small factories on the River Farset. But Belfast – the name means 'the mouth of the sandbank or ford' – remained a town whose wealth was based mainly on trade.

Belfast's initial surge of growth during the early nineteenth century was largely driven by a revolution in textile manufacture – first cotton and then linen. By the 1830s it was well on its way to becoming the world's leading linen producer. The rapid growth of its textile mills and clothing factories continued into subsequent decades. This was due in part to the entrepreneurial flair of local businessmen. Also the American civil war in the early 1860s disrupted the output of cotton firms in Britain and elsewhere because imports of raw material supplies from the slave plantations in the southern United States collapsed. As a consequence, the international market for linen cloth expanded accordingly. The fact that on the eve of the First World War women made up nearly two-fifths of the city's total labour force was due to the continued overwhelming dominance of its linen industry.

Meanwhile, the establishment of a railway network and of three major banks from the 1830s had boosted Belfast's regional role and fostered its growth. Rising confidence and the availability of capital led to improvements in its shallow river approaches, which were transformed into a major port and harbour by 1849. One economic development provided stimulus for the next; from the early 1860s, it was the shipbuilding and ancillary engineering industries – both had grown out of the linen industry – which were to provide the key stimulus to continuing expansion, and to propel Belfast from being a busy market town into one of the major industrial cities in the British Isles. Though other important industries had developed by the late nineteenth century – notably whiskey distilling, rope manufacture, and tobacco products – its prosperity rested principally on textiles, engineering and shipbuilding.

In 1901 these three industries alone employed almost one-third of its work force, which then numbered 164,000. At that time the city contained just one-fifth of the population of Ireland, but it produced one-third of the total manufacturing output of the entire island, and accounted for two-thirds of its industrial exports. Amongst other things, it could boast the largest shipyards in the world (Harland and Wolff's), the largest spinning mill (Mulholland's mill, York Street) and the largest ropeworks. At around 1850, shipbuilding had transferred to Queen's Island in east Belfast. The Ballymacarrett area received further stimulus from the construction and improvement of the bridges over the Lagan. The Queen's Bridge, Charles Lanyon's first commission in the town, was constructed in 1843, and the Albert Bridge was rebuilt after it had dramatically collapsed in 1886.

Thus, during the nineteenth century, Belfast was transformed from being a small, insignificant and predominantly Presbyterian town, heavily reliant on commerce, into a large, ethnically mixed, industrial centre. Throughout these years, its rapid economic and demographic expansion was dependent on the migration of labour from the surrounding countryside and beyond. In 1901, only one-fifth of the householders living in Belfast had actually been born there; one-half had originated in Counties Antrim and Down, and 30% from elsewhere in Ireland or Britain, or from abroad. Until the 1860s one striking consequence of this was a rapid increase in the proportion of Catholics living in the town; it rose from 8% to 34% between

1784–1861. Thereafter, the percentage fell – to below 25% of the population by 1901. During the 1870–90s, the influx of rural Ulstermen and women into Belfast was predominantly Protestant (from Antrim, Down and Armagh). Most of the Catholics who arrived then were female; Catholic men tended to emigrate, mainly to the United States.

In the early nineteenth century, the bulk of the Catholic population had lived in the Hercules Street – now Royal Avenue – area, and Smithfield (at that time the Falls Road and Andersonstown were staunchly Protestant, largely because of the religious identity of the local mill owners). Thus, the first chapel in Belfast, St Mary's, was built in Chapel Lane in 1784. In response to the growing number of worshippers, St Patrick's in Donegall Street, was built in 1815, on land leased from the Donegall family; one-third of its construction costs was provided by the local Protestant community.

Over the years following, this distribution changed. In the aftermath of the famine in the 1840s rural migrants poured into Belfast; 90,000 arrived in the 1850s–60s alone. Most came from Tyrone and Armagh, having travelled along the Lurgan–Lisburn corridor, attracted by the prospect of work in the industrial sites clustered on the lower Falls. A high proportion was Catholic and thereafter this area became a predominantly Catholic one (i.e. the 'Pound', Barrack Street, Divis Street, Durham Street, Albert Street). Others settled in Waring Street, and Corporation Street.

In addition, substantial numbers of Catholic migrants settled in tenement blocks in the Cromac district and in the lower markets area. At this time, the 1850s–60s, the affluent commercial gentry were moving out of their large town houses in the former and into the 'Malone Ridge' area; many of the premises that they vacated were bought by speculators and turned into cheap lodgings. This demographic change is evidenced by the completion of St Malachy's Church in 1844; it was originally intended to be the town's Catholic cathedral. A further movement of population resulted from the decision to replace Hercules Street by Royal Avenue in the 1870s. As a consequence, the Catholic population living there was scattered widely – into the lower Falls, North Queen Street, Short Strand, the Shore Road, and the area adjacent to the docks at Garmoyle Street.

Meanwhile the political life of Belfast changed in line with its evolving religious composition. In the early part of the nineteenth century, it had a three-fold politico-religious division. Members of the Church of Ireland had tended to be conservative, Presbyterians generally supported the Liberals and regarded the established church with suspicion, whilst Catholics strove for full political rights and had broadly nationalist sympathies. Over subsequent decades, the politico-religious divide between Protestants and Catholics steadily sharpened. The huge influx of migrant labourers into the town during the 1840s–70s, mostly from rural Ulster, had brought with it the quarrels of the countryside – the age-old hostility between the Catholic native Irish and the Protestant immigrants from Britain who had settled in Ireland from the sixteenth century on. Moreover, the sharp rise in the proportion of Catholics in the population of the town caused tension as the level of competition, in particular for jobs and living accommodation, rose.

In addition, when, from the 1880s, W.E. Gladstone's Liberal Party threatened to grant Home Rule (self-government) to all of Ireland, Church of Ireland members and Presbyterians set aside their differences and combined together in the Unionist movement. Its solitary aim was to defend the Union intact. R.B. McDowell, perhaps the most eminent historian of the Church of Ireland, states that its members were virtually 'unanimous in their determination to resist Home Rule'; 1,190 out of 1,218 vestries protested against it when it was being debated at Westminster in 1893 and, in April 1912, the General Synod opposed it by 398 votes to 5. Largely as a consequence of its Home Rule initiatives, Protestant support for the Liberal Party in Ireland collapsed.

Meanwhile, the Catholic minority had retained a distinct identity of its own; it was unified by its shared religious practice and increasing identification with the goal of Irish independence. The sectarian division was geographical as well as political. By the end of the century, recurrent inter-communal rioting and violence, 'holy war in Belfast' – in 1813, 1832, 1835, 1841, 1843, 1852, 1857, 1864, 1872, 1886, and 1912, had resulted in almost total residential segregation, especially in working class neighbourhoods. The riots in Belfast in July 1886, which were sparked off by debates at Westminster on the terms of the First Home Rule Bill, were the worst single episode of violence in nineteenth century Ireland. Roughly fifty people died; more blood was spilt than in the 1803 Robert Emmet Rebellion, or the 1848 Young Ireland rising, or the Fenian rebellion of 1867, or in the Land War of the 1870s–1880s. On the eve of the First World War, the city seemed to be tottering precariously on the brink of civil war. Two large paramilitary forces had been formed. The pro-Union, Ulster Volunteer Force had over 22,000 members in the city by late 1913. In March 1914, a Belfast branch of the nationalist Irish Volunteers was formed; within six months it had over 3,000 men.

Until well into the nineteenth century, North Belfast remained a thinly populated, rural area. At around 1800, the town was small and narrowly confined – its northern limit was Frederick Street, its southern boundary was where the City Hall now stands, and it extended as far as Upper Library Street and Millfield in the west and the River Lagan in the east. In 1659, the Donegalls had leased the townland of Skegoneill and part of Lowwood to Thomas Waring. The terms contained what were described as 'the usual additions' – for example, that the tenant should provide the landlord with 'fat hens', perform labour on his estate on 'duty days', and bring grain for 'compulsory grindings at the mills in Belfast'. The land leased by Waring, most of which is now in St Peter's Parish, was at that time open and unenclosed, and the whole area bare of houses. Before 1700 further leases relating to adjacent land, also in what was to become the parochial area of St Peter's, were agreed; for example, Jane Pegg, a widow, rented Ballyoghagan, George Martin held land at 'Listillyard' and Greencastle, etc.

It was not until the last decades of the eighteenth century that a number of 'big houses', set in extensive private grounds, began to be erected on the northern outskirts of the town; their names live on in those of the estates built in more recent years, such as: Mount Collyer, Jennymount (later named Castleton), Sea View, Mount Vernon, Parkmount (out of which the districts of Donegall Park and Ashley

Park were carved) and Merville (beyond Greencastle). By the 1830s, others had been added – the Grove, Lilliput, Lowwood, Macedon and Cliftonville, which is named after a villa built on the present Cliftonville Road during the 1830s, and still standing (adjacent to Belfast Royal Academy). Its design was inspired by the Clifton area of Bristol, and it has been described as 'one of the most important examples of suburban development in Ireland'.

Some of these 'big houses' were set in substantial areas of parkland. Lowwood had seventy acres, and Parkmount one hundred, running from the Lough up into the hillside; for over sixty years, it also had a notable heronry set amongst the great oaks which lined the avenue. Though these houses or villas have largely disappeared, a number of the prominent families who occupied them are still remembered – amongst them, the Langtrys of Fortwilliam (Lily was one of the mistresses of Edward VII); Boomers of Sea View; Adairs of Mount Vernon, Thomsons of Jennymount; Coeys of Merville and MacNeills of Parkmount.

By 1820, Belfast had spread out a little further – mainly on its north side, along the two roads leading to Antrim, the county town. On one, via Shankill, shops had by then reached as far as Peter's Hill. On the other, the main route, which passed along the shores of the Lough – via Millfield, Carrick Hill, Carrick Street, Carrick Road (now North Queen Street), Greencastle, Whitewell Road, Glengormley, Mullusk, and Carrickfergus – there were a number of small houses, as well as a military barracks. In addition there was the poorhouse (built in 1774), a mill on York Lane, and there were some substantial terrace houses on York Street.

The growth of North Belfast in the nineteenth century was largely initiated by the further migration into the area of the affluent upper and middle class. They had built up their wealth mainly in industry, commerce, and the professions. Historically, members of this social group had lived in opulent, centrally located town houses, and their abandonment of these was a gradual process. Even in 1843 it was said that roughly half of Belfast's 'nobility, gentry and clergy' still lived around the White Linen Hall (now the City Hall, Donegall Square area), College Square, Great Victoria Street and the Dublin Road. Nonetheless, from the 1830s the moneyed elite was gradually relinquishing the crumbling grandeur of the town centre, and escaping from the increasing noise and pollution resulting from the rapid growth of industry there. They began to migrate to the Malone area, and also to North Belfast – increasingly, their large houses and mansions were to be found in the area between the present-day York Road, Shore Road and Antrim Road. In the process, the businessmen, financiers, doctors, solicitors and architects concerned, separated their domestic lives from their professional activities – their homes ceased to serve also as shops, warehouses, offices and surgeries. At the same time, the ownership of some of the 'big houses' built there in the late eighteenth century changed hands, and their very large estates began to be broken up. For example, the wine and spirit merchant, Frederick Kinahan bought Lowwood for £6,000 in 1882, along with 17 of the 70 acres which had made up the original demesne. Parkmount became the home of Sir Robert Anderson; originally from Monaghan, he was chairman of both Anderson and McAuley, Ltd, and of Arnott and Company, Ltd, two of the city's leading retail premises.

At the time, the entire area north of the old town had much to offer. It still retained its rural character. It was spacious, airy, almost deserted – to live there was to evade the foul smells emanating from the tanneries, sugar refineries, tobacco curers, factories and shipyards, found almost everywhere else. Over time, mills were built at Milewater and Jennymount (late 1850s), but such intrusions into these northern outskirts were rare – possibly it was the lack of reliable supplies of water which prevented them from becoming an industrial adjunct to Belfast. Though a railway was constructed in the 1840s – a line which eventually linked Belfast, Ballymena and Londonderry – it was unobtrusive. There was little to divert the eye from the splendours of the Cave Hill, still unspoiled, and the deerpark – intimations of which still live on in local place names such as Old Park and New Park. Below lay the relatively unpolluted waters of Belfast Lough, on which the new residents could observe ships under full sail beating their way backwards and forwards from the waters of Garmoyle.

The area possessed an immense variety and profusion of plant life, reflecting the contrasts in the physical environment – from the moorland, basaltic scarp and woodland of the Cave Hill, to the salt marshes found along the old sea wall at Fortwilliam. In addition, it has been suggested that in an age of horse drawn transport the relative flatness of the area on the northern shores of the Lough and under the line of today's Antrim Road may have added to its attraction. The exclusivity of the area is suggested by the creation then of Belfast's first 'gated community' at Fortwilliam – a private road with gates at either end, built in the late 1860s, behind which resided some of the town's wealthiest and most prominent citizens.

This spate of house building on the town's northern fringes was facilitated, crucially, by the steady break up, due to bankruptcy, of the Donegall estate from the 1820s; beginning then, land for construction was available on perpetual leases and easy terms. As noted, a further factor was the opening in 1832 of a new route leading northwards from Belfast – the Antrim Road. It was one of a number being constructed then, which radiated out from the expanding industrial centre into the surrounding countryside (others included the Lisburn, Ormeau, and Crumlin Roads). It skirted the foot of the Cave Hill, carving its way higher up the hill-slopes than the older road by the shore. It is likely that it followed closely the line of one of the most ancient track-ways in the entire area. This had followed a path from the crossing of the Lagan at Belfast, proceeded via the fourteenth century English fort at Fortwilliam, and on to the castle at Carrickfergus built some two hundred years earlier. Over time, additional new roads were opened up, which connected the Antrim and Shore Roads.

As the nineteenth century progressed, North Belfast ceased to be the preserve of the wealthy elite. This was primarily a consequence of dramatic improvements in the local transport system, which transformed the accessibility of the area, and stimulated further waves of settlement. In 1840 the town's first horse-drawn omnibus services began and, by the 1860s, operated as far as Fortwilliam. In 1872, horse trams were introduced; these ran on iron rails or tramlines, and were provided by the Belfast Street Tramways Company until it was taken over by the Corporation in 1904; the first route linked Castle Place and Botanic Gardens. Gradually the network spread along the main arterial roads – on the Antrim Road, it at first stretched as far as Skegoneill Avenue, and later to Chichester Park. Because the Tramways Company resisted pressure to extend its provision still further northwards, an independent group (the Cavehill and Whitewell Tramway Company) was established. It was responsible for the construction of a line from the Chichester Park terminus to Glengormley in 1882.

By the early 1900s, the Corporation Tramways Committee was even considering an extension of the tramway system as far as McArt's Fort. Andrew Nance, the main sponsor of the proposal, was full of enthusiasm for the project. He stated: 'I venture to make the proposition that this immense boon [the Cave Hill] given to Belfast by nature, shall by the agency of the Tramway Committee be made accessible to the feeblest and oldest citizen of Belfast for the small payment of three pence ... The ease with which the ascent will then be made in our comfortable and easy-travelling cars will induce persons, even those in delicate health, to visit a place where the wonderful air will put new life into them. I have fully endeavoured to give some small idea of the value which the utilisation of this free gift of nature will be to everyone, and the great credit and advantage which will accrue to the city which makes itself the agent by which the benefit is bestowed'. Nance's vision was never realised; the line was never built.

Nonetheless, in the final decades of the nineteenth century, the aspiring lower middle classes also began moving into the northern suburbs – just as far as the tramline system provided a service. Already, in the 1850s–60s, a new residential development was constructed at Carlisle Circus, comprising spacious houses set out in luxury terraces. During the 1861–1914 period, Belfast experienced five construction booms; the greatest of these was in the 1890s; by the end of that decade, middle class housing in the north of the city had extended along the Antrim Road as far as the entrance to Belfast Castle. Housing areas such as Mount Vernon, Parkmount and Duncairn, and the Lough side estates of the Grove, Fortwilliam and Skegoneill had grown up by 1900 (they were formed by the breaking up of the estates of the 'big houses', or villas, which had been built there from the late eighteenth century; this 'parkland' was parcelled out into attractive, and more modest, sites). Along the Antrim Road itself, houses had by then been allocated numbers as far as Fortwilliam Park on one side, and Chichester Park on the other (shortly after St Peter's was built it was given the postal address of 697 Antrim Road). Between 1900–1910, the area beyond this was being built up rapidly, with new houses being constructed on the Antrim Road, and new streets appearing off it – Glastonbury Avenue, Parkmount Road, Waterloo Gardens, Downview Avenue, Gray's Lane, Chichester Road and the Old Cavehill Road. Belfast street directories indicate that the typical occupants were commercial clerks, merchants, manufacturer's agents, professional people, the owners of businesses and company directors, as well as those employed on the Earl of Shaftesbury's estate at Belfast Castle. They were predominantly members of the various Protestant denominations.

By the end of the nineteenth century, the working classes had also moved into parts of North Belfast. Improvements in the city's transport system greatly increased their mobility also, especially after the Corporation had taken over the tramway network in 1904. It introduced a scheme whereby two pence was the maximum fare regardless of distance, and cheap workmen's tickets were issued during prescribed hours in the morning and evening. In addition, the rapid pace of Belfast's industrial growth, 1870–1900, fuelled the demand for labour, for housing, and the search for new sites for their construction. During these three decades Belfast's total stock quadrupled; 50,000 houses were built in the 1880s–1890s, with 4,500 in 1898 alone, the peak year. As a result, after 1870, the heavily built up edge of the city spread quickly, and the network of dense working class housing extended on the north side, well beyond its previous limit, North Queen Street.

In this period, 'kitchen' houses and 'parlour' houses were the typical accommodation provided for workingmen and their families. The former were more popular as they were cheaper and offered more sleeping accommodation; their numbers expanded around mills, foundries, engineering works, etc. In North Belfast they were constructed, for example, at Jennymount, in the area around York Street mill and in the Skegoneill district, off York Road. On the fringes of these, 'parlour' houses (distinguished by their small front gardens and decorative tiles) were built, for example in Clifton Park Avenue, Duncairn Gardens, and Alexandra Park Avenue.

During these years, North Belfast was distinguished by the addition of one further, unusually exotic, addition to the composition of its population. After 1882, it experienced a major influx of orthodox Jews from Eastern Europe. They had been driven out of Russia by a series of pogroms and by persecution, which had been orchestrated by the Tsarist government, and were attracted to Belfast by its booming economic prosperity and growth; the numbers residing in the town rose from 55 in 1871 to 1,139 by 1911. They settled mainly in the area around Carlisle Circus where they sought, as far as possible, to reconstruct their lives as in their country of origin. They did so in part because it was one of the poorer areas of the town, and property there was therefore more readily affordable. Also, it was less rigidly demarcated as being Protestant or Catholic than most other districts in the city. Moreover, it was close to the docks, their point of entry; for the same reason large numbers were also settling in London's East End at this time.

The newly arrived Jewish migrants to other parts of Europe also tended to concentrate in one area. This was partly from necessity – the precepts and practices of their orthodox faith required that they live within easy reach of the synagogue, the schoolroom, the ritual bath, the kosher butcher shop and kosher dairy. In addition, ignorance of the language of the new country, of its labour conditions, of its habits and ways of thought, as well as the natural timidity of the fugitive from a land of persecution, impelled them to settle in a colony along with their co-religionists. By 1904, their numbers were large enough to justify the construction of a synagogue in Annesley Street, near Carlisle Circus, and in 1907 Jaffa Public Elementary School was built nearby, on the Cliftonville Road. However, as the wealth of those who had settled in the area increased – just like their Gentile neighbours – they too migrated northwards to the more affluent, leafy suburbs, further along the Antrim Road.

II
The Birth of St Peter's Parish Church
1900–1914

Thomas McTear, writing in 1882, noted that at the beginning of the nineteenth century 'there was only one church in the Parish of Shankill [St Anne's, Donegall Street, built in 1776]. It was built to replace the old church at the foot of High Street which had gone to ruin by neglect and had been occupied as stables by troops'. He added that, apart from the meeting house in Rosemary Street (built in 1783) and St Mary's Roman Catholic Chapel (built in 1784), 'there was no place of worship for the entire distance (ten miles) between Carrickfergus and Belfast' except for the ruinous parish church in High Street and the Presbyterian meeting house at Carnmoney, which was located 'two miles at least from the direct line of the road'. However, at the time when Mr McTear made these comments, the circumstances which he described were already changing dramatically; there was a remarkable spate of church building in Belfast from the late 1860s.

A recent history of Connor diocese, edited by W.A. McCourt, observed that in the late nineteenth century 'a most striking change was taking place in Ulster – the growth of Belfast', and described it as 'the greatest challenge confronted by the Church anywhere in Ireland.' Between 1861–1911, the number of Church of Ireland members in the city almost quadrupled; it rose from 30,000, or 24.6% of its total population, to 118,000, or 30.5% (during this same period the proportion of Catholics fell by 10%, and of Presbyterians by 2%, whilst the Methodist figure rose by 2%). As a consequence, while the number of clergy in the southern dioceses was being reduced, there was a marked increase in the number serving in Belfast – from about fifty up to 1871, to approximately sixty-five in 1914, and eighty in 1926. Meanwhile, the number of Church of Ireland churches had risen from three in 1830 to ten in 1860 (see chronological list of parishes created in Belfast, 1776–1914, in the Appendix). By 1914, there were thirty-four parishes and thirty-seven churches (in 1901, there were 103,000 Church of Ireland members in the city with thirty-seven churches, 120,000 Presbyterians with forty-seven, 21,500 Methodists with thirty-seven, and 85,000 Catholics with fourteen).

The Church's physical resources did however lag behind demand; at around 1900, there were almost five times more church members than there was seating accommodation for them in the pews. Nonetheless, these statistics do provide evidence both for the claim made by the authors of the history of Connor that the 'Church felt acute concern about supporting the needs of the increasing church population in the Belfast area', and that it responded energetically to the 'challenge'.

This was certainly true of Rev Henry Stewart O'Hara (see Chapter VIII), who is regarded as having been the 'founder' of St Peter's. He was born in 1843, and educated at the Collegiate School, Leicester and at Trinity College, Dublin, where he graduated with honours in 1865. After serving as curate in Ballyrashane, and in Kildollagh, he succeeded his father as Rector of Coleraine, 1869–94, before becoming Vicar of Belfast, 1894–1900, after the death of Dr Robert Hannay in 1894 (father of Rev G.O. Hannay, the famous novelist, who wrote under the *nom de plume*, 'George A. Birmingham'). He was also appointed Chancellor of Connor, 1884–97, and Canon of St Patrick's Cathedral, Dublin, 1897–9, before becoming the first Dean of St Anne's Cathedral, 1899–1900.

Rt Rev Henry Stewart O'Hara, Dean of Belfast, 1899-1900, Bishop of Cashel, 1900–1919, who is regarded as having been the 'founder' of St Peter's Church.

This last appointment – as the first Dean of Belfast, and thus the representative of the Church in the life of Belfast – was entirely appropriate because he had himself initiated the replacement of the old St Anne's church by the present cathedral. Its foundation and erection were to a considerable extent due to his energy and zeal; its nave, raised around the old parish church, was consecrated in June 1904 with over 200 diocesan clergy in attendance. It was earlier in his ministerial career, when he was Vicar of Belfast that Rev H.S. O'Hara also had the idea of building St Peter's, and he helped guide this vision to its fruition. In a striking acknowledgement of their profound debt of gratitude to him, the parishioners of St Peter's presented him with his Episcopal Seal when he was made Bishop of Cashel, Emly, Waterford and Lismore in 1900. He occupied this position until his retirement in 1919; four years later, in December 1923, he died in Coleraine at the age of eighty.

But, with regard to the founding of St Peter's, some of the most vital initiatives were actually taken locally. Its erection largely reflects the dynamism and determination of its erstwhile parishioners, the lay members of the Church then living in the Antrim Road area. On 13th August 1890, a meeting was held at Clarence Place Hall, May Street (these Italian Gothic premises had been built in the 1860s, and provided accommodation for the Church of Ireland Young Men's Society). It was chaired by H.H. McNeill of Parkmount and, as a result of its deliberations, a committee was formed to consider the problem of providing for the more effective pastoral care of those living in the north of the city – between the four parishes of St James's, St Paul's, Carnmoney and Whitehouse. Though the area was then thinly populated, it was being developed rapidly, and included amongst its residents the Earl of Shaftesbury and many of the city's leading merchants and businessmen. Nonetheless, the committee's initial enquiries proved to be unproductive. After a year or so the idea of securing a site for the new church at the junction of the

Lansdowne and Somerton Roads was abandoned, and it was decided to leave the matter temporarily in abeyance.

However, on 31st December 1894, a new committee was formed, also charged with the responsibility of erecting a church to meet the needs of members in this district, and discussions were reopened. One of its most crucial meetings took place on 12th December 1895. On that occasion Mr James Stewart, a linen merchant who lived at Beechmount on Downview Avenue, proposed that the new church be called the Church of St Peter; his motion was seconded by Mr R. Garrett Campbell, of Coolgreeney on the Antrim Road. Over the years immediately following, some changes appear to have occurred in the composition of the committee. In his *Jubilee* history of St Peter's, Dr Breene provides a definitive list of those who were serving on it in 1896, and describes them as being the 'original committee'. It then comprised [addresses, where known, have been included]: Colonel J.L. Alison of Knocknamona, Fortwilliam Park; R. Lloyd Campbell of Kinallen, Antrim Road; Godfrey W. Ferguson of Royal Avenue, and Claun, Donegall Park Avenue; Colonel Gelson; F.P. Hughes of Thornleigh, Cavehill Road; Alex Johnston of Summerville, Landscape Terrace; R. MacMurray; Cecil MacFerran; G. Perry; Francis Robinson of Chichester Avenue; George Herbert Ewart of Firmount, Antrim Road, Honorary Treasurer; Francis Joseph Bigger of Airdrie, Honorary Secretary; and the 9th Earl of Shaftesbury, occasionally resident in Belfast Castle. It is evident that most, if not all, lived in the local area, many of them in the 'big houses' on or near the Antrim Road. They were also a highly disparate group, mainly drawn from professional, commercial and industrial backgrounds; the membership included a flax spinner, an architect with offices in Royal Avenue, a bran merchant, a teacher, a 'clerk of merchants', a solicitor, a linen manufacturer, etc.

Given their social class, experience and background, the committee would clearly have had influence, and was likely to be competent. It comprised some of the leading citizens not just within the embryonic new parish but in Belfast as a whole, and indeed throughout Ireland. For example the 9th Earl of Shaftesbury, the sole representative of the landed elite amongst its members, stood at the apex of Belfast society. His involvement with St Peter's, and indeed with the city at all, had come about entirely by chance – through marriage. George Hamilton, the 3rd Marquis of Donegall, had had just one son, Frederick Richard, Earl of Belfast. He was a romantic and popular figure – handsome, young and talented, he wrote poetry, composed music, and was an enthusiastic supporter of popular education. In 1853, however, he died of scarlet fever whilst at Naples, aged 25. On his death, his only sister, Harriet Chichester, became heiress of virtually all of her father's estate (except Islandmagee), and in 1857 she married the eldest son and heir of the 7th Earl of Shaftesbury, the eminent social reformer. As a consequence, when the 3rd Marquis died in 1883, almost all of the remaining Donegall property passed from the direct line, and became part of the Shaftesbury estates.

The Donegalls' revived interest in their connection with Belfast, which had prompted the 3rd Marquis to build Belfast Castle in 1868–70, was perpetuated by his daughter, Harriet, and equally by her son, the 9th Earl of Shaftesbury. In any case, the estate they inherited in Co. Antrim in 1883 was sufficiently large for them to consider it worth visiting every year. Perhaps their active involvement in local affairs was also encouraged by the spectacular growth of Belfast in the late nineteenth century, and the fact that they had no rivals in the city of similar rank to themselves to act as local patrons. Belfast had millionaires but no resident, leisured landed class. Consequently Lord Shaftesbury's household at Belfast Castle, with its retinue of nineteen domestic servants (according to the 1901 census), stood unchallenged at the head of society.

Certainly, the Shaftesburys did all that was expected of them and more. The 9th Earl became mayor of Belfast in 1907. In 1908, when Queen's College was raised to the status of university, he became its first chancellor. His last act of patronage was to present Belfast Castle and its grounds to the City in 1934 (exactly forty years earlier, he had added to it its distinctive, Italian style, serpentine spiral staircase – as a gift to his mother, Harriet). But throughout his long life, he had fulfilled the role his social position required – supporting local charities, opening the Castle grounds for garden fetes, etc. His benevolence towards the Church of Ireland is illustrated by the fact that he headed the subscription list for the construction of the new cathedral, St Anne's. His involvement in the original 'founding committee' of St Peter's was therefore entirely typical of his work on behalf of the citizens of Belfast.

The Committee's Honorary Treasurer, George Herbert Ewart, was a member of one of Belfast's most illustrious and successful entrepreneurial families. He was the grandson of Sir William Ewart, the founder of the firm of William M. Ewart and Son, Ltd. It was Sir William who had built up the family's fortune. He had begun his business career as a small-scale fancy muslin manufacturer in Rosemary Street in about 1820. By the 1840s, his firm was manufacturing linen and cotton, as well as sewed muslin. By the late nineteenth century it had become the most extensive concern for flax spinning and linen manufacturing that Belfast has known – the city was then the most important linen producing centre in the world. It had offices, factories and mills in Bedford Street, Crumlin Road and Ligoniel, and also had branches in Manchester, London, and New York. In politics, the family was staunchly conservative and unionist. Sir William himself had represented North Belfast at Westminster from 1885 until his death in 1889. His son, William Quartus (George Herbert's father) who succeeded him, was Chairman of Belfast Conservative Association, and also held numerous prestigious positions; he was a Justice of the Peace, a Deputy Lieutenant, a Sheriff, a member of the Town Council, the Harbour Board and the Chamber of Commerce, and a director of the Great Northern Railway; he was later knighted.

The Ewart family had not only made a vital contribution to Belfast's industry, commerce and political life, but also to the growth of the Church in the emerging city. In November 1862 a group of committed laymen (which included William Quartus Ewart), who were concerned at the lack of church accommodation in the City, held a meeting in the firm's offices – then in Donegall Place, chaired by the architect, Sir Charles Lanyon (who gave his services to the Church free). They subsequently launched a campaign, which resulted in the formation of the Belfast Church Extension and Endowment Society. Over the fifteen years following, 1862–77, eleven new parish churches were built in the city, including St Thomas's

(1870), St James's (1873) and St Jude's (1873); in addition, St Mark's, Dundela (1877–78), was under construction. In the words of a Church Commission report, 'what they planned they executed. The fruits of their faith and toil ... have been reaped'. The same might also have been said of William Quartus's son, George Herbert Ewart. He died on 26th March 1924, and his funeral took place at St Peter's two days later, the Bishop of the Diocese officiating. An inscription may be seen around the inside of the west porch screen of the present Church; it reads:

> To the Glory of God and that there may be had in Perpetual Remembrance the name of George Herbert Ewart ... A Founder of St Peter's Parish and a Generous Benefactor, he at all times gave of his best for its spiritual life and for the erection and adornment of this Church.

The building bears one other enduring legacy of his influence; it was Herbert Ewart who approached George Tinworth in the late 1890s and asked him to produce the beautiful ceramic reredos behind its High Altar (see Chapter VIII).

Arguably, Francis Joseph Bigger, Honorary Secretary of the original 1896 St Peter's Committee (a position he held for the next nine years) was its most historically significant member – it is said of him that he became a 'living legend' during his own lifetime. He was certainly its most controversial. He was a High Churchman, and an active and loyal member of the Parish, in its formative years at least. After its foundation, he became a member of the Select Vestry and, in 1903, a churchwarden. He made a number of lasting contributions to the adornments of the Church, and to its history. Dr Breene records: 'in our early days [Bigger] ... took a rubbing of a Shield with Crossed Keys on the back of one of the books in York Minster. He suggested that it might be adopted as our Parish Badge. The idea was approved at Whitsuntide, 1896. A block was made, and the badge has been in use ever since' (York Minster was itself dedicated to St Peter – by the Benedictine Archbishop, later Saint, Oswald in 637 AD. Westminster Abbey is also). In addition, he influenced the design of the McNeill Window in the east wall of the south transept, and the piscina on the south side of the sanctuary is inscribed: 'Joseph Bigger *in Christo Quievit* XIII February MDCCCXC' (13th February 1890). The Church also has in its possession a small alms dish, carved in oak, which bears the lettering: 'F.J.B. Easter MCMII' (1892).

In the words of a local poet, Joseph Campbell, Bigger was 'a short-built, thick set, brown-faced, eager man'; born on 17th July 1863, he could claim a remarkable ancestry. He was the 7th son of Joseph Bigger of 'Ard Righ' ('Height of the King'), who was the 7th son of David Bigger of Mallusk, a United Irishman (of which Francis Joseph was extremely proud), who was the 7th son of William Bigger, who owned a wool factory at Biggerstown, Co. Antrim. His family had come to Ulster from Scotland in the seventeenth century, and had developed business interests in High Street, Belfast. Though he was born in Belfast, Francis Joseph spent part of his childhood in Liverpool after his father had moved there for business reasons, but he returned to the city with his family when aged eleven. He attended the Royal Belfast Academical Institution (his grandfather was one of its founders and his father was a governor) and the then Queen's College, Belfast, before studying law in Dublin, and completing a four-year legal apprenticeship with an established firm of Belfast solicitors – Messrs Henry and William Seeds. He was admitted as a solicitor in 1887, and two years later set up in partnership with an 'Inst' school pal and lifelong friend, William Strachan. Their firm had offices in Royal Avenue.

Apart from his involvement in the birth of St Peter's and in the life of the Church, Bigger had an extraordinarily wide range of interests. He had a passion for all things Irish – its history, culture, folklore, place names, antiquities and language. This interest had flowered during the two years he read law in Dublin, in the course of which he had frequented the antiquarian bookshops and the old second-hand bookstalls located along the quays; this proved to be the genesis of what became one of the most notable local history collections in Ireland. He was particularly knowledgeable on such subjects as the 1798 Rebellion, the Penal peri-

Portrait of Francis Joseph Bigger, 1863–1926, a founder member of St Peter's, and its first Honorary Secretary.

od, the Gaelic revival, Belfast and its environs, and the theatre in Ulster. In addition, he was a keen Mason – drawn by the organisation's pomp and ritual – and also served as Honorary Secretary and Chairman (1900–03) of the Belfast Naturalists' Field Club, and became editor of the *Ulster Journal of Archaeology* (1894–1914) which he had helped to resurrect. In addition, he was a Governor at his old school ('Inst'), was elected to the Royal Irish Academy, and became a Fellow of the Royal Society of Antiquaries of Ireland in 1896, a member of the Belfast Natural History and Philosophical Society, and a Director of the Ulster Reformed Public House Association. He lectured all over Ireland, wrote books and frequently contributed to Irish newspapers as well as to archaeological journals. His published work was not only profuse but also exceptionally diverse, and included topics ranging from labourers' cottages in Ireland, St Comgall of Bangor, the 1770 Land War, the authorship of the ballad 'Kitty of Coleraine', and a description of ancient Irish bronze trumpets. His achievements were recognised by Queen's University when, in 1926, he was awarded an honorary Master of Arts; the citation referred to 'a lifetime of enthusiasm to researches in Irish archaeology and local history'.

Interior of St Peter's Church shortly after its original construction

Bigger was also an extremely philanthropic and socially responsible man. He gave liberally to those in need and even had homes built for a number of them – the six 'Sally Gardens' cottages at Carnmoney, named after Yeats's poem. From his own resources he contributed to the restoration of ruined castles (Jordan's Castle, Ardglass), churches (Raholp Church, Downpatrick), and various buildings of historic interest, as well as ancient gravestones. At Clifton Street cemetery he had the graves marked of leading figures in the 1798 rebellion (Mary Ann McCracken, Rev William Steele Dickson), and he was responsible for having a huge slab of Mourne granite placed at the presumed site of St Patrick's grave at Downpatrick. He also arranged for the re-erection of high crosses – for example, at Down Cathedral, at Dromore, at St Brigid's, and at St Colmcille's, and of a wooden cross at Cranfield, near Randalstown.

In addition, his own home at 'Ard Righ', on the Antrim Road – where he lived on his own – was a centre of public education as well as of Irish culture. Advertisements appearing in the local press publicised the meetings of the 'Musical and Literary Society' which were held there. These featured lectures on geology, botany, medicine, zoology, photography, travel, etc. They were invariably delivered by specialists, and often illustrated by lantern slides and/or specimens (with microscopes being provided to facilitate closer examination). The house also contained Bigger's private library of 3,000 books; it was entirely in keeping with his public spiritedness that this, along with his private papers (including 3,500 letters), was bequeathed to the Central Library in Belfast by his brother in 1930.

After Francis Joseph's death, 'Ard Righ', the house in which he had been born and spent almost all of his life, was occupied by the Nationalist politician, Joe Devlin; Bigger had been largely responsible for his election to Westminster, representing West Belfast, in 1905. It was demolished in April 1986 and replaced by modern housing – an apartment block named 'Ardrigh Court' (it is number 737 Antrim Road; in Bigger's day the houses along the Antrim Road had not been numbered this far out of the city).

Though widely respected and revered, Bigger was also a somewhat controversial and divisive figure. Initially at least he sought to bind Protestants and Catholics together in a new unity, rooted in their common heritage – Ireland's culture and mythology, and its language; he shared Patrick Pearse's vision of a Gaelic speaking, Irish nation state that would embrace both traditions in a united national identity. He became an ardent Irish nationalist – a passion partly inspired by his study of Gaelic and involvement in the Gaelic League – and a committed member of Sinn Féin (the movement then espoused non-violent, passive resistance to British rule as the only means to achieve Irish independence – much as Gandhi was to do later in India).

Such political views and interests were certainly unusual for a member of the Anglican Church, and they may have been rooted both in his own family's links to the United Irishmen, and in experiences during his childhood. It is possible that it was being brought up in North Belfast, under the shadow of the Cave Hill that first instilled in him a romantic interest in Wolfe Tone and the men of '98 – they had such intimate links with that area. But there can be no doubt that Bigger developed an almost obsessive interest in them. For seven years he kept in his home the alleged bones of Henry Joy McCracken (they had been discovered in 1902, and were eventually placed in the MacCracken family vault). 'Ard Righ' became not just a powerhouse of Irish music, learning and conviviality, but of revolutionary politics. In 1898, he played an active role in the centenary celebrations of the rebellion. Later, he was involved in the formation of the Irish Volunteers, and in the Howth gunrunning (July 1914); he regarded both as a legitimate means of counteracting the political influence of the Ulster Volunteer Force. Meanwhile, much of his writing was propagandist – aiming to remind particularly the Presbyterian descendents of the United Irishmen of their patriotic past and hoping thereby to win them over to Irish nationalism.

He became a close personal friend and confidante of Sir Roger Casement; Casement stayed at 'Ard Righ' during his frequent visits to Belfast before the outbreak of the First World War. When in Germany, 1914–16, attempting to raise an 'Irish Brigade' from Irish prisoners of war to assist in the planned rising in Dublin, he regarded Bigger as one of his main points of contact in Ireland. Both men appear to have undergone a very similar pattern of development. Both were Protestants, unmarried, and had initially supported moderate, non-violent nationalism, before becoming active in the Gaelic League, which proved to be a stepping-stone to involvement in Sinn Féin and the Irish Volunteer Force. By late 1914, because of his relationship with Casement and other Irish separatists, Bigger's activities were closely monitored by the Royal Irish Constabulary; they noted that 'his associates were all extremists', that he himself was 'said to hate British rule', and considered that he did 'not bear a good moral character'. RIC Crime Special Branch regarded him as 'one of … [Sinn Féin's] more violent and fanatical members … enthusiastic, emotional, unbalanced … though not lacking in a certain type of intelligence'. His views and activities were certainly not typical of the Protestant middle class in Belfast at the time – even though the nationalist leaders Isaac Butt and Charles Stewart Parnell were Protestant, and Douglas Hyde, a founder of the Gaelic League, was the son of a Church of Ireland clergyman. It may have been as a consequence of his political views that his involvement in the affairs of St Peter's Parish appears to have tapered off in the early 1900s – long before his death. He died in December 1926 at the age of sixty-one, and was buried at the old cemetery, Mallusk.

However disparate its membership, the 'original committee' of St Peter's proved to be sufficiently united in its purpose to honour its responsibilities and achieve its goal. It was agreed that the new church should be built of Scrabo sandstone with Giffnock dressings, and that the interior should contain no painted plaster. It was also decided that all of the seats should be free – there were to be no pews. After the church had been built, one of its first visitors was to observe, cynically:

> The seats are free, which, of course, does not mean that going to church here
> is any cheaper than in the rented pew church. On the contrary, it is general-
> ly more costly, for the clergy have more excuses for begging, and take every
> opportunity to remind the worshippers of their responsibilities.

Actually, the committee's decision was an enlightened one, and in keeping with the changing temper of the times. When St George's, High Street, had been opened in 1816, it was arranged that all subscribers of £100 and upwards should have pews assigned to them, with power to sell; those of £50 and upwards should have pews secured to their families in perpetuity, but without right to sell; while those of £25 and upwards should have pews allotted for their personal and family use. Just six seats were provided for the free use of the poor. But, by 1931, only six of the 38 parish churches in Belfast were still making charges for pews (three of these were in what might be defined as 'North Belfast' – St George's had persisted with the practice, as had St Paul's, and Whitehouse). By then they had come to be regarded as a barrier to attendance, and the Church Commission urged that all churches in receipt of support from the Church Extension Society should be free.

In addition, a decision was taken that a school – Skegoneill National School – should be built, and run, in connection with the St Peter's Church and district (the Parish bore the cost of the rates, repairs, insurance, heating, light, caretaker's wages, etc). The state system of non-denominational education in Ireland, initiated by Westminster in 1831, had by 1900 become, in effect, a state system of denominational education; almost all Ireland's primary schools (i.e. the National School system) were under denominational control. Though chiefly funded by the state and in theory non-denominational, in practice, control of all but a few was vested in the parish clergy. In a large number of parishes the incumbent managed and supported, or tried to obtain support for, a primary school or schools. By 1900, 1,330 schools in Ireland were under the Church of Ireland's management in the National Board system; in these, along with the study of secular subjects, children were provided with scriptural education, and instruction in the catechism and formularies of the church. (Historically, Church of Ireland vestries – the name deriving from the vestry or room in which the priest's vestments were kept – had raised funds for a range of local services, including poor relief, parish constables, road repair and even the provision of recruits for the army. The money which the churchwardens had spent of behalf of the parish had largely been raised from the parish cess, a local tax on householders and, to a lesser extent, from the sale of seats in the parish church).

In due course the sites for both church and school were chosen. St Peter's was to be erected on the Antrim Road, in open and thinly populated land adjacent to the gates of Belfast Castle, on property which had belonged to the McNeill family of Parkmount House. It was a more commanding and attractive setting than that originally considered – on the intersection of the Somerton and Lansdowne Roads. It was also decided to build the church in phases, and to begin by constructing the chancel, transepts, and the eastern section of the nave. The school was to be located nearby, on the opposite side of the Antrim Road. The two sites were acquired at a combined cost of £1,200, though a rather larger sum was borrowed from the Board of Works. Samuel P. Close was appointed as architect of the church, and Henry Laverty and Sons as its builders. Close was one of the leading church architects in the city, and could bring an immense depth of experience to the drawing up of the plans. He had designed the rectory for St Mark's, Holywood Road, in 1887; St Patrick's Church, Newtownards Road, 1891–3; St Columba's, King's Road, 1896; St Mary Magdalene, Donegall Pass, 1899; St Nicholas's, Lisburn Road, 1899;

Fisherwick Presbyterian Church, 1898–1901, and his subsequent commissions included St Mary's, Crumlin Road, 1903.

Skegoneill National School was constructed at considerable speed and with an evident sense of urgency at the junction of the Old Cavehill Road and the Antrim Road (its architect was G.W. Ferguson, and the builder, John Lynas). A memorial stone was laid at the site by Mrs Herbert Ewart, wife of the Honorary Treasurer of St Peter's committee, on 16th May 1896. Three months later, in August, the building was opened by the Countess of Shaftesbury; Rev H.S. O'Hara acted as Chairman at the ceremony (the parochial district of St Peter's had been placed under his superintendence). The school would appear to have prospered from the outset. On 19th November 1897, it received its first official inspection when Mr Dalton, a District Inspector of education, visited it; his report was highly favourable. He had examined eighty of its pupils and also its staff (then comprising the principal, Ernest Perry, and two 'assistants' – Harriet Kirkby and Mary O'Neill). He concluded that:

> the state of the school is very satisfactory for a first results [sic]. Not only have the difficulties experienced in establishing a school been completely overcome but the school work has already been raised to a high level of efficiency.

He added that the schoolrooms were 'comfortably kept' and that though the 'attendance is still lower than anticipated … a steady increase may be expected year by year'.

Mr Dalton was entirely correct in this prediction – as the density of housing in the district steadily increased, the number of pupils attending Skegoneill rose rapidly. By 1902, 209 children were examined in the annual school inspection, and the school's principal had by then the support of four assistants, as well as the help provided by some of the older, fifteen to sixteen year old, pupils (they were officially referred to as 'monitors' or 'pupil teachers'). In 1908, 303 schoolchildren were inspected, and 408 in the autumn of 1914. At this point the numbers attending appear to have stabilised, perhaps as a consequence of the lull in house building caused by the First World War. The pupils studied a bewilderingly wide range of subjects, extending far beyond those classified as being 'obligatory'; these included: singing, drawing, algebra, geometry, book-keeping, physical science, light, sound, magnetism and electricity. Those who had attended it in the 1920s later recalled also its 'rich ecumenical tradition' – with Jewish children enrolled, as well as pupils from the various Protestant denominations, and Catholics. Certainly, from the outset, most of its schoolchildren were not members of the Church of Ireland. According to the earliest surviving attendance register for boys at Skegoneill (it is dated 1912), of the seventy-five who enrolled during that year just nineteen were listed as being members of the Church; two-thirds of them were Presbyterians. Similarly, of the sixty pupils listed in its earliest register for girls (covering 1913) just seventeen were Anglican, whilst over half were Presbyterian. In contrast, the teaching staff in this period were mainly, though not exclusively, members of the Church of Ireland.

Until the construction of St Peter's Church was completed, the premises at Skegoneill National School were utilised to meet the spiritual needs of parishioners. On Sunday 1st November 1896, three months after the School had been opened, the first ever services in the history of St Peter's Parish were held in one of its rooms (in fact divine worship was to be held there on thirty occasions by the end of the year). The Right Rev Thomas James Welland (Rector of St Thomas's, 1870–92, and Bishop of Down, Connor and Dromore from 1892 until his death in 1907) preached at 11.30 that morning, over 120 parishioners attended, and Rev H.S. O'Hara at 6pm (the time of the evening service was moved to 7.00pm in December 1897). At 8.30am on the following Sunday, 8th November 1896, Holy Communion was celebrated for the first time. From the outset the congregations attending were surprisingly large; at the Sunday morning service they averaged about eight-five during November–December 1896. Thereafter, numbers rose significantly; by 1900, one hundred and ninety or so had become the norm on Sunday mornings, and one hundred and forty in the evenings. Parishioner morale must also have been raised when, on 25th November 1896, the first baptism in the history of St Peter's took place at the school (of Dorothy Mary Hughes, born on 6th October 1895, the daughter of Frederick Patrick, a 'merchant', and Mary Elizabeth Hughes, of Thornleigh, Old Cavehill Road); twelve more baptisms were to follow between then and St Peter's Day, 29th June 1900. The number of children attending the

Altar of new church shortly after its original construction

Church was sufficient to merit the holding of a special Harvest Festival Service at the school specifically for them.

It is evident from contemporary reports in the local press that the premises at Skegoneill National School also fulfilled an important and varied social role for the local community. Amongst the entertainments it recorded being held there were: meetings of the 'Irish Society'; dramatisations of parts of Jane Austen's novels, including *Northanger Abbey* and *Pride and Prejudice;* a variety of vocal entertainments and, most intriguingly, the presentation of 'Mrs Jarley's Waxworks'. Public lectures were also held at the premises on matters of popular interest – such as the description of episodes in the Boer War, etc. Occasionally the newspaper accounts indicate that these events were 'well attended', or note that the audience was 'very fashionable'. This was probably due in part to effective and subtle publicity; some of the concerts held at the school were described on handbills as being: 'Under the Patronage and [in the] Presence of the Earl and Countess of Shaftesbury'.

Thus, for the four years 1896–1900, Skegoneill School played a vital role in meeting the spiritual, educational and social needs of local church members. It did so at modest cost; at its opening ceremony it was announced that about £100 per annum would be required to cover its expenses. Meanwhile, progress with the construction of St Peter's Church was proceeding apace. On 28th May 1898, the foundation stone was laid. Enclosed with it was an inscription, written on parchment and signed both by the architect, S.P. Close, and the builder, Henry Laverty. It read:

> In the name of the Father the Son and the Holy Ghost This first stone of the Church of Saint Peter in the Parish of Shankill and Diocese of Connor in the Kingdom of Ireland is laid to the Glory of God by Marion Elizabeth wife of Frederick Kinahan of Lowwood in this Parish Esquire on the twenty-eighth day of May in the year of our Lord One thousand eight hundred and ninety-eight and the sixty-first year of the reign of Her Most Gracious Majesty Queen Victoria in the presence of The Right Reverend Thomas James Welland Doctor of Divinity Lord Bishop of Down and Connor and Dromore and the Reverend Henry S. O'Hara A.M. Canon of Saint Patrick's Cathedral and Vicar of Belfast.

The reference to the 'Parish of Shankill' relates to the fact that the earliest known Church of Ireland church in Belfast, or Shankill (meaning the old church or the white church) as the parish was called, was located on the Shankill Road on the site of the old graveyard. It predated the Reformation, and served as the parish church for an area almost identical to the present City of Belfast west of the Lagan. Probably as the result of the movement of the community towards the mouth of the Farset River – into the area of the present High Street – the old church fell into disrepair and was replaced by one of its six alterages or chapels, the 'Chapel at the Ford'; this now became 'The Churche att Belfast' and stood on the site of the present St George's. It in turn was replaced by the 'The Corporation Church' which occupied the same site, though the date of the change is not known (the Corporation of Belfast was formed in 1613); the names of the earliest clergy of this church have not been traced (but from 1622 there is a continuous list of the incumbents of the parish church of Belfast up to the present day). By 1774, it had become structurally unsound and, in 1776, was replaced by a new church, dedicated to St Anne, in Donegall Street. It was built at the sole expense of the 1st Marquis of Donegall, and he named it in honour of his first wife, Anne. An Order in Council, dated 1776, changed 'the parish church of Belfast, which is Shankill, to the town of Belfast'. Though then given the title of 'Parish of Belfast', clearly usage of the original name lived on – the 'Parish of Shankill'.

For Marion Elizabeth Kinahan, who had laid the foundation stone of St Peter's, the date of the ceremony had a particular poignancy. Her son, James, had died in India during military service exactly nine years earlier (on 28th May 1889 – see Chapter VII); this association almost certainly determined the date that was chosen. Her husband, Frederick Kinahan, JP, lived locally at Lowwood, Shore Road, and was an extremely successful businessman. His family were perhaps the biggest wine and spirit merchants

The Very Rev Henry Robert Brett, First Rector of St Peter's, 1900–1926, and Dean of Belfast, 1926–1933

in the city (Lyle and Kinahan, Ltd, Donegall Place), owned several public houses, and were substantial aerated water manufacturers, as well as operating a company of merchant insurance agents. He was to serve as Parish Nominator, 1900–1901, and both he and his family were perhaps the most significant benefactors of the new Church. This is suggested by the inscription on one of the two brasses dedicated to the Kinahan family on the south wall of the sanctuary in St Peter's; it reads: 'To the Glory of God and in Memory of the Family of Frederick Kinahan of Lowwood who erected this Chancel and who died 17th March, 1902'. In addition, three windows in the chancel are memorials to members of this family. Two are in its south wall; the third is the great east window, the centre light of which was the only stained glass in the entire Church when it was consecrated in June 1900.

Even whilst building work on the new church had yet to be completed, a minister was appointed, and the necessary ecclesiastical and administrative structures were instituted. Initially the parochial district of St Peter's had been placed under the pastoral care of the Rev Alexander George Stuart (he had been ordained as a priest in 1892, and had served as curate in Coleraine, 1891–4, and then at St Anne's, which was his base throughout the years 1894–98); he was supported by Rev H.S. O'Hara who acted as a highly energetic superintendent (evidenced by the fact that he preached 19 times at Skegoniell School during 1898). In 1898, the Rev Stuart left St Anne's and took up duties as Curate of Carlow 'for family reasons'. He was then succeeded at St Peter's by the Rev Henry Robert Brett, M.A., who was appointed Curate-in-charge of the district on 1st November of that year. He was thirty years of age, had been educated at Kilkenny College and Trinity College Dublin. Like Rev A.G. Stuart, he had served as Curate in Coleraine (1893–94), where Rev H.S. O'Hara had been Rector, and both clerics had come with him to Belfast when the latter was appointed Vicar of Belfast. Mr Brett also served as Curate of St Anne's (1894–1900).

Though there was as yet no church building and, for some time to come, no rectory – Rev Brett was living at 8 Chichester Terrace in 1900 – soon there was at least an officially designated parish and, at about the same time, a Select Vestry was formed. At a meeting held on 8th February 1900 the Diocesan Council formed the district of St Peter's into a separate parish; it was legally constituted as such with effect from 1st April 1900. This new unit was carved out of the Parish of Belfast, Shankill. It included part of the town lands of Ballyoghagan, Lowwood, Greencastle and Skegoneill, and covered some 1,600 acres. Meanwhile, the first list of Registered Vestrymen in St Peter's had been compiled from the St Anne's Register; this was done at a meeting of St Anne's parishioners, held at the Cathedral on 12th March 1900. Next day, on 13th March, the first meeting of the Registered Vestrymen of the new Parish of St Peter's was held at Skegoneill School. The eleven members of the Church's first Select Vestry (at Easter 1900) were Colonel James L. Alison; F.J. Bigger (Honorary Secretary); James Campbell; A.C. Capper; G. Herbert Ewart (Honorary Treasurer); Henry Hughes; James MacDonald; Cecil MacFerran; Richard Nevin; Francis Robinson and Samuel Smith (Honorary Auditor). Five of them had served on the 'original committee' of the church formed in 1896.

Two weeks later, on 27th March 1900, Rev H.R. Brett was unanimously appointed incumbent of St Peter's by the first Board of Nomination (he was to serve as its rector for the next 26 years). It was, as he himself said, an 'eventful year'. By then, construction work on the first phase – the eastern section of the church – was nearing completion. The entire building, when finished, was considerably smaller than now; a small notch indented into the wooden flooring of the present-day nave marks where the door into the porch of the earlier structure was located. From the outset, the church was adorned and beautified by generous gifts from many families and individuals. For example, the chancel floor tiling was paid for by Rev H.R. Brett himself; the pulpit was given by C.J. Kinahan; the Litany desks and Vestry Wardrobe by the Earl of Shaftesbury; the rector's desk by the Berwick family; and the communion rails were provided by the builders, Messrs Laverty and Sons. The organ was erected by Edward Platt-Higgins, Rathcoole, Fortwilliam Park. Apart from the Kinahan windows referred to, the McNeill Window was erected in the south transept in 1907; it was dedicated to the memory of Henry Hugh McNeill of Parkmount, on whose land St Peter's was built. In addition, the parishioners made substantial donations of plate to the new church: the Kinahan family gifted a silver paten in 1900 and a silver flagon in 1902; the Misses Montgomery and Macauley a silver flagon in 1899; the Spiller family two silver chalices, and three silver patens in 1902; and Ms B.A.M. Leach a silver baptismal shell.

At 3.30pm, on St Peter's Day, 29th June 1900, the Church was licensed and opened for public worship by the Bishop of the Diocese, Rt Rev T.J. Welland, (as was required by law, official approval had been given by His Excellency, the Lord Lieutenant of Ireland). It was entirely appropriate that on this most auspicious occasion the Church's acknowledged 'founder', Bishop H.S. O'Hara, should have preached the sermon (he had just been made Bishop of Cashel; at Christmas 1896 he and his wife had gifted to St Peter's a silver paten and, twelve months later, a silver chalice). He must have been gratified by the size of the congregation; its affluence is suggested by the fact that the offertory totalled over £500 – a detail which was duly recorded in the Preachers' Book. When the first services of St Peter's parochial district had been held in Skegoneill Schoolhouse on 1st November 1896, the collections had totalled just £20.

The last Sunday services to be held in Skegoneill School took place on 24th June 1900; an entry in the Preachers' Book records that the weather that day was 'wet' in the morning, and 'hopelessly wet' in the evening. The first Sunday services to be held in St Peter's Church took place on 1st July 1900. Shortly afterwards, in a letter dated 17th July 1900, the Register General in Dublin 'begged to acquaint' the Mr Brett that, as the church had been officially licensed, it might now be used 'for the solemnization of marriages'; its 'name had been duly entered in the Books of this Department', and the necessary register books and forms were being dispatched in 'this day's post'. In fact, the parish's marriage register indicates that the first wedding to be solemnised in the history of the parish did not take place until 13th June 1901 – the marriage of Francis Edward Smith, a 'florist, nurseryman', and Sarah Elizabeth Johnson. The first baptism had taken place on 18th July 1900 (of Marie Enid, daughter of John McCormick, a 'merchant', and Agnes, of Abbey Park, Belfast); it was the first of five to take place that year.

On St Peter's Day, 29th June 1901 – the first anniversary of the church – the preacher was Rev G.O. Hannay, the well-known novelist and Rector of Westport, Tuam. From reports in the Belfast press it is evident that, even within its first year, St Peter's was already establishing a reputation for fine music. Thus, on 27th December 1900, the *Evening Telegraph* had described how

> at midnight on Christmas Eve the residents in the districts of Fortwilliam Park, Chichester Park, Ashley Park, and Antrim Road were awakened by a choir singing lovely Christmas Carols. It subsequently transpired that the choir of the Parish Church of St Peter's, so noted for their excellent music, were the good people who so kindly favoured their friends and neighbours in such an appropriate way on Christmas morning.

On 4th February 1901 the *Belfast News Letter* gave an account of a memorial service conducted by Mr Brett at St Peter's two days earlier, following the death of Queen Victoria; it confirms the content of the *Telegraph*'s report. It stated that parishioners filled the building almost to capacity 'to testify to the sincerity of their grief at the death' of their monarch. It noted that 'the church was not draped in black … [as] it was evident throughout that an attempt was being made to give prominence to the triumphal note … the note of hope'. It concluded by praising the quality of the music, noting that the 'organist conducted the musical portion of the service with much ability'. A new organ was installed two years later, and first used in early April 1903.

By far the most detailed description of the early days at St Peter's was contained in a journal called the *Nomad's Weekly*; it had a second, more revealing and strictly accurate title, the *Belfast Critic*. The publication had a substantial circulation; its manager, Alfred S. Moore boasted: 'we guarantee that ten copies of our paper are sold in the streets of Belfast alone for one of any of the penny papers – weekly or daily.' One of its most popular features was a couple of pages it devoted each week to 'Pen and Pulpit'. The author of this piece was William J. Livingstone, who wrote under the *nom de plume* of *Erastus*. He was in the habit of visiting one of the places of worship in Belfast each Sunday, and in the following issue describing what he had seen and heard, and offering his comments, whether favourable or otherwise. He had a pungent pen, a cynical eye and a capacity for the telling insight and detail.

Number 85 in the 'Pen and Pulpit' series dealt with St Peter's, and was published on 30th June 1906 (it was reprinted in full in Dr Breene's *Jubilee* history of the church; one reviewer described it as 'one of the best things in the book'). Livingstone's language is somewhat pretentious and flowery – suggesting a concern to impress rather than instruct. But he does convey some impression of the experience of worshipping at the church, and of the nature of its congregation. He seems to have been unaware that the Sunday morning he had chosen to attend, 24th June, coincided with the St Peter's Day services that year. Thus, on arriving, he records his surprise at seeing 'a notice in the porch [which] informs me that I have struck another special collection – the Anniversary Services. But', he continued,

> it also proclaims the glad tidings that the distinguished Bishop of Derry will preach. Not that I would have any objection to the Rev Mr Brett, the rector. Indeed I went out for the special purpose of hearing him. He will keep though, as they say in the classics, our Dr Chadwick is something we cannot have every day.

[Rt Rev Dr George Alexander Chadwick had been Rector in St James's, 1870–72, and Armagh, 1872–96, and was Bishop of Derry from 1896–1916, after which he retired. He had published extensively; Dr Breene described him as 'eloquent and gifted'.]

Livingstone had travelled out to St Peter's by tram, and alighted at the terminus close by the church. Throughout his visit what appears to have impressed him most was the affluence and elevated social class of the congregation. He observed, for example, that despite the 'midsummer' weather, a mixture of

> stifling heat with a series of torrential showers, just dropped in when least expected, … the ladies have bravely donned their summer costumes, and the Antrim Road this Sunday morning in June is like an animated fashion-plate clad in all sorts of gauzy materials. In the distance they appear like the maidens of Ancient Greece, but a closer acquaintance reveals the modernity. The lightness of the picture is regulated by a mere male thing in frock coat and silk hat here and there, like punctuation marks in this poem of picturesque piety, this song of silken softness, this march of *mousseline de soie*. I must, perforce, ferret my way through this perfumed … pageant … I join a few whose unintelligible enunciation proclaims their high breeding … The strains of the opening hymn can be heard even over the noise made by my fellow travellers and myself on the gravel walk as we make for the impromptu porch. They are far enough away from the city to be honest out here, sitting as they do under the everlasting frown of the Cave Hill, and so the ladies hang their costly wraps in the vestibule ere they set forth in search of a seat …

Livingstone's initial impressions were confirmed and reinforced when he entered the church itself. He wrote:

> it is a slice of a cathedral! There is the carefully laid floor, the chairs, the pray-
> ing cushions, the fancy desk, lectern, and pulpit that you will find in a larger
> form in the more mature church. On every side we see the familiar faces of
> the merchant princes of Belfast. There is a distinct flavour of petrol in the air,
> while every male – and some of the females – bear evident traces of the golf
> links in their weather-beaten, sun-brown faces. There are men who have made
> so much money in trade as to despise trade, and men with sufficient blue
> blood in their veins to enable them to wear badly cut clothes with an air of
> distinction. There are men who have arrived at that interesting part of their
> career when attendance at public worship is absolutely necessary.

Surprisingly, Livingstone was somewhat disappointed with the performance of the
choir, and attributed its lack of accomplishment in part to the affluence of the congregation. He wrote:

> the choir is not as good as it ought to be. This is not Mr Gifford's fault, I feel
> certain, for he has the reputation of being an enthusiastic musician, and there
> is no doubt it takes many years to build up a choir, especially in aristocratic
> suburbia [A.M. Gifford, LRAM, was organist from 1903 to 1916]. People of
> good breeding ... who are possessed of voices do not consider it "form" to take
> part in such work. It cannot be made exclusive.

Nonetheless, Livingstone did make some positive comments about the music during the service. He noted that though

> there was an inclination to "rush" the psalms ... some of the other items were
> distinctly creditable. The *Te Deum* was well rendered, yet I thought, the dif-
> ference between the loud and soft parts was not sufficiently marked. When
> they came anywhere approaching "piano" the general effect was beautiful, but
> they very seldom got below "mf".

However', he added encouragingly, 'under such guidance as they have there is no
doubt of their ultimate perfection'.

In the remainder of his account, Livingstone focused mainly on the presiding clergy. He protested that he had

> heard Mr Brett so often that I could almost write him a "character" [i.e. ref-
> erence] without another sample of his abilities. When senior curate of the old
> church of St Anne's he was wont to command the respect of all by his master-
> ly sermons. [He was] as famous for his attention to detail as for love of the
> unorthodox.

In somewhat barbed comments, Livingstone suggested that the cleric was well suit-
ed to his position as rector of the new church, writing:

> he must have realised one of his greatest ambitions when he was appointed ...
> It is close to the Castle, and there is always a chance of "tone" in the suburbs,
> for Mr Brett is undoubtedly the man for a swagger congregation. And if you

want to see such a church in the making you should visit the unfinished building on the Antrim Road. Mr Brett conducts the early part of the service with that preciseness for which he is famed. Every word and every syllable gets its full measure of attention and the thin sharp lips come down like a guillotine on the end of each word and chop it off clean and clear …

Livingstone did provide a highly favourable description of Dr Chadwick. He observed that the Bishop first

'began to take an active part in the proceedings with the commandments … and [that] the magnificent voice of the visitor rolled round the little building and seemed to gather beauty in its progress. I cannot remember having heard him since he was connected with Armagh – a long time ago now – but the voice retains all its fascination. He has changed in appearance since we last met, but the machinery of thought still works as freely. His text is commonplace! Yet he announces it in such a way as to give the impression it is something new and wonderful, and suggests things never before thought of. St Matthew iii, 2: "Repent ye for the Kingdom of Heaven is at hand." The attention of the congregation is arrested. It is held. It is imprisoned until he cares to release them'.

The sermon certainly appears to have 'imprisoned' Mr Livingstone, for he provided a detailed summary of it in his report.

Next, he described the lifting of the collection. He described how Dr Chadwick, at the conclusion of the sermon, 'after pointing out how absolutely necessary the church was to a man's salvation … asked for their support to clear off the debt on the building'. According to Livingstone, the effect was dramatic. He writes:

Even this hackneyed subject was brightened under the Bishop's treatment. You considered it an honour and privilege to associate yourself with anything recommended in such beautiful language. You changed the coin you intended to give for one of greater value.

Having considered his own reaction, Livingstone scrutinised the impact of this appeal on the members of the congregation, and he concluded his account with some wry humour at their expense. He wrote:

Looking round the wealthy members I wondered if they ever saw coppers in the collection plates of St Peter's; I feared to look when one came my length! I felt that my eyesight would be endangered by the glitter of the gold. I put out my hand! Heavy! I drop in my modest contribution, and, in passing the plate to my neighbour, glance down. *A study in brown! I am* surprised. Just a few tiny water-lilies of silver in a pond of coppers. Then the congregation file out into the glorious sunshine, wearing the air of people who had set out for a distasteful task and were glad after all that they had faced it.

Though fluently written, Livingstone's account was more facetious and cynical, than it was strictly accurate. The offertory that Sunday morning (it was for 'parochial endowment') actually totalled over £30 – a remarkably large sum, and much more than was usual for the church at that time (the average St Peter's collection at this service during 1906 varied between £3–5). Moreover, according to Dr Breene, by the end of 1910 the members of the Parish had raised for all purposes a sum of about £22,000, and a substantial endowment fund had been built up, and the overall financial position of the church was reasonably secure. Meanwhile, the congregation was continuing to increase slowly but steadily as new housing was constructed in the neighbourhood. At the 11.30am Sunday service attended by Livingstone, it had numbered 316 – the highest figure of that year, apart from the Harvest Festival held in early October (when it was 340). The average number to attend divine worship at St Peter's on the Sabbath between 1901–1914 was *c.* 220 in the morning and 150 in the evening (the figures are recorded in the Preachers' Book, the totals having been 'reckoned by coins' at the end of each service). Overall, the period following the opening of St Peter's and preceding the war was one of quiet, solid, sustained growth.

III
St Peter's, 1914 –1933:
The Completion of the Church

Rev H.R. Brett's entries in the Preachers' Book for the Parish, particularly during his first years as Rector, read rather like those of a monastic chronicler; they comment not only on events in St Peter's but also frequently on noteworthy developments in the wider world. For example, he makes reference to decisive episodes during the Boer War (1899–1902), to the coronation of Edward VII, and to the deaths of Scott and Oates during their South Pole expedition (16th February 1913). On Sunday, 14th April 1912, he recorded:

> 'The *Titanic*, 46,382 tons, the largest ship in the world, built in Belfast, struck an iceberg … on her maiden voyage to New York, and sank at 2.20am. Of 2,340 souls on board, 1,639 were drowned' [the final figure was actually *c.* 1,500].

Later that year, on Saturday 28th September, he made reference to the 'Ulster Day' service held at 11.00am in St Peter's; he reflected on the 'great enthusiasm' that had been shown, and stated that 'on this day 137,368 Ulstermen [had] entered into a Solemn League and Covenant' in which they pledged to resist Irish Home Rule by all means that might prove necessary. In July–August 1914, he listed the declarations of war which were exchanged between the greater and lesser European powers (28th July–12th August 1914), and later observed that it was the 'murder of Archduke Ferdinand at Sarajevo' that had been 'the spark that set Europe on fire' (28th June 1919).

The calm progress being made by the new church was shattered by Britain's entry into the war in Europe on 4th August 1914. But the conflict did at least bring one benefit or consolation – it forestalled the prospect of civil war in Ireland; both Sir Edward Carson and John Redmond, the respective unionist and nationalist leaders, immediately and unreservedly gave their full support to Britain's war effort, and agreed to postpone the resolution of the Irish question until after hostilities had ceased. With palpable relief and evident surprise, Sir Herbert Asquith, the Prime Minister, observed: 'God moves in mysterious ways'. His foreign minister, Sir Edward Grey, whilst noting that 'the lamps [were] going out all over Europe', added that Ireland had now become 'the one bright spot'.

The dark shadow cast by the First World War is evident in a request which Mr Brett received from the Rt Rev Charles Frederick D'Arcy (former Dean of Belfast and Vicar of St Anne's, and Bishop of the diocese, 1911–19), in August 1915, after the first year of the conflict. It provides some sense of the sombre atmosphere at the time. The Bishop proposed that the clergy of the diocese 'keep Sunday the 8th of August as a day of Special Prayer for our Country and her Allies, and for all their forces, and also as a day of dedication to that supreme task which God in His providence has laid upon us'. In addition, he instructed them to read the following message from their pulpits:

> My dear brethren, on the 4th August last year Great Britain declared war. During the months which have elapsed since then we have learned something of the tremendous nature of the conflict in which we are engaged, and also how vast are the sacrifices which must be made if we are to do our duty. We face the future with the confidence that springs from conviction as to the righteousness of our cause, and with determination to go on to the end which is set before us no matter what the cost may be. Many a dear head has been laid low in death, and many are the sorrowing hearts in our land … Never was there a more heroic age than that in which we are living. It is terrible to live at such at time, but it is also glorious … The Navy and Army are the strong right arm of the nation, striking for God and the right.

Four years later to the day – on 8th August 1919 – Lord French, the then Lord Lieutenant of Ireland, arrived at Belfast Castle to take the salute at the victory march-past of the 36th (Ulster) Division, which had been arranged for the following day.

In total, 206,000 men from Ireland served during the Great War, all of them volunteers. There was an initial surge of enlistment. In 1915 alone, 14,000 men were recruited to the British army from Belfast; of these 10,000 were Protestant. Members of the Ulster Volunteer Force joined up virtually *en masse* – 30,000 of them – forming the 36th (Ulster) Division, a British army unit, raised specifically for them by the War Minister, Lord Kitchener. In October 1915, it transferred to France. On 1st July 1916 (the date on which the Battle of the Boyne had traditionally been celebrated) it had its first experience of 'total war', when deployed at the Battle of the Somme. On that fateful opening day, the British army suffered the largest number of casualties in its history. Within the first two days, 5,500 men of the 36th were reported dead, wounded or missing. In total, an estimated 30,000 Irishmen lost their lives in the 'Great War'.

In the words the historian, R.B. McDowell, its parishioners regarded the War as a 'fight [by Britain] for freedom and civilization against unscrupulous aggression'. Already, by late 1916, some 21,000 Church members – drawn from all four provinces – had enlisted. The lengthy war memorials found in every parish church attest to their loyalty and their sacrifice. Though the membership of St Peter's Parish was still small, eighty-one young men and women from the congregation answered the call to fight for King and Country (see Appendix 1). Eleven made the supreme sacrifice. They died at Loos, the Somme, Ypres, Cambrai; the very name of each battle evokes overwhelming images of the unimaginable horrors and indescribable slaughter of the Western Front (in the Great War, the proportion of British soldiers killed and wounded, in relation to the numbers who were recruited, was much high-er than in the Second World War).

The names of those members of the congregation of St Peter's who made the supreme sacrifice in the First World War were:

> Lieutenant FRANCIS MAPLETOFT LEONARD, 8th Royal Inniskilling Fusiliers, killed in action at Loos, 29th April 1916
>
> Lieutenant LAWFORD BURNE CAMPBELL, 12th Royal Irish Rifles, killed in action at the Somme, 1st July 1916
>
> Corporal ERIC HILTON STEWART, 20th Royal Fusiliers, killed in action at the Somme, 16th July 1916
>
> Chief Steward JOHN MEHAFFEY, 'Bray Head', torpedoed, 14th March 1917
>
> Lieutenant STUART SIMON FAUSSETT, 9th King's Liverpool Regiment, killed in action at Ypres, 31st July 1917
>
> Second Lieutenant ROBERT KELLY POLLIN, 1st Royal Irish Rifles, killed in action at Westhock, 31st July 1917
>
> Lieutenant WILLIAM SHIELDS, Royal Air Force (5th Squadron), killed in action at Ypres, 5th September 1917
>
> Lieutenant EDWARD LAWSON McDONALD, 12th Royal Irish Rifles, killed in action at Meouvres, Cambrai, 23rd November 1917
>
> Private THOMAS CHEDDY, 10th Royal Irish Rifles, died at Sunken Road, Cambrai, 14th December 1917
>
> Private JOSEPH GREER, 14th Royal Irish Rifles, died at Etretat of wounds received near Cambrai, 14th December 1917
>
> Captain JAMES THOMPSON ROBINSON, 24th Royal Welsh Fusiliers, killed in action at Ploegsteert, 8th September 1918

Throughout the conflict, Rev H.R. Brett had duly recorded its decisive strategic events and battles in the Preachers' Book – the sinking of the *Lusitania* (7th May 1915), the Battle of Jutland (31st May 1916), the entry of the USA into the war (6th April 1917) and also such developments on the home front as the internment locally of enemy aliens (13th May 1915). On 11th November 1918, he noted the 'surrender of Germany and signing of the Armistice' and, five days later, referred to the service of 'solemn thanksgiving for the complete victory of our arms', which was held in St Peter's five days later, on 17th November. A further 'Service of Thanksgiving for Peace' was held in the Church on 28 June 1919 – the date on which Germany had signed the post war peace settlement, the Treaty of Versailles. The Rector also noted a two minutes silence being observed in St Peter's on the first anniversary of the Armistice – at 11.00am on 11th November 1919 – in 'Remembrance of the Glorious Dead'.

After the Great War was over, the parishioners of St Peter's decided to erect a 'Victory Window' in the south transept of the church (see Chapter VII). It was intended not just as a memorial to the fallen and to those who served, but also as a remembrance of the patriotic services of every kind performed by the men and women of the Parish both at home and abroad. Its scale was and remains impressive.

It covers some 200 square feet; its six main lights are each 14 feet 6 inches in height and 21 inches wide. It was the work of the nationally renowned firm, Messrs James Powell & Sons, Whitefriars Glass Works, London (this same company had been responsible for the Kinahan 'Motherhood Window' in the chancel of the church, and for the McNeill Window in the south transept; it was also given commissions for the stained glass both in the aisles and in the great west window of St Anne's Cathedral). The total cost of its manufacture and erection was roughly £1,100. That over £900 had already been raised before the window had been produced is eloquent testimony to the commitment of the congregation of St Peter's to the project. Below the window is a framed tablet, with an inscription panel composed of glass tiles; it contains the names of the eleven members of the congregation who died in the Great War, and the dates of their death, and bears the inscription: 'Their name liveth for evermore'. Nearby, on its north side, is a richly carved memorial tablet of oak. Amidst the pierced tracery and other decorative work on its panels (including a shield bearing the Cross Keys, the arms of St Peter's), is a list – gilded and in raised characters – of the fifty-nine men and women from the Parish who served overseas during the First World War. Alongside this is a dedicatory inscription, which reads: 'To the Glory of God Who gave us Victory and in Remembrance of the War Services of Men and Women of this Parish of whom those named Served Overseas this Window is Dedicated'. Eleven others, whose names do not appear, were engaged in Home Defence or were in training for military service at the date of the Armistice, 11th November 1918 (see Appendix I).

The Victory Window and the memorial tablets were dedicated by the Bishop of the Diocese of Down, Connor and Dromore, Rt Rev C.T.P. Grierson (1919–34), on Sunday, 21st November 1920, almost exactly two years after the armistice. A congregation of almost five hundred had crammed into the little church; it was filled to bursting point – far in excess of its seating capacity. The order of service used provides some insight into the mixture of emotions felt by parishioners at this climactic moment in the history of the church – intense feelings of thanksgiving and gratitude, of relief, and also of celebration. The Processional hymn, with which the service began, opened with the triumphal verse:

> Ten thousand times ten thousand
> In sparkling raiment bright
> The armies of the ransomed Saints
> Throng up the steeps of light;
> 'Tis finished! All is finished
> Their fight with death and sin;
> Fling open wide the golden gates
> And let the victors in.

Similar sentiments were expressed in the scriptural readings; these were taken from Psalm CXII and from Ecclesiastes XLIV, and included the verse: 'The righteous shall be had in everlasting remembrance. Their name liveth for evermore, and their glory shall not be blotted out'. Afterwards, the choir sang the anthem: 'Blest are the departed, who in the Lord are sleeping, from henceforth for evermore. They rest from their labours and their works follow them.'

In the course of the prayers which followed, the priest expressed the congregation's feelings of profound gratitude to God for victory, and of remembrance – especially of those from the parish who had served. He prayed for 'those who mourn their loved ones killed in the War', and continued

> We thank Thee for Thy manifold and great blessings to our Nation through-out the long years of war, and for having crowned our Arms with victory. We thank Thee that in the day of calamity the people of this parish offered them-selves willingly for duty in the field of battle and in various fields of National Service [as sailors, soldiers, airmen, merchant seamen] ... We thank Thee for our brothers who were faithful unto death, and whose sacrifice allows the peace we now enjoy.

He also expressed sentiments of hope – for lasting peace – no doubt echoing the deep yearnings within his congregation that the recent conflict really would prove to be the war to end all wars. He pleaded:

> O God, Who makest wars to cease, and by Whose mighty aid the violence of our enemies has been restrained, remove, we pray Thee, all hindrances to peace and concord, that being delivered from the terrors of war we may serve Thee in settled freedom and holy quietness, through Jesus Christ our Lord.

During the act of dedication, Bishop Grierson, a renowned scholar who had been Dean of Belfast throughout the war, spoke movingly of those who had served their country with such courage. He too spoke of hope – the hope that future congrega-tions might learn from the immense sacrifices made by their own. He said:

> We dedicate this Window and these Memorial Tablets to the Glory of God and ... in remembrance of the many patriotic activities of men and women of this Congregation during the Great War. Holy Father, we remember before Thee our dear ones who have passed within the Veil. We know that neither life nor death can separate us from the love which is in Christ Jesus our Lord; and therefore we leave them with Thee, assured that Thou wilt not pass by those who laid down their lives for duty and for righteousness. Have compas-sion on those that mourn, and draw them in their sorrow nearer to Thyself. And grant that these memorials of self-sacrifice and courage may ever lead those who worship in this Church to walk more diligently in the path of duty and to trust more fully in Thy redeeming love ... It may truly be said of St Peter's that, from its earliest days, its aisles have echoed and re-echoed to 'sup-plications and thanksgivings, to lamentations and paeans of triumph.

During Lent 1921, Rev H.R. Brett gave a series of seven sermons which had been directly inspired by the Victory Window, and were published in Belfast later that year. Both during and after the war, his record of service to the Church had been recognised and extended by his appointment to various prebendary positions both within the Down diocese (1917–26), and at St Patrick's Cathedral, Dublin (1919–20). Meanwhile, he had also been made Diocesan Registrar of Down, Connor and Dromore (1917–26), and Archdeacon of Connor (1920–26). Sunday, 4th April 1926, was, he noted, his 'last day in St Peter's'. The Dean of Belfast (Very

Rev T.G.G. Collins) joined him in conducting the morning service, and the church was filled to overflowing. He left to take up an appointment as the new Dean of Belfast and Vicar of St Anne's (1926–32). In so doing, he was following in the footsteps of the acknowledged 'founder' of St Peter's, Rev H.S. O'Hara, and returning to the church where his ministerial career might be said to have begun. At the Cathedral, he worked for the enlargement and beautification of the building and, in the words of Dr Breene, 'added lustre to its services and prestige to the Church in the city'. In addition, he served as one of the Chaplains of the Northern Ireland Parliament, established in 1921.

Rev H.R. Brett retired in September 1932; he died two months later. Under his stewardship St Peter's had flowered. He secured the finances of the parish and, by 1931 it had a 'church population' of 1,800 – a figure far removed from the small numbers who had attended the earliest services held in Skegoneill School during the 1890s. His distinguished record of ministerial service is commemorated in the present church. A memorial window erected in the south porch by his wife and sons is inscribed: 'In Memory of Henry Robert Brett, Rector of this Parish, 1900–1926. Dean of Belfast, 1926–1932'; its themes were aptly chosen – 'Hope' and 'Fortitude'. It was dedicated by the newly appointed Bishop of the Diocese, Rt Rev J.F. McNeice, at 3.30pm on St Peter's Day 1935; the fifteen other clergy present swelled the already large congregation. In addition, the lettering around the base of the communion table in the side chapel reads: 'This Table and Rail were placed here in Memory of Henry Robert Brett. First Rector of this Parish, by Parishioners and Friends. St Peter's Day, 1937' – the date on which they were dedicated.

Rev H.R. Brett was succeeded at St Peter's by the Dr R.S. Breene, who was instituted as Rector by Bishop C.T.P. Grierson on 14th May 1926. Though he was then forty years of age, it was a position which he was to occupy for the next 37 years; he remains the longest serving rector that St Peter's has known. He was privately educated at home with his brother, before entering his first paid employment – in the Imperial Civil Service, the Customs and Excise branch, in Londonderry. His tenure there was a brief one – the position never really appealed to him; consequently, he enrolled in extramural studies at Queen's (graduating with a BA in Arts and Law in 1910) and commenced his theological studies. He was ordained priest in 1912; his first clerical appointment was as curate of Ballynure and Ballyclare parishes (1911–13). It was here that he met his future wife, Rebecca Louisa Denison, then aged 16. She was just 17 when they married on 24th September 1913. Many years later their daughter, Molly, recalled how her mother's parents had not permitted her to wear her engagement ring until she had passed her school certificate!

Dr Breene's next appointment was as curate in Glenavy, Co. Antrim (1913–15). With the outbreak of war, he joined the army as chaplain (1915–20). Whilst in service he was posted to Egypt and India, and was employed on the Hospital ship *Olympic* (sister of the *Titanic*, launched by the White Star Line in Belfast in 1911) during the allied troop evacuation from Turkey after the disastrous Gallipoli campaign. He was mentioned in Dispatches in 1918. He had meanwhile persisted with his academic studies at Queen's – completing an MA in Modern History in 1914,

The Very Rev Richard Simmons Breene, Rector of St Peter's, 1926–63, and Dean of Connor, 1956–63.

an LLB in 1918 and an LLD (he was the last student to be awarded it by examination) in 1919; he was already beginning to emerge as one of the Church of Ireland's most distinguished scholars. However, his most fervent wish after the Armistice was to remain in regular military service. But this proved impossible as he failed the optical test owing to a visual impairment. Nonetheless, after the termination of his full-time appointment in 1920, he continued to serve as Honorary Chaplain to the Forces (a position which he continued to hold when he came to St Peter's in 1926).

At first Dr Breene had difficulty in acquiring an ecclesiastical appointment in Ireland after the war, and so remained in England. However, in 1920, he received a telegram from the Bishop offering him the Rectorship of the combined parishes of Killinchy, Kilmood and Tullynakill, Co. Down. There he remained until he was appointed to St Peter's in 1926. His daughter, Molly, then a child, later recalled the dramatic nature of the change in the family's circumstances resulting from their transfer to Belfast. There was as yet no rectory, so they moved into a four bed-roomed, rented town house. It was much smaller than they had been used to, but was equipped with electricity and with a telephone, both of which were new and unfamiliar to them. As money was in short supply, holidays were arranged by organising exchanges with other rectors in the north – in Ballynahinch, Strangford, Annalong, and elsewhere. They did not acquire their first car until 1931.

For the congregation of St Peter's, as for the Church in the city as a whole, the interwar period was one of sustained growth and consolidation. This steady expansion represented a return to the trends which had been disrupted by the Great War, but it was now set against a backdrop of persistent economic recession. Nonetheless, the parishioners of St Peter's sought bravely and successfully to improve both the structure of their church and its amenities. One highly significant development was, in effect, forced upon them by the changes in the local political context from 1921 – the formation of a new regional government located in Belfast. As a consequence of the Education Act, introduced by Lord Londonderry in 1923, Skegoneill School was amongst the first to be transferred from Church control to the Local Education Authority, (it had continued to thrive – over 430 of its pupils were examined in each of its annual inspections during the mid twenties). This process was completed without St Peter's receiving any financial compensation. To replace the facilities that had been lost as a result, it was decided to erect a parochial hall for the recreational use of the congregation when working hours were over (other churches in the diocese – St Mary Magdalene's, All Saints', Carnmoney – also built halls at about the same time). Its construction cost £3,300, and it was initially intended to serve only as a temporary structure.

The new premises were dedicated by Bishop Grierson on 8th October 1927. After welcoming the Bishop to the service (he had 'taken a real and factual interest in our hall') and the Rev H.R. Brett ('former rector of our parish … he will always be welcome'), Dr Breene expressed his 'great happiness to see this work completed'. He also thanked those members of his congregation who had been directly involved in bringing the project to fruition, and complimented the architect and the builders who

> have done all that could be done to give effect to the wishes of the building committee … [It is] just what we wanted in this parish', he added. He then spoke movingly and directly about how he envisaged the new accommodation being utilised. He said: 'We intend to use the Hall for the purposes of feeding the Church, of drawing our parishioners more closely together, of providing accommodation for our junior organizations – guides, scouts … [the 11th Belfast Company of Girl Guides and 57th Belfast Boy Scout Troop provided a Guard of Honour at the ceremony], and of developing our Sunday School work. I hope that our parishioners will regard their Parochial Hall as their own, and that they will literally make themselves at home in it. I pray that God's richest blessing may rest upon everything that is said and done within these walls and upon all who, in any capacity, work for the extension of His Kingdom in the shadow of this roof.

In conclusion, he indicated that, as a result of the construction costs incurred, the church now had debts 'in the neighbourhood of £1,800', and stated – with justification – that he was 'sure the parishioners of St Peter's will soon wipe it out'. Major G. Ewart, acting as spokesperson for the Churchwardens, then asked the Bishop 'on behalf of the clergy, churchwardens, and select vestry … to dedicate this Hall to the glory of God, for the purposes which it is intended to serve'.

As the congregation of St Peter's continued to grow – to over 300 families by the early 1930s, it was inevitable that its next clear objective should be to at last finish the construction of the church itself in the manner envisioned by its founders in 1900. But immense practical difficulties stood in the way. To complete it, including the lower part of the tower – a tower had been included in its original plans – a sum of £10,000 would be required. But in 1931 Church Extension (the central body responsible for encouraging the physical expansion of the Church of Ireland) could provide only limited financial support; it was prepared to make a conditional contribution of just £2,000. This was due to the extent of its other innumerable commitments, at a time when the City's industrial economy was in the grip of the Great Depression; of its thirty-seven parishes, only five were without pressing financial problems. Some of the newer and poorer ones had built up substantial debts, and their need was thought to be greater than St Peter's. There were a number with churches still uncompleted – such as St Columba's and St Simon's. Considerably more were in need of parochial halls – seventeen were required in Belfast as a whole. But, to many church members, the greatest priority was to make spiritual provision for the City's rapidly expanding suburbs – Cregagh, Finaghy, Stranmillis, etc.

In addition, St Peter's itself still had debts outstanding from the costs incurred in constructing its hall, and was still without a rectory. Moreover, the nature of the parish itself had evolved since its foundation, reflecting post war trends in the social composition of North Belfast. A Church Commission report, produced in 1931, noted that 'the district [St Peter's] has changed. From the Church standpoint it is stronger, and it is weaker. It is stronger in that the population has increased, and, in the long run, that is the thing of importance; it is weaker in that there are now very few people of means'. Also, though the parish had indeed grown, it was by no means one of the bigger ones – even within North Belfast. St Peter's had at the time a 'church population' of about 2,000, but St Matthew's had 10,000, and St Mary's, 12,000.

The option finally adopted by the parishioners of St Peter's was to finish the construction of the church, including: the extension of the nave by two bays (which enabled the new building to seat a congregation of 450–500); a respond (required to support the arch); porches; a baptistry, and the completion of the west front. But it was decided to abandon plans for the building of a tower. As a result of this decision, total costs were reduced to about £8,000. According to a General Synod Report, the Church Commissioners (the Representative Church Body) provided £2,000 of this in 1933, and the diocese a further £2,000. The remaining £4,000 had to be made up from parochial contributions. One not insignificant, if improbable, source for this portion was the Font and Baptistry Fund. It had been initiated – with considerable foresight – soon after the first section of the Church had been built in 1900, comprising the subscriptions made by parents after each christening (by 1908, it already totalled almost £150). In addition, in 1901, Rev S. Baring-Gould had sent the then Rector, Rev Brett, an autographed copy of his well-known hymn, 'Now the day is over', indicating that it was to be sold and the proceeds placed in the Fund (it realised £5). Gradually, its value had accumulated. Thus, in 1933, some £600 of the cost of the Church's new baptistry and font (£1,000 in total) was contributed from this one source. By 1934, the level of the debt owed by St Peter's had already fallen to £1,000 (the Parochial Hall had by then been paid off). No doubt the parishioners were more willing to make the sacrifices required as they watched (in the words of a Church Commission's report in 1934) their 'really noble parish church' emerge.

It was highly appropriate that R. Mills Close should have been given the commission to design the extension. He was the son of Samuel Close who had been responsible for the first section of St Peter's in 1900, and he himself had immense experience. He had worked on St Anne's Cathedral, 1922–24; was the architect of St Simon's, Donegall Road, in the 1920s; of St Columba's, Knock, completed by 1931; and in the late 1940s was to provide the plans for the rebuilding of St James's, Antrim Road, after it had sustained bomb damage during a German air-raid. The builders were Messrs J and R Thompson (who donated the floor of the south porch). The extension to St Peter's had almost been finished by mid 1932; a stone in the wall at the west end of the Church is inscribed: 'To the Glory of God and to Commemorate the Completion of the Western End of St Peter's Church This Stone was laid by Mrs Herbert Ewart on Saint Peter's Day, 1932'. The preacher at the ceremony was Very Rev Herbert B. Kennedy, the Dean of Christ Church Cathedral, Dublin. Exactly twelve months later, on St Peter's Day, Thursday 29th June 1933, the completed church was consecrated by Bishop Grierson. Up to, and including that day, it was the tenth place of worship which he had consecrated in Belfast during the period beginning 24th May 1930 – a remarkable record and a dramatic illustration of the speed with which the Church was continuing to grow within the city. The preacher was the Most Rev C.F. D'Arcy, Primate of All Ireland (1920–38) and a former Bishop of the diocese. According to the Preachers' Book, the congregation numbered 725, probably the largest in the history of the church, and an offertory of £336 was collected – further evidence, despite the Church Commission's observations, of its continuing affluence. On this most auspicious of occasions, the choir of St Peter's was robed for the first time.

The Church had begun at last to justify fully William J. Livingstone's description of it in 1907 – as being a 'slice of a cathedral'. His sentiments were echoed by the

Painting of the façade and south side of St Peter's Church, executed shortly after the extension of the nave had been completed in mid 1933.

Belfast News Letter in a report dated 29th June 1933. It stated:

> 'When St Peter's Church was designed, about 35 years ago, it promised to be one of the most beautiful in Belfast. The completed building … shows that promise fulfilled. St Peter's has the dignity and spaciousness and perfection of detail that ought to be found in a daughter church of St Anne's Cathedral … To see [it] … on a quiet afternoon, with the sun making lights and shadows on old stone and new stone and old oak and new oak, is to receive an impression of growth, to feel a sense of maturity, an atmosphere of effort and sacrifice and achievement that a building wholly new cannot have … The general effect of the whole building is of unity, variety, and restraint … There is nothing second-rate in conception or execution. When St Peter's was first planned, in more prosperous days, a large and beautiful church was visualised, and those who have completed the building have kept this ideal uppermost in their minds'.

On the following Sunday, 2nd July 1933, Holy Communion was celebrated in the completed church for the first time. Bishop Grierson was the celebrant, and the preacher was Rt Rev J.F. MacNeice, Bishop of Cashel, Waterford and Lismore (1931–34), a former Archdeacon of Connor, and father of the famous Ulster poet, Louis MacNeice. In his sermon, he reflected on the early history of St Peter's. He referred to the 'venture of faith' which had been embarked on almost forty years before – by those who had 'felt that the district should have a church'. He continued:

> they resisted the temptation to take short views, or to build cheaply. They knew well that a church, such as they contemplated, could not be completed just then, but they felt that their successors could be trusted to approve of a design which had in it the promise of spaciousness and beauty. The portion of the church built by them was sufficient for the needs of the district for almost a generation. You have had the crowning joy of consummating what was begun by them in faith. While their fine conceptions made possible your achievement ...

He added,

> it is also true that apart from your sacrifices and exertions their work could not have been perfected ... You, well led by your Rector, have had the great joy of finishing the nave of a very beautiful church.

But Bishop MacNeice concluded with a warning that 'the Church's battle has [not] been won. The times are critical.' By way of illustration, he cited the suppression of the church in Stalinist Russia, and noted that in Hitler's Germany 'surrenders [were being] demanded which loyalty to Christ would forbid His followers to make'. In his final remarks, he expressed his deep personal commitment to, and pride in, the Church of Ireland, stating that

> of all the institutions in Ireland ... [it] is the most Irish. She, holding the Catholic and Apostolic faith in its fullness and purity, and being in communion with other Churches all over the world who hold the same faith, is yet not subject to any. She recognises no authority beyond the shores of Ireland, and no Head but Christ.

There was much cause for celebration in the Byford family on the following Sunday, 9th July 1933. The first wedding to be solemnised in the completed church took place then, when John Nelson Hamilton, an 'agent', married Muriel Lucile Byford. That same day the first baptism in the new baptistry also occurred – of Neville Griffith, the son of Frederick John Byford, a 'district manager', and his wife, Dorothy Elizabeth.

IV
St Peter's Church:
From 1933 to the Retirement of
Very Reverend R.S. Breene, October 1963

The range and quality of the donations and bequests to St Peter's throughout its early history provide eloquent testimony to the generosity of its congregation, and was a reflection of its continuing growth and the affluence of its membership. Though the attractions of the Malone area were increasingly drawing the wealthy middle class away from North Belfast, St Peter's still retained amongst its parishioners some of the city's leading commercial, industrial and professional families. The Kinahans and Ewarts sustained their intimate connection with the Church. Both Sir James H. Norritt, LLD, JP, FCIS, and Frederic T. Lloyd-Dodd, DSc, were churchwardens, members of the Select Vestry and Diocesan Synodsmen. Noritt became Deputy Lord Mayor of Belfast in 1950 and was Mayor, 1951–51 (another parishioner, the 9th Earl of Shaftesbury, had held this office in 1907). Lloyd-Dodd was a university professor and a Unionist MP at Stormont from 1949. Henry Johns was also a Diocesan Synodsman and Parochial Nominator in the early 1920s. He was a solicitor, a JP, and a Director (and later Chairman) of the Belfast Banking Company; he marked the death of his sister, Maria, by providing for the carving of the Pillar of Agriculture in St Anne's Cathedral.

It was the first of that church's pillars to be carved, and it was designed by Peter Macgregor Chalmers and carved by Morris Harding (who was responsible for the font in St Peter's baptistry, and reredos in the side chapel). Other Church Officers included Sir Arthur Scott Queckett, the highly esteemed Parliamentary Draftsman for the Northern Ireland government from its foundation; he had, for example, drawn up the final draft of Lord Londonderry's Education Bill in January 1923. In addition, from that year, the Bishop's House for the Diocese of Connor had been located on the Antrim Road (at Number 603, virtually opposite the site of Skegoneill School; the gates of the 'See House', or 'Bishop's House', still survive). As a consequence Bishop Grierson had resided in the parish and was a parishioner at St Peter's throughout his Episcopate, as was a successor – Bishop Charles King Irwin.

The completion of St Peter's in 1933 provided an additional stimulus to this pattern of lavish expenditure; it provided new opportunities, and reinforced the impulse, to adorn and beautify the building still further. Between 1933–1950, no fewer than six new memorial windows were added to the Church (on 13th May and 29th June 1934 respectively, the Pearson Window in the north wall of the baptistry, and the Berwick Window in its west wall; on 29th June 1935, the Brett Window in the west wall of the south porch; in 1944, the Megaw Window on the north side of the west door, dedicated on 19th October, and the Taylor Window in the west wall of the baptistry, dedicated on 17th December; finally, in 1950, the Handworth Window between the baptistry and the west door; see full details in Chapter VII).

During these years there was also a succession of modifications and refinements to the fabric of St Peter's, which facilitated and enhanced worship, as well as adding to the church's beauty and its comfort. The donors were varied – mainly parishioners, clergymen and their families, and Church organisations (such as the Mothers' Union and Guides); in his *Jubilee* history, Dr Breene also includes an anonymous benefactor, whom he refers to as a 'Presbyterian friend'. The names of some are evident from a close reading of the tablets and plaques on the Church's walls and furnishings. Thus, a small plain tablet on the west wall reads: 'The Original Electric Light Installation of St Peter's was presented by the Misses Taylor, Ardeen, in Memory of their Brother Edward. It was modernised and extended by them at the Completion of the Church in Memory of his Wife Janie'. The outside doors in the south and west porches have an inscription on the back: 'In loving memory of a devoted mother. St Peter's Day, 1933'; they were the gift of Mrs Gerald Ewart in memory of her mother, Mrs Collins.

The conduct of divine worship was further facilitated by the furnishing of the south transept as a side chapel – it was dedicated by Bishop Grierson on 29th June 1935. Two years later, on St Peter's Day 1937, the Bishop dedicated the Brett Memorial Communion Table there, and the Ellen and Mary Ferguson Memorial Reredos in the south transept. These timely additions enabled weekday services to be held more conveniently and effectively (Holy Communion was first celebrated in the side chapel on 30th June 1937). On 19th April 1935, new carved, oak, centre choir stalls (on both sides of the aisle) were dedicated; they were the gift of Annie and Clara Taylor (some years earlier, Susan Spiller had funded the erection of the front choir stalls). According to Dr Breene's account, they made it possible to bring boys back into the choir – they had made up a significant proportion of its membership during the earliest days of the Parish. Perhaps as an additional inducement for them to join, it was also decided to allocate the moneys being accumulated in the Baptistry and Font Fund to the provision of a bursary or scholarship at some future date for the education of a choirboy. In addition, the Preachers' Book records that on 16th May 1936 the Church's choirboys were each given two shillings and sixpence by Lady Queckett and Mrs Hugh Pearson – in celebration of the coronation of George VI (on 12th May).

The Ewart family were undoubtedly amongst the most generous benefactors of the Church throughout the years preceding its Jubilee. Its members gifted commodious and comfortable choir vestries which were located in the Crypt, and amongst other items – altar linen cloths (for many years the family also laundered these); a carved and gilded oak Aumbry door; sanctuary mosaics; pulpit stairs; a chancel railing; a carved oak lectern; an alms dish; the west screen; and a massive oak vestry wardrobe. Other notable gifts to St Peter's included a pulpit donated by C.J. Kinahan; a Bishop's Chair by the Robinson family; a Bishop's Desk by J. McDonald;

and a lectern by A.C. Capper and the Misses McFerran. In addition, members of the congregation provided vases, collection plates, a stand for the Colours, steps for the chancel, hymn boards, books, veils, and a wide range of monetary gifts and legacies. Given the huge number of donors, it would be impossible to provide a full list.

Several other developments of profound significance in the history of St Peter's occurred during the years immediately preceding the outbreak of the Second World War. At last, in 1937, a rectory was purchased by the Parish (number 697 Antrim Road) under a scheme of annual payments, which extended over thirty years and was arranged with the Representative Church Body. In mid 1938 the Chapel of the Resurrection was presented to the Church of Ireland – in effect, to St Peter's – by its owner, the 9th Earl of Shaftesbury. The 9th Earl also contributed to a fund (along with the Bishop of Connor, Rt Rev J.F. McNeice, and others), the purpose of which was to cover the costs of some urgently needed renovation and decoration work to the building. On Sunday 18th September 1938, the Bishop officiated at the first service to be held in it for many years.

Also in 1938, the Parochial District of St Katharine's was formed, within St Peter's Parish. At the Jubilee Service held in St Peter's in 1950, Archbishop J.A.F. Gregg, Primate of All Ireland, accurately described this development as 'an interesting sign of the growth of Belfast and of the corresponding growth of the Church of Ireland'. The Church had grown in North Belfast especially; a Church Commissioners' Report, produced in 1931, stated that the area comprised fifteen parishes and churches and two mission districts, cared for by 32 clergymen, and that it had a total 'church population' of 51,140. It was then larger than either South Belfast (with fourteen parishes and churches, 25 clergymen and 46,850 church people) or East Belfast (with nine parishes and churches, one mission district, 18 clergymen and 40,500 church people).

As a first step towards meeting the needs of St Katharine's parishioners, a Church Hall was constructed on the high ground above the Shore Road, at the corner of Dunlambert Park and Fortwillliam Park; this was the approach favoured by the Church authorities at the time when establishing a new parish. The building was dedicated by Bishop MacNeice on 3rd September 1938. Full Sunday and weekday services were initiated immediately, church officers appointed, the usual parochial organisations established, and successive Curates from St Peter's given the responsibility of running the new district (Rev G. Freeman, Rev R.P. McDermott, and Rev R.W.T.H. Kilpatrick). An altar and a magnificent lectern of carved and gilded oak, which had been first used at the Chapel of the Resurrection immediately after it was consecrated, were transferred to the new premises. That the congregation there thrived is suggested by the fact that on 1st January 1944 the Parochial District of St Katharine's was separated from St Peter's, and became a fully independent parochial unit – a daughter church. But, as Dr Breene noted in 1950, 'the war and post-war conditions … made the task of those who are handling its affairs one of very great difficulty' – in particular, the bomb damage caused by enemy aircraft, and the displacement of population due to mass evacuation. Eventually the construction of St Katharine's Church was completed. It was consecrated on 24th November 1956, and the Rev T.E. Beacom, who had been Curate-in-charge from 1st January 1944, was instituted as Rector in 1958, and remained until his retirement in 1982. The church was one of a number erected in Belfast at that time (others were located in Ardoyne, Upper Malone, Highfield, Whitewell, etc.) with funds raised from the parishes directly concerned, support from the diocese, and loans provided by the central Church authority (i.e. the Representative Church Body).

Inevitably, the outbreak of the Second World War impinged heavily on St Peter's Parish as well. On Wednesday, 6th September 1939, prayers of 'intercession' were held in the church and, on 23rd March 1941, the congregation participated in a 'National Day of Prayer'. During the months immediately following, Belfast sustained four enemy air assaults lasting ten hours in total. The most severe were on the nights of 15–16th April (Easter Tuesday) and 4–5th May 1941; at the time both were referred to by Dr Breene as 'heavy raids' in his entries in the Preachers' Book. Up to 1,100 people died, and 56,000 houses were damaged (one half of the city's total stock). These successive Luftwaffe attacks were followed by a 'crash evacuation' by its civilian population who feared further onslaughts; by late May, one government official estimated that as many as 220,000 had left temporarily, and had scattered throughout Ulster and beyond. Meanwhile thousands of others 'ditched' during the hours of darkness; they left their densely packed and vulnerable houses and streamed along the main arterial roads to the suburbs, to shelter in parks, ditches and hedgerows until first light, when they thought it safe to return home.

With the exception of East Belfast, North Belfast suffered more from wartime destruction and disruption than any other part of the city. It was heavily and repeatedly bombed from the Antrim Road to Whitewell, causing death, destroying housing and businesses (incendiaries at York Street Flax Spinning Mill caused the biggest conflagration of the entire blitz), and dislocating transport (e.g. at the LMS Railway Station). St Peter's was near the heart of the maelstrom. As Dr Breene notes in his *Jubilee* history, the head quarters of the Royal Navy and Air Force in Northern Ireland were located inside the boundaries of the Parish for much of the war, and both the church and the new Parochial Hall were in increasingly frequent use by the Services as the number of forces' personnel based in the city rose (for example, the church's archives indicate that there were twenty-five 'military' services held in the Church, between 28th December 1940 and 22nd March 1941). He adds that 'very many of our parishioners who were not in the Forces were engaged for the duration in Civil Defence and other war duties'.

Though Dr Breene does not mention it in his *Jubilee* history, his own family led by example. He himself was appointed chaplain at Victoria Barracks, North Queen Street; back in uniform, he wore the same jacket as he had done in 1919. His wife volunteered for service as an Ambulance Driver. Their son, Arnold, who was then in his twenties and in the Territorials, was called up in September 1939 – on the day of his parents' wedding anniversary. He was posted to the gun emplacement at Greypoint, near Marino. His sister, Molly, later recalled that 'this was directly opposite the village of Kilroot, Co. Antrim, where there was another garrison also staffed by the Territorials. They formed the protection against unauthorised ships entering Belfast Lough. If a ship entered the Lough without giving the correct signal, the Territorials would open fire'. Meanwhile, Molly herself joined the WRNS. At the beginning of the war, the Headquarters of the Flag Officer Commanding, Royal Navy (who was in control of shipping), was at the Customs House, in the city centre. But after severe bomb damage in this area during the April–May blitz, it was evacuated to Belfast Castle, 1941–46, where the ballroom was converted into a signal office. Many years later, Molly recalled:

> It was very convenient for me to just walk up to the Castle [from the rectory] to go on watch, and I slept two or three nights a week up there … It was nice to get signals from the Coastguards saying "HMS …" entering the Lough and look out of the window to see them sailing up.

Molly also had clear recollections of the blitz; she wrote:

> we all spent a few nights under the stairs (which had been reinforced) at the Rectory. We had a few rocks through the ceiling of my father's study, but nothing too serious … I always remember when the sirens went and I was at home, my father took off to the church to keep an eye on things and we didn't see him till the "all clear". The rest of us waited till things got a bit noisy, and then I got my cocker spaniel puppy (a 21st birthday present), wrapped him in a rug and joined the others under the stairs. The Sexton, George Morrow and his wife, always joined us on such occasions [he had been sexton at St Peter's since 1920]. They used to live at the gate lodge of Fortwilliam Park. I expect they came up by tram and felt safer with us all at the Rectory'. She adds – correctly – that there was 'no damage to the church as far as I can recall.

Other churches nearby were less fortunate however; St Peter's Parish records state that; 'St James's parishioners [were] present' at the Sunday services on 20th April 1941, 'the parish church [on the Antrim Road] having been destroyed in the raid of the 15th' (only the church's steeple remained standing). The others totally devastated within the neighbourhood included Holy Trinity, Clifton Street; St Barnabas's, Duncairn Gardens; and St Silas's, then on the Oldpark Road. There was also bomb damage to the Chapel of the Resurrection; St Katharine's church hall; and St Paul's, York Road. Elsewhere in the city, St Aidan's, Blythe Street; St Luke's, Northumberland Street; and St Mary's, Crumlin Road, were amongst those extensively damaged.

As in the First World War, there was no conscription in any part of Ireland during the Second World War. However, 38,000 men and women from Northern Ireland volunteered for military service; some 5,000 were killed in action. The experience of 1914–18, when huge casualty levels were sustained at the Somme, was not repeated; during 1939–45, the death toll was more evenly spread over the course of the conflict. After virtually every major military engagement, names appeared in the obituary columns of the local newspapers. The final Roll of Honour for St Peter's Parish contains the names of 183 young men and women who volunteered for one or other of our fighting services, and also one who joined the United States Army (see Appendix I). It would appear that there was not a significant theatre of war in the entire conflict in which some member of the congregation was not involved.

Eighteen made the supreme sacrifice. Amongst the decorations awarded to parishioners by His Majesty King George VI, were the DFC; AFC; MBE; MC; and MM In addition, thirty-one enlisted from St Katharine's District during the conflict, two of whom were killed in action.

The names of those parishioners from St Peter's Parish who made the 'supreme sacrifice' in the Second World War are recorded on the commemorative plaque located on the north wall of the north transept. They are:

LINDSAY ARMSTRONG, RAF
ROBERT MICHAEL GODFREY CLARKE, RAF, missing
ROSEMARY ELIZABETH COX, RAF
IVOR DAVID CROZIER, Army
JOHN DERMOT CAMPBELL
ROBERT GRATTAN GURNEY GRIFFEN, RAF
CLAUDE LOWRY HANDFORTH, Army, missing, prisoner-of-war
WILLIAM CHARLES HENDERSON, RAF
PAUL TREVOR KINGSTON, RAF
THOMAS DUNWOODY MAYNE, RAF
GEORGE ALBERT MCGARVEY, RAF, missing
HUBERT FRANK OVER, RAF, missing
JACK DONNELLY PRINGLE, RAF
DERRICK EDWARD REAY, RAF
GEOFFREY NORMAN REAY, RAF
WILLIAM ARTHUR ROBINSON, RAF, missing
ARTHUR NORMAN TAYLOR, RAF, missing
JOHN JOHNSTON WAITE, Army, Major, killed at Tobruk

The names of those from St Katharine's District who made the supreme sacrifice were (the roll of the names of parishioners in St Katharine's District were included in St Peter's Roll of Honour up to the end of the year 1942, after which St Katharine's Roll was compiled independently):

GEORGE FURNEY, Army, killed in action
JAMES GREEN, RAF, killed on service

The intensity of the emotions experienced after Germany's defeat is evident from the text of the 'Thanksgiving for Victory' Order of Service, which was held in St Peter's at 8.00pm on 'VE Day', Tuesday 8th May 1945; three hundred and twenty parishioners were present, including uniformed contingents from the Red Cross and the St John's Ambulance Society. The introductory 'Bidding' forcefully expressed a deep gratitude to God for victory, a keen remembrance of the immense sacrifices that had been made, and a fervent hope for the future. It read:

> Brethren, we are met together on this day to pour out our hearts in fervent thanksgiving to the God and Father of us all, and to dedicate ourselves afresh to the service of His kingdom. We desire to thank Him for deliverance from the hand of our enemies; for the devotion, even to death of those who for the five years past have stood between us and slavery; and for the hopes of a better world for all His people. I bid you, therefore, lift up your hearts that you

may tell the praises of our God, and pray that His wisdom may lead us and
His Spirit strengthen us in the days that are to come.

During the prayers, the Rector led the congregation in giving thanks

> for the trust and cooperation between the allied nations, for the mighty help
> of Russia and the United States of America, [and] for the wholehearted loyal-
> ty of the Dominions and Colonies.

His words also fully acknowledged the dark shadow still being cast by the persistence of war in the Japanese theatre, when he declaimed:

> O Lord, God and Father of us all, we commend to Thy almighty keeping our
> kinsfolk and our allies in the Far East, who still bear the suffering and bitter
> pain of war. We ... pray thee to crown their endeavours with final victory.

On Sunday afternoon, 20th November 1949, a 'British Legion Service of
Dedication of the Standard of the Cavehill Branch' was held in the Church. As had
happened after the 'Great War', the parishioners in St Peter's again felt it appropriate permanently to commemorate the shared experience and sacrifice of the Second
World War. Initially, after it had ended, priority was given to the renovation and
repair of parish property (the cleaning of the church, reconditioning of the organ,
decoration of the Parochial Hall) as essential maintenance had necessarily been neglected during the period of the conflict. It was not therefore until February 1951,
that the Select Vestry first considered what sort of memorial would be most appropriate. At first, some members favoured the construction of a new hall but, by June
'51, they had decided on the erection of a commemorative window in the north
transept, to balance that unveiled in the south transept after the First World War,
but only if it was evident that the congregation would be willing to raise the approximately £2,000 required. This proposal was subsequently debated at two meetings
of parishioners, held on 5th February and 29th May 1952, and from these it was
immediately evident that sufficient funds could be raised. The Select Vestry then
invited the leading competing firms to submit designs for this commission and, in
due course, it opted for that submitted by the highly reputable, London based studios of Messrs W.M. Morris; the firm had an office in Belfast. At 2.30pm on
Remembrance Day 1955 (celebrated on Sunday, 5th November), the new 'War
Memorial Window' to 'those who fell and those who served' was unveiled by Mrs
Margretta Elizabeth Reay, JP, and dedicated by Rt Rev Charles King Irwin, Bishop
of Connor. The sermon was preached by Rev B.D.M. Price, Chaplain to the Forces,
and Deputy-Assistant-Chaplain-General, Northern Ireland District.

The essential theme of the Memorial Window is of Christ's victory over death,
made manifest by His triumphant ascent from the tomb. This directly inspired the
words written by Dr Breene in the Order of Service for the dedication; these highlighted how the message of the New Testament had triumphed over the travails and
devastation of war. He wrote:

> Our thoughts naturally turn back lovingly and gratefully to our people, some
> now beyond the veil, who joined the fighting services, the principal temporal

instruments of victory in the struggle that we commemorate. The symbols, however, point too to a loftier plain, reminding us of the Victory, which is also our Victory, of Him who is crowned with many crowns. They lead us finally to the contemplation of the glorious truth that Prevailing Divine Love over-rules all our designs and destinies, and lives and reigns, eternally at the heart of existence. They lead us, in fact, to the Doctrine of the Trinity, which is simply stated in St John's words, "God is Love". Love, at the last, is over all. "*Amor vincit omnia*". To God, so revealed to us in Jesus Christ, we lift our hearts in penitence, in prayer, in hope of healing, in gratitude, in praise, on this our day of Remembrance and Thanksgiving. We say, as we set up our Memorial, "Glory be to the Father, and to the Son, and to the Holy Ghost".

The opening words of the Anthem chosen by the choir reiterated these sentiments:

> 'Give us the wings of faith to rise
> Within the vale and see
> The saints above, how great their joys
> How bright their glories be.
> We ask them whence their victory came;
> They, with united breath,
> Ascribe their conquest to the Lamb.
> Their triumph to His death'.

There is much to suggest that, despite the loss of life and the destruction of war, and the hardships and austerity of the post war years, St Peter's retained its energy and dynamism. Thus, when in 1948 the church was fitted with a new electric, under floor heating installation costing £1,400, the debt incurred had been repaid in full by late 1949. Moreover, in 1950, Dr Breene was able to draw up an impressive list of groups and societies attached to the Parish:

> a flourishing branch of the Mothers' Union [it had been founded in 1910, and its banner had been designed by the mother of one of the curates, Rev J.R.B. McDonald]; ... for many years, latterly ... a strong Young Wives Group; ... it has always had a Literary or Men's Society; ... a Dramatic Society that, over a long period, has presented to appreciative audiences, winter by winter, an interesting series of excellently produced plays by George Shiels, Ruddick Millar [and others]; ... [and] two Badminton Clubs, Senior and Junior. The former, founded in 1927, has a long list of League successes to its credit, and has won many cups and trophies.

Mention might also have been made of St Peter's youth organisations – the Youth Guild, Brownies, 11th Belfast Company of Girl Guides, Rovers, Wolf Cubs, 57th Belfast Boy Scout Troop. Contemporary parishioners recall upwards of a hundred attending Senior Sunday School, with as many as 75 in the Kindergarten. The Select Vestry minutes record that, in September 1953, it was necessary to transport additional chairs to St Peter's from the Chapel of the Resurrection, as there were insufficient numbers in the church to cater for the size of the congregation. In addition, the church choir retained its enviable reputation and tradition, and its youth section had recently been revived; the choir had first worn robes in 1933, and these were replaced in May 1953.

Throughout these years its musical renditions were frequently broadcast on the BBC.

Throughout its history the major events in the life of the nation have been marked in the worship of St Peter's. On 26th January 1936, a Memorial Service was held for George V; on the previous day, Dr Breene noted in the Preachers' Book that he had 'prayed for King Edward VIII for the first time. God save the King'. On Sunday 10th February 1952, a Memorial Service was held for King George VI, and Accession Prayers were said for Her Gracious Majesty, Queen Elizabeth II; a full congregation were present. Almost exactly one year later, on 1st February 1953, a Memorial Service was held to mark the sinking of the 'Princess Victoria' (on the afternoon of 31st January 1953, the British Railways, roll on-roll off ferry, travelling from Stranraer to Larne, sank in gales off the coast of Donaghadee, with the loss of over 130 passengers and crew).

St Peter's Brownies posing outside the Parochial Hall in 1943. The group includes: Rosemary Playford (Tawny Owl); Cicely Pollitt; Pat Lee; Margaret Dunlop; Betty Rogers and Maureen Pearson.

Notable dates in the life of the Church itself have also been suitably acknowledged. On Sunday, 3rd November 1946, St Peter's parishioners celebrated the fiftieth anniversary of the congregation's first service (held in Skegoneill National School on 1st November 1896). But it was not until 1950 that the church officially marked its Golden Jubilee. The highlight of the year was the Golden Jubilee Service held on St Peter's Day, 25th June, and conducted by Dr Breene, assisted by Rev T.G. McAlister, curate of the Church since 1945. The preacher was Most Rev Dr J.A.F. Gregg, Archbishop of Armagh and Primate of All Ireland (1939–59), who had served as Curate in the diocese, and was one of the Church's leading scholars. In his sermon, he reflected back on the various milestones in the history of the Parish over the preceding 'creative, formative fifty years' – the opening of the eastern section of the church in 1900; its enlargement and consecration in 1933. Overall, he stated that his deepest impression was of

the vitality of the people … What surer sign could be shown of liveliness than that a district like St Peter's should become a parish, and, in turn, give birth to a new district [St Katherine's] which itself speedily became a parish?

The Youth Leaders at St Peter's in *c.* 1950 [1950 Booklet, page 20] (Front Row, left to right): L.H. Roberts; Mrs Warnock; Rev T.H. McAlister; Rev Dr R.S. Breene; T.W. Gordon; Miss M. Hegan; Miss S.A. Jackson (Back Row, left to right): A. Sewell; Miss J.M. Rogers; E.T. Ward; Miss M. Patterson; A. Donaldson; Miss I. Warnock; B.W. Boyd

The fact that St Peter's choir, assisted by the Youth Guild Choir, led the praise, and that the offertory was for the organ renovation fund, served to underline the veracity of these observations. Moreover, the service was attended by the Rev J.R.B. McDonald, who had been ordained for the junior curacy in St Peter's on the Feast of St Philip and St James, 1941, and had since been working as a missionary in Uganda. Between 1900–50, a total of five men and one woman had gone from the Parish to serve as missionaries overseas – two to India, two to Western Canada and two to East Africa (see Chapter VIII).

The 'vitality' of St Peter's persisted as it faced the challenges of the 1950s. The existing Parochial Hall, built in 1927 and regarded then as temporary, had become overstretched; the accommodation it afforded was no longer adequate to meet the needs of the thriving congregation – in particular the requirements of its expanding

St Peter's Cubs, *c.* 1960 [1960 Booklet, p 6]

St Peter's Junior Organisations, at Church parade, November 1948, outside the Parochial Hall. The photograph includes:
(*On steps with flags, left to right*): Jacqueline Patterson (with guide flag); Cicely Pollitt (with King's flag); Billy Neely (later a Church of Ireland clergyman); Lexie Fulton and David Hall.
(*In the larger group*): Maureen Patterson (Brown Owl); Florence Warnock (Guider); Dorothy Hall; Sally Bennett; Julie Bradford; Betty Rogers; Margaret Dunlop; Pixie Baker; Pat Wood; Maureen Pearson.
(*Amongst the boys*): Henry Ward; George Dobbs; David Pollitt; John Bennett and George Hall (twin brother of David Hall).

youth organisations – the scouts, Sunday School, etc. In November 1951, the Select Vestry considered purchasing one of the army surplus huts, then being sold off, and the following year agreed in principle to erect a hall. This difficulty was resolved, and the facilities of the church further enhanced, in June 1954 when a hall was purchased from Townsend Street Presbyterian Church at a cost of £225. Having been

St Peter's Scouts, *c.* 1960 [1960 Booklet, p6]

St Peter's Brownies, *c* .1960 [1960 Booklet, p5]

inspected and passed by the City Hall authorities, it was dismantled, transported to St Peter's, and then assembled, and named the 'Norritt Hall'. The driving force behind its construction had been the church's Scout Group Parents' Committee, which had been founded in 1947 on the suggestion of Sir James Norritt, the Group's second Scoutmaster and an extremely active church member. Its objective had been to raise funds in order to provide accommodation primarily for the use of the Baden-Powell organisations attached to St Peter's; it succeeded in raising £300 towards building costs. According to Dr Breene, who presided at the opening ceremony (held on Saturday 18th September 1954), in total, the hall cost £1,000, the remainder being provided from church funds. The service of dedication was con-

St Peter's Girl Guides, *c*. 1960 [1960 Booklet, p5]

St Peter's Church in 1960, viewed from the north-west [1960 Booklet, p3]]

ducted by the Bishop of Connor, Rt Rev Charles King Irwin, who said of the new building that it had become 'essential', and expressed the hope that it would 'encourage recruiting for all branches of the Group;' Some 150 of its members were present, and on parade, to mark the occasion.

Though most of the costs of construction were quickly paid off, there was still a small sum outstanding six years later. Because of this and other debts and expenses, the Select Vestry called in fund raising consultants from England in June 1958, and two years later agreed to accept, and act on, their recommendations. As a consequence, a new initiative was launched in the Parish in 1960 – 'a Campaign for planned giving'. At the time, the Church's financial requirement over the next three years was estimated at about £26,500. This sum was made up of £4,500 per annum for normal operating costs; in addition, £2,000 was urgently needed for essential maintenance and repairs, £1,000 to defray debts still outstanding, and £10,000 for proposed improvements to premises – specifically, the construction of a new vestry. Also, the Parish had a continuing obligation to support foreign missions, and to contribute towards the expenses of the diocese. The objective set therefore by the Select Vestry was to raise £30,000 over the next three years (1960–63), with £21,000 regarded as the 'first step' – it was referred to as 'the canvass target'.

The 'Campaign' entailed leading laymen from St Peter's calling with parishioners, and asking each to sign a pledge to give an agreed sum at regular intervals to the church (it was an approach which was being adopted elsewhere, and which has since become an integral part of the life of the Parish). It was introduced in order to generate a steady and assured income; at its conclusion every family who had given its consent was to 'receive a year's supply of weekly offering envelopes for the pledged amount' (these were referred to as 'covenant subscriptions'; a 'monthly envelope scheme' had been introduced much earlier – in 1929). When introducing the

The interior of St Peter's Crypt, *c.* 1960. It was then in an extremely dilapidated state, but was still used by the choir for robing; its members walked around to the west door of the Church before each service and made the same journey back afterwards whatever the weather [1960 Booklet, page 9]

scheme, Rt Rev R.C.H.G. Elliott, Bishop of Connor (1956–69), also highlighted its spiritual benefits. He stated that 'in every case where a congregation has had a Campaign … there has been a notable rise in the spiritual temperature … a genuine quickening of religious life'. He also suggested that 'the whole subject [of church giving] has tended to be treated in too haphazard a fashion'.

Likewise, Dr Breene described the initiative as 'a great adventure in Christian stewardship', and reminded parishioners of the motto of the founders of St Peter's: 'I will not offer unto the Lord that which costs me nothing'. But he regarded it as essential and unavoidable as well. Writing with complete candour, he stated:

> In the sixty years of our parochial existence we have never been able to keep pace with the calls that have been made upon us. It has been a continual struggle to make do on inadequate means.

In retrospect, it is tempting to regard the 'Campaign' also, at least in part, as an attempt by Dr Breene to ensure that the affairs of St Peter's had been placed on a secure footing – for his successor. If so, he was entirely successful; in March 1963, the fund raising scheme was described in the Select Vestry as having 'greatly improved church finances'.

But Dr Breene's final years as rector were also tinged with sadness. In October 1961, George Morrow retired as sexton 'after forty years of unfailing service to St Peter's'. Until her death in 1950, he had been ably assisted by his wife; in a fulsome tribute to her, written at the time, Dr Breene referred to her 'life of devoted personal service to St Peter's, the Chapel of the Resurrection, Skegoneill School (when a

Members of the congregation of St Peter's during a tour of the Holy Land in the late 1950s or early 1960s. The group includes:
Rt Rev Cyril Elliot, Bishop of Connor; Dr R.S. Breene, Rector of St Peter's; John Hesten; M.M. Hoggs; Janet Chamberlain; Helen Jordan;
Agnes Fordyce; Blanch Smith; G. Smith; Lily Smythe; H. Dinsmore; Dorothy Charnock; Nancy Ireland; Ivy Dick; E. Harris; Edward Hayes;
Ida Brown; David Monkton; Pauline Monkton; David Strong; Ellie Copeland; Kathleen Baird; N. Earls; Mell Stewart; G. Hall; E. Summers;
V. Shepherd; J. Shepherd; N. Francis; T. McDonald; Doreen Clipson; A. Clipson; Amy Dougall; E. Summers; Jo MacKellan; E.S. Bierhaugh
and Salim Dakleak

Parish institution) and our Parochial Hall'. When George himself died, in February 1962, the Rector described him as having been 'faithful and devoted.' In the summer of that year, the death also occurred of Henry Evelyn Wood (brother of the eminent composer, Chris Wood) in the most tragic of circumstances; he had been knocked down by a motorcar outside the church on a Sunday after Evensong – he was a tenor in the church choir. In the words of the 1962 Annual Report, he had 'served the parish with honour and distinction during his long life', and had been an 'honoured member of the Select Vestry'. When its members next met after the accident, on 6th September 1962, the minutes record that 'many spoke in very moving terms.' Just over a year later, in early 1964, Sir James Norritt – after whom St Peter's new hall had been named – also died.

Dr Breene officially retired on 7th November 1963, having conducted his final Sunday services in St Peter's as incumbent on 27th October 1963, and last celebrated Holy Communion there on the 30th. He was then 77 years of age, and had been Rector of the Parish for more than half of its existence. Not only was he much loved by his own congregation but also, in the words of a colleague, he was 'highly esteemed by his brother clergy' and, as a consequence, 'elected to practically every position of responsibility in the diocese' (see list in Chapter VIII). In addition, he had been from 1944 a valued member of the Faculty of Theology at Queen's University, Belfast. As for his other passions – the Masonic Order was what has been described as 'an absorbing interest in his life'; he was a 'foundation member of St Peter's Lodge'. In addition, he was a prolific writer; he served as editor of The *Irish Churchman* for fourteen years, and was Church of Ireland correspondent for the *Belfast News Letter*, contributing for over four decades the weekly *Viator* column, so exercising an impressive ministry through the printed word. At the time of the Golden Jubilee celebrations in 1950, he of course also wrote his *St Peter's Church Jubilee Book*, which the present author has found to be an invaluable source. One newspaper review at the time described it as being 'well produced', and 'out of the usual run of such publications in that it includes a comprehensive account of the history of the district'.

That it was a labour of love for Dr Breene is evident from the dedication inscribed on its title page; translated from the original Latin, it reads: 'Lord, I have loved the habitation of Thy house and the place where Thy honour dwelleth' (Psalm 26, verse 8). The book was characteristic of the man; it is a comprehensive record of half a century of church life, contains a wealth of information about the history and geology of North Belfast, and bears eloquent testimony to the skill and erudition of its author.

In addition, Dr Breene was an accomplished poet. In 1958 a collection of his poems, *Songs of the Nativity and Other Verses*, 1946–1958, was published in Belfast. Its thirty-six pages contained twenty-five poems, which he had brought together in book form in memory of his first wife, Louisa, who had died on 27th January 1957. Speaking to the Select Vestry, the then Curate Assistant at St Peter's, Rev E. Leeman, said of her that 'her passing has left us the poorer … She won our trust, our deep affection and our love … Her life has been … a benediction to us all [and] … an inspiration to all' (Dr Breene married a second time – Vera Elizabeth Capper, a widow, on 23rd September 1958, after a brief engagement). Most, if not all of the poems in this collection were first written for the Christmas cards which he had dispatched to his parishioners over previous years, and which encapsulated the Nativity story in poetic form. One, which began with the line 'O Bethlehem is a Small Place and very far away …' was included in the *Irish Church Hymnal*, Carol Number 13 (this collection was the staple of Church worship at the time, along with the *Book of Common Prayer*; it was revised in 1960). Dr Breene's impressive output was conducive to the fostering of creative talent within the members of the Parish's congregation. Derek Mahon, one of Ulster's finest and best-known poets, grew up off Salisbury Avenue during the 1940s–50s; he has been described by one academic as being a 'child of St Peter's'. Mahon himself spoke of the 'source of his own poems [as] being in the hymns that he first learnt in the St Peter's choir'. One of his earliest, perhaps his first, was actually printed on a card produced by the Parish during the 1950s, for use as a Christmas greeting.

The Very Rev Richard Simmons Breene, MA, LLD, Dean of Connor, died on 4th February 1974. Three days later, his funeral service took place in St Peter's, where he had served for thirty-seven of his fifty-one years as ordained priest. It was fitting that the address should have been given by Canon T.E. Beacom, the rector of its daughter church, St Katharine's (1958–82; he had been Curate-in-chief, 1944–58). In the course of his remarks to the 250-strong congregation present, the Canon stated that 'three buildings loomed large in [Dr Breene's] life. Firstly, St Peter's Church – he was tireless in his endeavours to embellish and enrich this holy house with carvings in wood and stone, and in stained glass. Secondly, Lisburn Cathedral – when he was appointed Dean [of Connor] in 1956 he carried out his various duties there with meticulous care and attention to detail. Thirdly, Queen's University, Belfast – he was one of its most illustrious Alumni. He was also an enthusiastic member of the Faculty of Theology'.

The Canon continued:

> we shall remember him [Dr Breene] firstly as a priest of the Church, to whom the services of the sanctuary were of paramount importance. He was scrupulous in liturgical matters, as any one of his curates would have told you ... For him the acme of public worship was the Sacrament of Holy Communion ... He initiated the liturgical mould for the daughter church of St Katherine's – a tradition we are endeavouring to maintain. Secondly, we shall remember him as a pastor. To some he may have seemed a rather remote and austere figure, but to those who knew him and to his parishioners in particular, he was a warm-hearted pastor. I quote some words he wrote in 1955 – "It is a great privilege to be a pastor – to have the cure of souls"... Thirdly, we shall remember him as a poet ... At heart, Dr Breene was a poet ... [His poems] ... display a rare simplicity and sensitivity to things spiritual ... R.S. Breene may be forgotten as priest, as pastor, but posterity will remember him as the poet ...

Canon Beacom concluded his remarks by saying of Dr Breene:

> it is impossible to contain such a remarkable character, such a scintillating conversationalist, such a brilliant raconteur within the compass of a short address. Suffice it to say his passing leaves the church and the community all the poorer ... It was beneath the reredos here, which depicts the empty tomb, that on so many occasions he celebrated the Holy Mysteries. Here he strove to remind his people that they were met together to worship a living Saviour ...

The Canon ended his eulogy by quoting from the last poem in *Songs of the Nativity*; it was entitled 'Nocturne'. This, he described as 'a fitting recessional to one whose friendship we enjoyed, whose memory we shall treasure. This poem is for us an insight into the life of a man who was literally out of this world.' He then read the following, moving extract:

> Most gracious Lord, receive my soul
> And if I die tonight
> Grant me to share that bright abode
> Of love and peace and light,
> Where evermore Thy saint's glad host
> Praise Father, Son and Holy Ghost.

The chancel rails of the present Church and an inscribed tablet nearby, both dedicated by Rt Rev A.H. Butler, the Bishop of the Diocese, on 22nd March 1981, remain as a permanent and appropriate memorial to his years of service to the congregation of St Peter's Parish.

V

St Peter's Church, 1963–2009:
From the 'Troubles' to the Institution of
Rev A.T.W. Dorrian as Rector

Rev William E. Harris was Dr Breene's successor at St Peter's. He was born in Cahir, Co. Tipperary, on 28th May 1921, the son of Ernest and Isabel Harris. Until the age of six, he was educated at the Church National School, located inside the gates of the Bishop's Palace, Cashel. He was then sent to board at Bishop Foy's School, Waterford, and became head choirboy for a time at Waterford Cathedral; he was musically gifted – an invaluable attribute throughout his vocation. He entered Trinity College Dublin in 1938, but his studies were interrupted when he enlisted in the Royal Air Force in 1941. He saw active wartime service in North Africa, Malta and Gibraltar; this military experience was to provide him with a rich vein of illustrative and anecdotal material which he was to use with craft and skill to illuminate his sermons. After being de-mobbed in 1946 he resumed his studies, graduating with a BA in 1948, and MA in 1957.

After being ordained Priest in 1949, he worked in several Belfast parishes (see Chapter VIII) including St Matthew's and St Thomas's, and the Church Mission in Ballymacarrett; in 1959, he became the Incumbent of Annahilt, Co. Down. On 2nd July 1954, he had married Margaret Jephson of Waterford, and by the time of his appointment to St Peter's in 1963, they had three sons – Brian, Patrick and Michael, aged between three and eight years. His two daughters were born whilst he was rector of the Parish – Clodagh in 1964, and Sheila in 1967 – and both were baptised in St Peter's.

Canon Harris was instituted as rector of the Church – only the third in its history – on Wednesday, 18th December 1963, by the Bishop of Connor, Rt. Rev R.C.H.G. Elliot. During the first section of the service, immediately after the Processional hymn, the Rector-Elect was 'presented' to the congregation; this was followed by the

Canon William E. Harris, Rector of St Peter's, 1963–1990, and Canon of St Patrick's Cathedral, 1982–1990

'Administration of the Declarations' by the Diocesan Registrar, the actual 'Institution' itself and the reading of the 'Charge'. The address was then delivered by Canon R.A. Deane, who had been ordained priest in 1915 and served as Rector of St Thomas's for over thirty years; he had himself retired in 1963. At the outset, he set out for those present, in the clearest possible terms, the purpose of his remarks as laid out in the liturgy of the Church of Ireland. It was, he said, 'to declare the duty and office of those instituted to the cure of souls, and how the people ought to esteem them in their office'. He continued:

> by this direction we understand that the objective of our sermon is more general than particular. It is meant to be a kind of omnibus discourse about the relationship between the pastor and the parish anywhere, at any time. It is not on the one hand a fitting opportunity to look over our shoulders and estimate how ably and happily Richard Simmons Breene laboured as your rector for 37 years, nor is it on the other hand an occasion for looking into a crystal globe and making prophecies about how William Ernest Harris and St Peter's parish are likely to flourish in the years to come.

The congregation of the church may well have found the tone of what Canon Deane proceeded to say surprisingly pessimistic and somewhat discomfiting. In hindsight, however, it was also arguably both timely and incisive. He declared that 'however optimistic we may be at this moment the future is ominous ...' He described the current 'age [as one] when a rampant materialistic philosophy is driving in the outposts of Christianity all over the world ... The future presents the terrifying prospect of a world that has liquidated God and substituted science as the Saviour of mankind ...' He elaborated on this theme by stating that

> the enemies of religion are ruthless. They use literature and art; they infiltrate the theatre, the cinema, the dance hall, the press. The church itself is not exempt from this onslaught of the materialist philosophy – the ugly gods of money and sensualism push their bloated faces into the most sacred places and corrupt even the boys and girls before they know what they are asking from life or what life is able to give them. Parochial work and witness will demand all the loyalty, all the energy and all the cooperation that clergy and laity can bring to bear upon the common problem.

Canon Deane's remarks were in fact reminiscent of those that had been made by Bishop J.F. MacNeice at the dedication service held after the completion of St Peter's Church in July 1933. On that occasion, the Bishop had noted that

> in the big centres of population in England and Scotland, the Church is not in effective possession; there is widespread indifference. There is much hostility. At a recent meeting of the [Presbyterian] General Assembly it was stated that thousands of Protestants in Belfast had no Church connection and were in danger of lapsing into irreligion.

Nonetheless – overall – the first sixty years in the history of St Peter's had been ones of sustained growth and of justifiable optimism. Thus, Dr Breene, in his *Jubilee* history published in 1950, had written: 'Of course, the population [of North

Belfast] has grown very considerably but, even taking that into account, it is evident that there has been no very noticeable decay of institutional religion amongst us in the last century and a half'. As evidence of this, he pointed out that soon after the opening of St Peter's in 1900, Seaview Presbyterian Church, the Catholic Chapel on the Somerton Road, and a small Evangelical Church had all been built within the vicinity St Peter's.

But, by comparison, the years that followed – from the 1960s – were fraught with much graver and more wide-ranging difficulties. In part those which confronted the Parish were, as Canon Deane inferred, universal to the Christian Church through-out the western world. McCourt's history of Connor diocese, written in the 1980s, noted:

> we live in a secularised and increasingly materialistic society … the economic
> pressures of life, and an awareness of new attitudes to questions of social need,
> all challenge traditional Christian belief.

One symptom of this was a fall in church attendance. A Quaker survey conduct-ed into Northern Ireland during 1959–62 found that weekly church attendance amongst Protestants had already fallen to 55%. Other contemporary studies cited figures of slightly below 50%; these stood in sharp contrast to an estimated 90% for the Catholic population – one of the highest levels in Europe. By the early 1990s, these percentages had fallen for both communities; for Protestants it was then roughly 40%, and for Catholics 85%, with the proportion amongst young adults significantly below the overall average.

But St Peter's was also afflicted by other problems, some of which were specific to Belfast – notably the fall in its population and the considerable movement of Church of Ireland parishioners out of the city, from the 1960s. One causal factor, highlighted by the history of Connor, was that 'with the end of the war there were immense schemes of house building all around Belfast'. It noted that these develop-ments had 'involved the Diocesan Council in not only the nurture of "new parish-es" but the continuing creation of more new area Churches and Church halls … The challenge … was to produce new places of worship for the new housing areas … The policy was to build dual-purpose church-halls' (by 1985, ten had been built in the suburbs of Belfast – at Highfield; Rathcoole; Cloughfern; Upper Malone; Kilmakee; Glengormley; Greenisland; Derryvolgie; Mossley; and Muckamore). As a result of loans provided by central Church bodies and money raised by local parishes and through appeals, a number of churches had also been erected in this period, includ-ing St Katharine's, Fortwilliam (where worship had hitherto been conducted in a church hall), and others in Ardoyne, Upper Malone, Derryvolgie, Highfield, Kilmakee and Whitewell. In addition, a number had been built jointly with the Methodist Church (for example, at Glencairn and Jordanstown).

The history of Connor concluded that by 1985

> the policy of erecting new places of worship in development areas has been by
> and large effective; there is a visible church presence in the great housing
> estates with buildings to meet the spiritual needs of our people.

But it stressed that

> no one was under any illusion that we were catering for a vast influx of new members of the Church of Ireland. It was a matter of redeployment of church buildings to meet the needs of a shifting population ... which might otherwise have been lost to the Church.

In fact census data suggests that Church of Ireland numbers in Northern Ireland peaked in 1951 at 353,245, rising from 338,724 in 1926. By 1961, the figure had dropped by almost 9,000 to 344,800 (in contrast, the number of Presbyterians had increased by 3,000 between 1951–61, Methodists by 5,000, and Catholics by 26,000).

Clearly, as the Diocesan History recounted, the movement of the Church's parishioners in Belfast was affected 'by economic changes ... the re-development of a vast urban area'. But, as it also stressed, there were other factors as well. Amongst these, it listed: 'political and social unrest ... political unrest and uncertainty ... violence and terrorism.' During 1968–9, the province lurched into the worst phase of violence in its history – the worst indeed in the modern history of Ireland. The litany of milestones which followed is etched into the minds of those who lived through these turbulent years: the formation of the Provisional IRA in late 1969; internment, 9th August 1971; 'Bloody Sunday', 30th January 1972; the fall of Stormont, 24th March 1972; the fall of the Sunningdale Executive, 14th May 1974; the Hunger Strike, begun on 1st March 1981; the Anglo-Irish Agreement, 15th November 1985 ... the Provisional IRA's ceasefire, 31st August 1994. During these twenty-five years, 3,172 people died as a result of the 'Troubles' in Northern Ireland (dwarfing the figure for the early 1920s), 119 in Britain, 100 in the Irish Republic, and 16 on the mainland of Europe. There were 35,000 shooting incidents, 20,000 explosions and malicious fires, and 19,000 armed robberies. By 1995 the British government had paid out £1,100 million in compensation for personal injury and damaged property.

Inevitably these events impacted on North Belfast, and on the life of the Church there. Reflecting back over preceding decades Rev Charles J. McCollum, rector from 1996 to 2008, stated during the St Peter's Centenary celebrations in 2000,

> the political developments of the 1970s and '80s in Northern Ireland encouraged considerable movement of population and notably affected the life of St Peter's ... The church suffered.

On the same occasion, Rt Rev James Moore, the Bishop of Connor, reiterated these sentiments. He said:

> St Peter's has been in place during the growth years of the Antrim Road district when it attracted large numbers of people and families to its services and parish activities. In recent years it has had to weather the storms of the "Troubles"... The movement of population during these difficult years has reduced the number of parishioners.

In 1986 the population trends current in Belfast at the time were analysed by

Charles Brett, who was then Chairman of the Housing Executive. He stated that

> there are three main mixed districts [in the city which are] still principally
> middle-class areas of owner-occupation: all three [were] formerly mostly
> Protestant – the Antrim Road, the Ormeau Road, and the Malone ridge
> (including Stranmillis, the University area, and the Holy Land). In each of
> these a discernible pattern has appeared over the past decade. Catholic fami-
> lies have by degrees moved in, and Protestant families have by degrees moved
> out. This process is a complex one. It reflects in the first instance the greater
> pressure of demand on the Catholic side since so many other formerly mixed
> areas became 'unsafe' [for them] in 1969–72. It reflects also the fear of
> Protestants, especially those serving in the security forces, that their new
> neighbours may include unidentifiable members of, or sympathisers with, the
> IRA. So gradually and usually without overt intimidation or fighting, streets
> in the mixed areas have been changing complexion: thus providing, on the
> one hand, a very welcome and much-needed safety-valve for the hard-pressed
> Catholic population; but on the other, a loss of traditional territory, viewed
> with dismay and apprehension by many Protestants, even quite moderate
> ones.

Throughout the 1970s and 1980s, many Protestants who had the means to do so, moved out of Belfast into the suburbs or into commuter towns, or retreated into their own heartland areas within the city. Thus when on 11th February 1976, Most Rev G.O. Simms, the Primate of Ireland, met the then Secretary of State for Northern Ireland, Merlyn Rees (March 1974–September 1976), as part of a delegation of church leaders to discuss the current 'Troubles', this was the main issue that he raised with him. He is reported as saying that 'he and his colleagues recognised that the security forces faced a formidable task, to which there was no real solution'. But he added that 'he wanted to be reassured that adequate steps were being taken to deal with the security situation in North Belfast'. And he suggested that 'greater flexibility and awareness on the part of the security forces was required [there] to stem the expulsion of Protestants' and others from their homes.

The congregation of St Peter's Church was dramatically affected by these population movements. A recent academic study conducted at Queen's University has shown that in 1968 the whole of the area adjacent to the Antrim Road, from north of Carlisle Circus to Gray's Lane, was then predominantly occupied by Protestants, or was 'mixed' – with significant numbers of both Protestants and Catholics. The only exceptions to this were a number of little streets clustered around the New Lodge Road, and a much smaller area, south of the Limestone Road and centred on Atlantic Avenue, both of which were almost exclusively occupied by Catholics. But, by 1988, profound changes had already taken place. A substantial section of North Belfast along the west side of the Antrim Road – bounded by the Old Cavehill Road in the north, Alliance Avenue in the west and the Crumlin Road in the south – had become predominantly Catholic. So also had the east side of the Antrim Road – the district stretching from Clifton Street in the south to Skegoneill Avenue in the north. The two neighbourhoods in the north of the city which had undergone the most far-reaching transformation in their denominational composition during this period were Cliftonville, and a large area around Chichester Park. In 1968, the populations of both had been mainly Protestant. But, by 1988 Catholics, migrating from Ardoyne, New Lodge, etc, formed the overwhelming majority of householders in each.

Skegoneill Primary School was one of the first 'casualties' of these population trends. Following its transfer by the Church of Ireland to Belfast Education Committee in 1923 its numbers had grown slowly but steadily. So much so that on 4th May 1962, new school buildings were opened in Chichester Avenue (a little more than one hundred yards from its original site on the Old Cavehill Road) to cater for an anticipated enrolment of five hundred and sixty pupils. Dr Breene attended the formal opening ceremony, which was performed by Sir Francis Evans, the Ulster Agent in London, who had attended the school some fifty-five years earlier.

During the years immediately following, the decision to move to new premises appeared to have been fully justified; in the mid 1960s, over five hundred children were on its registers, and there were sixteen full-time members of staff. However, thereafter pupil numbers plummeted almost continually; in mid 1980, the Select Vestry at St Peter's discussed the speculation then current that it would close. By early 1988 it had just sixty-three children on its rolls (this was the lowest enrolment in its history – it had been over 80 in 1896–7, its foundation year); 20% of them were Catholic (a proportion which it was predicted would rise to 50% by the following September); and they were tended by two teachers. As a consequence, the Belfast Education and Library Board decided that the school was no longer viable, the Northern Ireland Office rejected parental pleas that it be granted 'integrated status', and its closure was announced on 31st May 1988. Four weeks later – on 29th June, it had its last roll call. At the time, the *Belfast Telegraph* commented that 'dramatic demographic changes in North Belfast were largely to blame'; the newspaper's report then proceeded to list some of its more illustrious former pupils – including Raymond Piper, the noted local artist; John Cole, the son of an electrician, who after eleven years at the *Belfast Telegraph*, became Deputy Editor of the *London Observer*, and later Political Editor at the BBC; and two former Unionist cabinet ministers at Stormont, Herbert Kirk and William Fitzsimmons.

The problem of falling numbers of parishioners experienced by the Church of Ireland in North Belfast was accentuated by decisions that had been taken by the church authorities in the aftermath of the Second World War. The *History of Connor* states:

> With the ending of the War the immediate task facing the Diocese ... was the rebuilding and repair of churches which had been destroyed or damaged in the German air raids of 1941.

It lists those that had been extensively damaged and then been fully restored: St Paul's, York Road; St Aidan's, Blythe Street; St Luke's, Northumberland Street; and St Mary's, Crumlin Road. It continues:

> Totally destroyed were St James's, Antrim Road; Holy Trinity, Clifton Street; St Barnabas's, Duncairn Gardens; and St Silas's, Oldpark Road ... The

rebuilding rights of Holy Trinity, Clifton Street, were transferred to the site of St Bride's, Joanmount, Ballysillan Road; Holy Trinity, Joanmount, was erected there. St Barnabas's, Duncairn Gardens, was rebuilt. St Silas's Church, Oldpark Road, was moved to a new site on the Cliftonville Road, quite close to St James's Church.

But, in its conclusion, it stated candidly that

> in retrospect, particularly with the exodus of Church of Ireland people which has accelerated in the troubled years since 1969, it was a mistake to rebuild so many churches in that area.

This adverse context is starkly reflected in the numbers regularly attending divine worship in St Peter's Church. As already noted, during the years immediately preceding the Great War, the average turnout on Sunday mornings was about 220, with around 150 going in the evenings (though the figures show considerable variation – they were significantly higher on Remembrance Sunday, the Harvest Festival, the Carol Service, and for confirmation services). By the mid 1930s, this had risen a little – to approximately 250 in the mornings, but the numbers attending in the evenings had dropped to 80–90. Peak figures were recorded in the 1950s, when the normal congregation was 350–400 at the 11.00am service, and still about 80–90 at 7.00pm. By the 1960s, there are already indications of a measurable fall in numbers in the mornings – to c. 220, with 80–90 continuing to attend in the evenings. These downward trends persisted; by the 1990s, the average Sunday morning attendance was c. 70–90, with roughly half this number going to church in the evenings.

This worrying context was of course discussed at length by the Select Vestry at St Peter's. On one occasion, Canon Harris had advised its members as to their role, stating that it was often perceived as being the '3 F's – furniture, fabric and finances'. But he stressed that their remit was in fact much wider: 'to underpin the work of the parish – namely to worship God, and to proclaim Him in the church, parish and wider community'. Nonetheless, it was the '3 F's', and indeed the continuing viability of St Peter's which absorbed much of their time and energy throughout these decades. In May 1971, for example, the Minutes record that 'a somewhat lengthy discussion' took place 'concerning the rationalisation of the church in the area and possible future trends of population movement.' In May 1972, one member expressed the view that – locally – 'too many churches [had been] built after the war, and this had increased the financial problems in St Peter's and other churches.' In October 1973, when the Vestry was discussing launching an appeal to raise funds for organ restoration, the then Curate, Rev S.N.M. Bayly,

> spoke at length. He questioned the principles involved and the wisdom and advisability of going ahead with the scheme to collect so much money for [its] … renovation. He questioned whether the church would be in existence in St Peter's in ten or fifteen years time.

After a 'long intense discussion', a vote was taken, and the initiative was carried – unanimously, apart from the abstention of the Curate. Mr Bayly was, in fact, to be the last curate at St Peter's until now (when he left in 1974, he was not replaced);

there had hitherto been an unbroken succession of curates dating back to 1920.

The acute difficulties which were confronted by St Peter's are also all too evident from the Church's Annual Reports and Statements of Accounts. In 1973, for example, Canon Harris stated:

> The population of the parish tends if anything to decline, which means that in terms of finance the burden has to be borne by fewer people … Your Select Vestry … has been anxious to find out where expenses could be cut and also how income might be increased.

One consequence he highlighted was the Parish's 'inability to be as generous as we would like to be … [with regard to our] obligations to the diocese and to the work of the church overseas.' He also emphasised that 'in order adequately to maintain our extensive buildings we should in fact be spending far more than we do'. The Church Treasurer, in his report for 1981, spelt out

> the financial disciplines within which the parish has to operate … [These, he stated] require it to be entirely self-supporting and to bear its own costs for maintenance of the clergy, employment of sexton and organist, upkeep of buildings which are insured for £800,000 [a figure inflated by the 'Troubles'], energy costs, and to contribute to charities and the work of the church in the wider field. There are no subventions, no support grants. We have an overdraft.

In the late 1940s, St Peter's had had a small favourable balance of c. £3–400 but, by 1980, it had an overdraft of c. £5,000 and, by the time Canon Harris retired in 1990, this was to rise to c. £20,000. Thereafter the financial difficulties of the church were eased by the sale of the Chapel of the Resurrection.

The marriage of Christine Bentham and Robert Marshall, held at St Peter's on 8th April 1978; the bridesmaid was Valerie McKnight, and Robert Dennison was best man.

However, some major items of expenditure were unavoidable; after Dr Breene's retirement in 1963, the Church authorities – the Vacancy Commission – had inspected the rectory, which had been acquired by the Parish in the 1930s (697 Antrim Road), and concluded that its structure was gravely defective. This verdict was confirmed by an independent architectural survey subsequently commissioned by the Select Vestry in St Peter's, which concluded that the cost of its repair and renovation would be prohibitive. In December 1963, Vestry members therefore decided to purchase a new rectory and, whilst a suitable property was being sought, to procure temporary accommodation for Canon Harris (73 North Circular Road). But because of the difficulty in acquiring alternative permanent premises, they resolved instead (in October 1964) to demolish the Antrim Road rectory, and build a new one on that site. By 1967, the construction work had been completed, Canon Harris moved into the re-built rectory, and the North Circular Road house was sold. Meanwhile, in March 1965, a house was purchased (19 Ophir Gardens) for the use of the Curate of St Peter's (it was sold ten years later, in March 1975, after Rev S.N.M. Bayly had left the Parish).

The costs incurred in these purchases were partly defrayed by the sale of the sexton's house – Fortwilliam Gate Lodge (located at the Antrim Road end of Fortwilliam Park). This L-shaped, sandstone-built property, constructed in c. 1850, may originally have been owned by the Ewart family (they had lived in the adjacent property, Firmount, 581–3 Antrim Road, until the early 1940s). Certainly George Morrow had occupied the lodge from the early 1920s. In 1951, it was bought by St Peter's – in Dr Breene's words, 'on advantageous terms' – with the sexton being permitted to remain in it throughout his lifetime, which he did. It was sold in December 1965 for £1,228.

St Peter's Cubs forming a guard of honour at Christine's wedding; both Christine and her bridesmaid, Valerie McKnight, were Cub leaders.

In 1973, Canon Harris indicated that 'any major item of repair or replacement constitutes a crisis situation which has to be met by special means'. There were many such 'items' throughout the 1970s–80s – major restoration work to the organ was required (in March 1971, expert consultants estimated that this would cost £10,000); major repairs were needed to the church roof which was leaking, and new guards for its windows; and the renovation, painting and rewiring of the Parochial Hall was a matter of urgency (it had been extended in late 1963). In addition, the problems associated with the Chapel of the Resurrection were then ongoing, increasingly acute, and difficult to resolve, with any solution likely to be costly.

The Rector and the congregation responded with energy and flair. For example, in October 1973, an 'Organ Fund' was launched, spearheaded by Professor K.J. Ivin who had volunteered to take on this role. By early 1974, £2,473 had been raised – through donations, the proceeds of an auction sale, the sale of tea towels, the collection of waste paper (in some years, this source alone brought in £1,000), a 'coppers in a bottle' initiative, a Christmas concert and the sale of Christmas cards, and numerous other functions. On 3rd June 1975, a service of dedication was held for the restored organ at Choral Evensong; the preacher was the Rev E.F. Darling, Rector of St John's, Malone, and later Bishop of Limerick. By 1977, the target amount had been raised, and the appeal was declared to be over. Moreover, in 1980, the annual Report for St Peter's detailed how by then major repairs to the leaking church roof had been completed and new guards put in place to protect its windows, and the Parochial Hall had been painted and rewired. Meanwhile, determined efforts had been made to raise the church's regular income. When addressing St Peter's 'financial problems' in his 1976 Report, Canon Harris stated 'we have acted on the general principle of giving away a tenth of our income.' In his 1977 Report, he noted that the Parish's annual income was then £13,000; he suggested that the congregation should strive to raise this sum by £2,000 – to be achieved by each family contributing fifty pence per week. Overall, though the Church's deficit was tending on trend to increase, it nonetheless remained at a manageable level.

From the outset, the context of rising political tensions from the late 1960s impinged directly on the life of the Parish – and not just through their impact on local population movements, and the resulting strains on the church's finances. On 15th December 1968, a service of 'Special Prayers for Northern Ireland' was held in St Peter's. On 4th September 1969, the Select Vestry Minutes first mention the 'recent troubles in the city'; they record that members at this session provided 'detailed accounts … of the meetings held, leaflets prepared and distributed, food, clothes and furniture collected and delivered, relief centres, peace groups' in the area, and 'unanimous approval was given' to these initiatives. In December 1969, it was noted that the North Belfast Friendship Committee was 'not so busy because the immediate threat [of] refugees, etc, was over.' At subsequent meetings, the involvement of church representatives in local inter-communal groups was discussed, and there are references to explosions in North Belfast, and to the sending out of letters of condolence to local victims of the violence. In September 1971, members agreed that when locking up church property, a 'check should be made for explosive devices'. Parishioners' concern with regard to security steadily increased during the years that followed. Both Parish Notes and Annual Reports make repeated reference to the problem of vandalism in relation to church property – windows broken, motorcars damaged, the petty theft of cloths, carpets and kneelers, graffiti etched on to doors, break-ins, etc – much of it attributed to 'roaming gangs at night.' In 1978, Canon Harris commented that it was 'a sorry reflection on the climate of our times.'

Some of the congregation did of course experience personal tragedy as a result of the 'Troubles'. In November 1971, a chemist shop (located at 502 Antrim Road) owned by a parishioner, Mr J. Lord, was destroyed by a terrorist bomb. On Friday, 21st July 1972, Stephen Parker, a 14 year-old member of St Peter's, who had been preparing for confirmation in the church and was a member of the Belfast Youth Orchestra, was killed by a car bomb. It exploded outside a busy row of shops on the Cavehill Road, Belfast, and resulted in the deaths of two other innocent victims – Miss Bridgetta Murray and Mrs Margaret O'Hare (on that day, 'Bloody Friday', the Provisional IRA exploded twenty-six bombs in the city, killing eleven people and injuring one hundred and thirty). Stephen was posthumously awarded the Queen's Commendation for bravery for his valiant efforts in trying to forewarn people about the device. His father, Rev Joseph Parker, Chaplain of the Mission to Seamen at the port of Belfast and a prominent peace campaigner, subsequently founded the 'Witness for Peace Movement'. Along with a local priest, Father Hilary Armstrong, he conducted a memorial service held at the scene, on 27th July 1972, which had been organised by local residents and was attended by several hundred people of all religious denominations from the Cavehill Road area. During this act of worship, he took two pieces of wood from the debris caused by the explosion and formed them into a cross. This was subsequently given into the care of the Rector of St Peter's, and

> [a] plea was made that it should be moved annually to each church in the neighbourhood as an act of witness to future generations of the tragedy which follows when men continue to ignore the light of Christ and pursue instead their own selfish aims.

It endures as a poignant symbol of the triumph of Christian faith over violence and death. The 'Cavehill Cross' is now shared between neighbouring churches. When at St Peter's, it is displayed in the north-west corner of the baptistry. On Friday, 20th July 1973, a 'Remembrance Service' was held in St Peter's to mark the anniversary of 'Bloody Friday'.

Consistently, throughout the 'Troubles', Canon Harris – a committed member of the inter-communal group, PACE (Protestant and Catholic Encounter) – provided strong and unwavering Christian leadership. At a meeting of the Select Vestry, on 18th April 1969, he 'referred to the importance of the church in politics', stating that both 'Christianity and politics concern people.' He is quoted in the Minutes as saying: 'at present the church is being challenged and the Rector felt strongly that it was a time for hope and for showing love of our neighbours'. On 4th May 1973, he began his Annual Report to the Vestry by stating that the 'Troubles' were 'still with us and during the last year everyone has been influenced directly or indirectly'. Then, reflecting back on the death of Stephen Parker, he once more 'urged that we should not compromise but should be a Christian community in this place and agents for peace in our area.' In an article in the Parish Notes for September–October 1975, entitled 'Ulster Now', he discussed how parishioners might best respond to the current, apparently unending sequence of vicious atrocities. He stated:

> the present wave of appalling violence should give us all to think furiously, and to pray fervently … In recent days we have before us the example of Sam Llewellyn, a Protestant from the Shankill, who went up the Falls to help people in trouble and who was horribly murdered, and [the example] of all those people, Catholic and Protestant, who have suffered violent bereavement, and who yet appeal for no reprisals or retaliation.

He ended with an appeal:

> we in this district are fortunate in many ways. We can say with the psalmist "the lot is fallen unto me in a fair ground". Surely the least we can do in return is to display in our words and actions the love of God in relation to our neighbours.

[The death of Sam Llewellyn was one of the most shocking events of the 'Troubles' during these years. On 15th August 1975, he had driven three times to Clonard, West Belfast, to deliver building repair materials in his van after a car bomb had exploded in that area. On the third occasion, he was murdered by the IRA; he was twenty-six years of age. At the time a local newspaper aptly described it as the 'good Samaritan' shooting.]

At the Select Vestry meeting on 29th April 1981, Canon Harris again discussed the 'continuing violence and division in the community'. He stated categorically that:

> these could not exist if we were all truly practising the Christianity we claim to serve. He paid tribute to those who in the face of difficulty were working for reconciliation. He paid a warm tribute to his brother clergy of all denominations in the area between whom the closest cooperation and friendship existed.

[In January 1980, during the Annual Week of Prayer for Christian Unity, Father Hilary Armstrong, from St Theresa's, Somerton Road, had been invited to preach in St Peter's; according to the Parish Notes, it was the 'first ever occasion' in which a Catholic had done so in the church]. After the infamous Remembrance Day bomb at the Cenotaph in Enniskillen, on 8th November 1987, in which eleven people – all Protestants – were killed, Canon Harris once more appealed to the members of St Peter's Vestry: 'may it move us to devote ourselves all the more to peace and reconciliation.' Canon Harris led by example; the strength of his personal commitment to ecumenism was courageous, given the temper of the times, and was an indication of the depth and sincerity of his Christian faith.

Given the nature, scale and persistence of the 'Troubles', it was always likely that at some point the Church would itself suffer direct physical damage. It was located beside major commercial premises – the Lansdowne Court Hotel – which lay adjacent to the north transept (separated from it only by an insubstantial fence), and had been a target for terrorist action on a number of occasions. At 2.30pm on Friday, 31st July 1987, the worst fears of the congregation were realised. At that moment, a 200-pound, IRA 'car bomb' exploded in the car park of the Hotel devastating the building; it also caused much collateral destruction to surrounding property, including St Peter's and its halls. On the evening of the explosion and during the following day, parishioners spontaneously conducted a preliminary 'clean up' operation, gathering up the shattered glass and fallen masonry. They were at least reassured to find that nothing had been removed from the church in the immediate aftermath of the incident.

During the days and weeks that followed, it was the Select Vestry which spearheaded and coordinated the Parish's response. It at once appointed a restoration sub-committee from amongst its own membership to organise and oversee the repair work; over succeeding months it worked tirelessly to restore St Peter's to its former glory. Its members included Derek Noblett, Sam Hargrove, Harold Jacobs (honorary treasurer), Basil Jeffers (quantity surveyor), and John Cross (solicitor). A number of important decisions had to be taken quickly. For example, a firm of solicitors (McKinty and Wright, Belfast) was instructed to apply to the Northern Ireland Office for compensation for malicious damage to church property, in the name of the Representative Church Body, Dublin (since shortly after its disestablishment in July 1869, this body had held property and other assets in trust for the use and pur-

Some of the young people confirmed at the Confirmation Service, conducted by Rt Rev William J McCappin, Bishop of Connor, and held at St Peter's on 9th February 1986. The full list of those confirmed was: Diane Margaret Marshall; Irene Florence Martin; Deirdre Elizabeth Barton (daughter of the author); Janice Victoria Jeffers; Anne Katrina Dunlop; Andrea Margaret Beattie; Sarah Hootor Mitchell; Robert James McKay; Peter Stanley McDowell; Tanya Marie Hutchman; Tanya Clair Conville and Adrian William McCormack.

St Peter's Church showing some of the damage caused to the Chancel roof by the car bomb which exploded at the Lansdowne Court Hotel on Friday 31st July 1987.

The 31st July 1987 car bomb also damaged the Vestry and clerestory windows.

poses of the Church of Ireland). An architect, Gordon McKnight, was also appointed to work out the details of the claim on behalf of St Peter's. Mr McKnight worked in close cooperation with the chartered loss adjusters selected by the Northern Ireland Office (from the firm of Thomas Howell, Selfe, Ltd). The loss adjusters' function was to monitor the cost of the restoration work, and make recommendations with regard to the level of compensation which the government should pay. Basil Jeffers recalls that they were sympathetic in their response – for the good reason that it was immediately apparent to them that the work of restoration was being planned and implemented in a prudent, economical and professional manner.

Clearly the precise extent of the damage that had been caused to parish property could not be fully assessed without detailed inspection, which would require the use of scaffolding. Initially its gravity was not fully appreciated, but some of it was immediately evident. After a preliminary, visual inspection on 11th August, Sam Hargrove and Derek Noblett compiled a list. With regard to the church, they found slates had been removed from its roof and damage done to some of its supporting woodwork (especially on its north side elevation, which was closest to the seat of the explosion); structural repairs were needed to stonework, both interior and exterior; and stained glass windows and some of the doors had been either totally or partially destroyed. Likewise, in the main Parochial Hall, windows, doors, the kitchen wall, the electric water-heater and light fittings had all suffered extensively from the blast; so also had the windows and the emergency door in the scout hall. The immediate priorities were therefore to secure the entire church premises against possible break-in, as far as possible to provide them with temporary, waterproofing protection against the elements, and to restore the heating system. A contractor was appointed with responsibility for carrying out this short-term remedial work; it had to be completed with immense care in order not to jeopardise the claim for compensation.

During the following months, detailed investigations conducted by engineers (Taylor and Boyd) and members of the Select Vestry established the full extent of the damage, and of the repair and restoration work required. St Peter's Church is stone built with pitched and lean-to slated roofs, supported by timber trusses, which in turn sit on the external walls and internal stone pillars and arches. After thorough inspection, it became obvious that the complete area of the roof had been lifted by the force of the blast, sufficient to disturb or dislodge the slates; as a consequence, engineers reported that all the slate fixings were suspect. The church roof therefore had to be stripped and retiled (at a cost of almost £30,000). In addition, this lifting action caused by the explosion had adversely affected the roof timbers (the trusses, purlins, etc); some on the north side and in the sanctuary had been dislodged and opened. Also, because of damage to the tiling, guttering and drainpipes, water had entered the church; this too detrimentally affected the timbers (especially, in the chancel, nave, aisles, and porches). They required to be checked by a timber specialist, and extensive sections had to be replaced; similar action was necessary with regard to the guttering itself and the 'lead valley'. The external stonework and rendering needed to be repaired, though in fact this had escaped major damage; there was no structural damage to the walls. Two of the seven stone crosses which stand at the apex of the finials (or gables) in St Peter's had to be replaced by experts (one on the south transept and the other above the east window), and the others were checked to ensure that they were securely fixed to the masonry walls.

Considerable damage had also been done to the interior of the church – the force of the blast caused a slight dislodgement of the stones at the apex of one of the arches; some of the joints were opened and required to be tightened; there were hair-line cracks in the rendering; and the internal stonework was shaken and the pointing disturbed and needed to be repaired. The door frames at the western and southern entrances to the church were both sucked in by the explosion; the main door itself was damaged beyond repair and a new oak one had to be fitted. Also, electrical installations had to be rewired, and the heating system made operational again. The bomb damage sustained by the church organ – its chamber, etc – was such that it had to be dismantled and rebuilt (at a cost of c. £15,000), and another one hired (from Crymbles, Belfast) whilst this work was in progress. It suffered not only from the direct effects of the blast, but also the damage caused to the roof, which had permitted rain and dust to permeate it. The delicate work of repair was delayed by the need first to ensure that the church was entirely dust free.

But, predictably, it was the stained glass windows which had suffered most from the blast – thus, temporary glazing had to be installed. Of all the restoration work that required to be done to the church they were the most expensive single item to repair; some of the estimates for this work totalled over £40,000. It was not just that the glass in the windows had been shattered. In a number of places stone tracery had been removed by the force of the explosion (e.g. in the north transept). Also two dressed stone mullions – the upright strips between the panes of tall windows – had been damaged (one on the north and one on the south side), and others forced out of their vertical alignment; these had to be repaired by stonemasons who, in some instances, made new pieces to suit. In addition, the areas around the windows had been scaled, and extensive re-pointing work was necessary. Those most severely damaged were located in the north transept, along the north nave, and in the chancel and choir area. Amongst them was the huge 'War Memorial Window', in the north transept erected after the Second World War, and designed by the firm of W.M. Morris.

Other church property was also damaged. Repairs were needed to the kitchen area of the Parochial Hall. Its large Gothic window had also been badly shaken and had to be replaced (its central supporting mullion had been destroyed). In the scout hall, the centre section of the external wall had been sucked out by approximately two inches, and a number of doors and their frames had been destroyed. In addition, the roofs of both halls had been severely affected, and their paintwork and plastering needed to be restored.

Even this list, however, does not cover the full extent of the repair work that was required. During the minute examination conducted after the explosion, other structural defects with the buildings were uncovered; these predated it, and had hitherto been unknown to the Select Vestry. For example, in November 1987, an inspection of the external rendering of the church and halls – where it had been removed by the blast – showed decay in the timber walls bearing on the brick, and evidence of a severe attack of wood beetle, which had reduced some sections to dust. Also the metal had expanded in places, and the steel stanchions (upright supporting bars or posts) were badly rusted – probably due to lack of insulation and the intermittent use of the heating system. As a consequence, the decayed timbers had to be renewed before re-rendering, and more effective provision made for insulation. In addition, during a survey (carried out by Denis Agnew from the offices of Gordon McKnight – the supervising architects) it was discovered that the ends of most of the floor joists were suffering from rot. Where necessary these were replaced, and measures were taken to provide the existing ones with increased support. The cost of these additional works had, of course, to be borne by the Parish, as they were unrelated to the damage caused by the bomb, and they inevitably inflated the total repair bill. Figures provided by Basil Jeffers indicate that St Peter's received compensation for malicious damage amounting to almost £128,000 from the Northern Ireland Office, and the further monies added to this by the Parish to carry out remedial work (i.e. for property repairs which had not been caused by the blast) amounted to almost £7,000. Other, later, estimates suggest that the Northern Ireland Office grant amounted to £150,000, with St Peter's itself having to find an additional

£15,000 for repair work. The inevitable effect was that the church's finances were further strained – after several years (1986–88) in which they had been showing a steady, if modest, improvement.

The congregation displayed much imagination, ingenuity and verve in its efforts to raise the funds necessary. In retrospect some felt that, out of their shared adversity and tribulation, 'a sense of togetherness erupted amongst the parishioners after the bomb' (perhaps an additional factor was the fact that from May 1978 Canon Harris had initiated an 'after-church coffee experiment' in St Peter's – in a conscious effort to foster a 'real spirit of fellowship'). For example, a number designed and embroidered new 'tapestry kneelers giving a sense of colour' to the church. Each one was 'completely different': some depicted scenes in celebration of the birth of grandchildren, whilst others were produced in memory of loved ones who had died, or were produced to represent organisations attached to St Peter's (the kneelers in use before the explosion had to be replaced owing to the difficulty of extracting the glass shards from them). For a fee of £10, the names of parishioners were painted on to an individual roof slate by Bob Beattie, the esteemed artist and a member of the congregation; approximately £700 was collected by this means alone. Also, to help raise funds, a supper dance and benefit night was held at the Lansdowne Court Hotel on 3rd June 1988, the meal and sherry reception having been donated by Mr David Magill of the Hotel in a gesture much appreciated by the Parish. It was an immense success, raising – according to the Parish Notes – some £500. During the evening there was a tombola table and a ballot, and the music was provided by Dave Glover and his band. Other initiatives included a 'talent drive'; coffee mornings, dinner parties and bridge nights held in the homes of parishioners; the making and sale of goods varying from pots of marmalade to bird feeding boxes, a 'bring and buy' sale, a Christmas sale, a book sale; and a Sunday School concert held in the Lansdowne Court Hotel, with members from the wind section of the Ulster Orchestra. Wilson Knipe, the famous Ulster tenor, was also present at this event and sang accompanied by the late Edgar Pierpoint, whilst Bob Beattie did sketches of those present, each priced £5.

In due course, despite the severity of the damage, the restoration work to St Peter's was successfully completed and paid for. Already, by July 1988, the church roof, masonry work and windows had been repaired, and also the structural damage to the halls. By the following December, the restoration of the organ was almost finished, and it could by then be played. Reflecting back afterwards Margaret Harris, the Rector's wife, commented to a newspaper reporter that the 'church [was] … looking good and', she added proudly, 'we managed to keep going right through all the work' (services had taken place in the southern portion of the church, the rest being roped off). She paid an especially warm tribute to the Select Vestry's sub-committee who had done such 'a tremendous job' in overseeing the repairs. She took particular pride in the fact that the Second World War Memorial Window, which had needed to be replaced, had been 'restored to exactly the same style'; the repair costs for this alone had been in excess of £30,000. Those involved in the work of reconstruction must have been further energised, and their commitment re-affirmed, by a letter which Canon Harris received from the Department of the Environment on

25th November 1987. This informed him that the church had been placed on its list of buildings of special architectural and historical interest as and from that day (as with the Chapel of the Resurrection in November 1974, the DoE had classified the premises as being 'Grade B+'). It stated that

> buildings such as yours make a particular contribution to Northern Ireland's heritage and to the character of our communities', and added that such action was taken in order 'to ensure that they receive special consideration whenever proposals for development are contemplated.

On 14th October 1989, the *Belfast Telegraph* declared that St Peter's had 'been restored to its former glory.' With the restoration work completed, a service of dedication, thanksgiving and celebration was held there at 8pm on Wednesday, 18th October 1989, with 250 parishioners in attendance. Canon Harris performed the introduction, and it was presided over by Rt Rev Samuel G. Poyntz, the recently appointed Bishop of Connor, who performed the 'Act of Thanksgiving' and pronounced the Benediction. The preacher was Very Rev John Shearer, Dean of Belfast from 1985, and Choral Evensong was sung by the church choir. It was an uplifting experience, witnessed and shared by a large congregation; Margaret Harris had appealed to former members and friends of the Parish to attend. After the service supper was provided in the Parochial Hall, Bishop Poyntz cutting a cake made to mark this auspicious occasion.

Meanwhile, Canon Harris's services to the Church over almost forty years had been fittingly acknowledged in 1983 when he became a Canon on the Chapter of St Patrick's, Dublin; he was elected by his fellow clergy to the Prebend of St Audoen. It was an honour which he greatly appreciated, relishing in particular the connection with the Cathedral; he was installed on 12th February 1983. The Parish Notes for St Peter's (December 1982–January 1983) formally record that 'the rector has been made a Canon', adding, by way of explanation, that 'St Patrick's is the National Cathedral of the Church of Ireland, and as such it draws its Chapter from all over Ireland'. The entry concluded reassuringly: 'The Rector remains here in St Peter's – the commitment to St Patrick's involves two weeks residence in the year in Dublin.'

Canon Harris retired on 7th July 1990, shortly before his seventieth birthday. He had served the Parish faithfully for twenty-seven years, despite recurrent illness, and through what was until then the most difficult and challenging period in its history. Against the background of the 'Troubles', his strong support for ecumenism had impressed his many admirers. His love of music had blended well with the musical traditions of St Peter's, as had his enthusiasm for the scout movement. His rich fund of anecdotes, drawn from his wide and varied experience, had added lustre to his sermons. He died in 1996; his funeral took place in St Peter's Church on 24th June (the Bishop of the Diocese and Rev S.R. McBride officiated at the service). The large numbers who attended are a measure of the esteem in which he was held by the congregation, as also was the Select Vestry's decision to purchase a lectern for the church as a permanent memorial to his ministry. (Margaret Harris had pre-deceased her husband; given her record of tireless service to St Peter's, it was appropriate that her funeral should have been held there – on 8th March 1993).

In September 1990 Rev Stephen Richard McBride was appointed as Canon William Harris's successor; he was instituted by the Rt Rev Dr Samuel Poyntz, as the fourth Rector of the Parish of St Peter's two months later, at 8.00pm on Friday, 9th November 1990; the invitation list included local MPs and councillors, representatives from neighboring schools, the RUC, and the Jewish community. He was then in his late twenties, and had grown up in a neighbouring parish – Holy Trinity, Joanmount. He had been educated at the Royal Belfast Academical Institution and at Queen's University, from where he graduated in 1984 with a BSc (Hons.) in Architecture. Subsequently he gained a BTh and MA at Trinity College, Dublin, where he was also awarded Downes Divinity premiums, and the Elrington Prize in 1989, both of which were competed for by theology students. During the period of his Rectorship at St Peter's, he was working on his doctoral thesis.

The Venerable Stephen Richard McBride, Rector of St Peter's, 1990–1996, and Archdeacon of Connor since 2002

Apart from this impressive academic record, he had in addition a distinguished athletics career, gaining colours at both Queen's (where he was Captain of the Athletics Club) and Trinity, as well as winning representative honours for Northern Ireland at both junior and senior levels.

Rev McBride had been made deacon in St Anne's Cathedral (21st June 1987) by the Rt Rev William McCappin, and served his title as Curate Assistant in Antrim Parish (1987–1990) under the direction of Canon Leslie Forsythe. His ordination to the priesthood, by the Rt Rev Dr Samuel Poyntz, had taken place in St Patrick's Parish Church, Ballymena (26th June 1988). He had married Helen Mary Clyde, BSc MA, daughter of the Rev Dr John and Mrs Jean Clyde, and an 'old girl' of Belfast Royal Academy, on his twenty-sixth birthday (28th September 1987) at Holy Trinity Church, Belfast. Before coming to St Peter's, they had one child – Rachael Sara, born on 12th September 1990, and baptised in Antrim. Alexander (Alex) Richard John was born on 22nd July 1993, and baptised in St Peter's.

There were a number of important milestones in the history of St Peter's during Rev S.R. McBride's period as Rector there. Two months before Canon Harris vacated from the Parish, the members of the Select Vestry had applied – successfully – to the Diocesan Council for permission to procure a new rectory. As a consequence, the McBride family had moved into the old one (697 Antrim Road) for a period of just six months, when it was sold – in June 1991 (for £101,000); they then transferred to temporary accommodation (in Fortwilliam Grange) for eleven months whilst suitable, alternative, permanent premises were acquired. After several options had been examined, number 17 Waterloo Park South was purchased (for £102,000), and 'blessed' in August 1992 – a smaller, more manageable and younger house (it was built in 1970) than the Antrim Road rectory. Thus the new Rector had to make three successive house moves inside a period of just eighteen months. It was, as he himself recalled, 'not the ideal beginning to an incumbency but', he added, 'the new rectory had much to recommend it with its spectacular views of Belfast Lough and its quiet location'.

During the five years of his incumbency, the Parish also embarked on several major construction projects, which were initiated to improve the fabric of St Peter's, and were urgently required; income generated by the sale of the Chapel of the Resurrection helped ease the resulting financial strains. As the under-chair heating system installed in 1948 was not able adequately to heat the building (despite utilising 1,600 feet of tubes), and the Church's lighting levels were also poor, the Select Vestry carried out investigations into replacing both. In the end, it was decided to choose an overhead heating system; it was almost £30,000 less expensive than the alternative oil-fired installation, and almost twice as powerful as the tubular heating system already in operation in St Peter's. Moreover, it allowed for much greater flexibility, as selected areas within the Church could be targeted, without the necessity of heating the entire structure. After a brief closure of about twelve weeks, a service to mark its re-opening was held on Sunday, 5th April 1992, followed by a buffet lunch in the Parochial Hall. In the same week, a BBC 'Songs of Praise' broadcast was hosted, with members of congregations from other churches in the locality also in attendance.

The year 1992 was also significant in other ways. The lighting system of the Church was replaced, and the entire church rewired. At the same time, a new flood-lighting scheme was acquired which illuminated one of its most striking and best-known features – its beautiful façade. The total cost of all of these renovations, including the heating system, was c. £56,000. Also in late 1992, the sexton of the church, Tommy Young, retired from full-time work; he was much loved by parishioners. He had fallen gravely ill in the February of that year, been unable to work for thirteen weeks, and been advised on medical grounds that he was no longer physically able to fulfill the duties of the post. He was originally from Irvinestown, Co. Fermanagh, and had initially been appointed to St Peter's on 2nd May 1961, at an agreed wage of eight shillings per week. Though his health was not robust, thankfully, he remained as 'Honorary Sexton' for several more years, and was ably assisted by the 'Holy Dusters' rota of volunteers which was immediately put into operation and helped in cleaning the interior.

Other important initiatives were taken during Rev S. McBride's period as rector. These included improvements to the sound system at St Peter's (in July 1994), through the installation of microphones and speakers, and using funds provided by the Lily McClure bequest. In 1995, it became evident that the lead-work of the entire church was in a state of advanced deterioration. A photographic display highlighting examples of its gaping holes and weakened flashing was mounted in order to illustrate to parishioners the extent of the problem. The overall cost of its replacement was almost £50,000. Alongside this work, the slates on the south transept were replaced. To help raise the necessary funds, members of the congregation were once more encouraged to buy a slate. Bob Beattie painted the names of those who did so on the reverse side of each one purchased (as he had done in the aftermath of the bomb damage in 1987), and provided a certificate; by September 1995, £600 had been raised by this means.

Canon Harris had been fervently committed to ecumenism, and his successor preserved and fostered this tradition. During the early 1990s, it was widely believed that the churches could and should provide examples of cross-community activity and worship, though many at the time still harboured considerable reservations about such initiatives. Rev S. McBride records that the clergy in the Antrim Road Clergy Fellowship came together on a monthly basis, and that 'such was the trust between the members that they were able to discuss many difficult and sensitive theological and political issues in a non-threatening environment. 'This', he adds, 'enabled them to build relationships between themselves and their churches which were significant at a time of hope for a new political future'. One of the practical outcomes resulting from these clerical gatherings was the holding of combined Holy Week services – the parishioners of St Peter's joining those from the neighbouring Fortwilliam and Rosemary Presbyterian Churches. In addition, lunchtime services were held in Fortwilliam Presbyterian Church during each December, with local clergy of all denominations leading the worship, and the singing led by pupils from nearby schools.

There were further examples of ecumenism in action. During the autumn of 1993, the parishioners of Holy Family Church joined others drawn from Cavehill Methodist Church, Rosemary and Fortwilliam Presbyterian Churches, and St Peter's Parish in a 'United Festival of Faith.' Moreover, on a Sunday afternoon in September 1993, over two thousand homes were visited by the members of local churches. Their purpose was to advertise a four-day mission, being led by Canon David Mcinnes, assisted by a team from St Aldate's in Oxford. Those involved in this group also visited local schools during their stay and, each evening, combined services were held. Mr McBride states that

> this united event was the catalyst for a re-examination of the Christian Aid and Unity Week services. "Issues Facing Christians" was the umbrella title for the new combined services, in which worship was combined with discussion and fellowship in a less formal environment.

In September 1995, Rev S.R. McBride was appointed to Antrim Parish, where he had served as Curate Assistant. 'It was', he writes, 'a time of mixed emotions as it had been a most enjoyable five years in St Peter's, and it was very difficult to say goodbye to so many faithful parishioners'. The date for his institution in the new church was arranged for All Saints' Day, 1st November 1995. But, he recalls, this had to be postponed as he had injured his back whilst moving house, and his farewell sermon was delivered by Canon R.E. Turner, the Diocesan Registrar. Thankfully, there was another, later, opportunity for him to say goodbye and express his thanks; according to the Preachers' Book, he himself conducted his last service as incumbent in St Peter's on 19th November 1995. At the final meeting of the Select Vestry which he chaired (on 2nd October 1995), Daphne McClements paid fulsome tribute to his ministry in the church, saying that 'his kindness and compassion would never be forgotten'.

In a personal contribution to this church history, Rev Stephen McBride made the following perceptive and gracious observation:

> Parish histories can be written and read as if they are a record of the singular feats of the Rector. No parish history is ever complete without reference to the efforts of so many dedicated, yet often anonymous, people within a parish who give of themselves to enable the work of the church to thrive. I wish to thank all the parishioners who supported me during five very special years of my ordained ministry, and who helped to mould me with their encouragement and prayers.

Whilst at St Peter's, Mr McBride had carried out research into Rt Rev Richard Mant, Bishop of Down and Connor (1823–48), and nineteenth century ecclesiastical architectural trends in the Church of Ireland. During the year after he had left the Parish, he was awarded a PhD by Queen's University for this work. His expertise in this field was further acknowledged, when he was invited to contribute a joint chapter with Paul Larmour, entitled 'Buildings and Faith: Church Building from Medieval to Modern' in *The Laity and the Church of Ireland, 1000–2000 All Sorts and Conditions*, published in 2002. In the same year, Bishop Alan Harper appointed him as Archdeacon of Connor, and Precentor of St Anne's Cathedral – so preserving the links between St Peter's and its mother church.

Four months after Rev S. McBride's departure, on Friday 29th March 1996, the Rev Charles J. McCollum, the fifth incumbent of St Peter's, was instituted as Rector

of the Parish. He was born into a farming family near Cavan town on 1st September 1941, the eldest of five children. He attended the local Roman Catholic primary school, and then Cavan Royal School, one of the five Royal Schools of Ulster, founded in 1608. Before entering the priesthood, he had had a successful teaching career, training for the profession at the Church of Ireland Teacher Training College in Dublin. His first teaching post was in Monaghan Model Schools (1963–1975), where he was appointed principal teacher in 1970. In 1975, he was appointed head of the Practising School in the Church of Ireland Teacher Training College. This post he held for the next ten years, during which time the school's growing reputation was reflected in the lengthening waiting lists of those wishing to enrol.

In Mr McCollum's own words, however, a 'vocation to the priesthood was never too far

Rev Charles James McCollum, Rector of St Peter's, 1996–2008

away throughout his career in education'. In1985, he commenced his training for the ministry, entering the Church of Ireland Theological College, and during his time there being awarded the Downes and Ebrington prizes. At the end of his third year, he accepted an invitation from Trinity College, Dublin, to forgo ordination, and undertake further theological study. During the period which followed, he focussed on the study of 'Faith Development in the Adolescent and Young Adult', and was duly awarded a BTh (Hons). In 1989, he was ordained to serve a curacy in Larne Parish in the Diocese of Connor and, in 1991, was appointed to the Parish of Whiterock in West Belfast, where he served for five years. After being appointed to the incumbency of St Peter's he applied his earlier educational training through the various services and commitments he fulfilled in the wider diocese and church. For example, he served for five years as Chairman of the Church of Ireland Youth Department; he undertook tutorial and teaching work (in Christian Ethics) with candidates for the Auxiliary Ministry, and with candidates in training as diocesan readers (in liturgy, spirituality and contemporary issues); and he served on the boards of several local schools (including St Therese of Lisieux). In addition, he was Chaplain to the Mater Hospital in Belfast.

Outside parish and church life, he has maintained a strong interest in motor sport and rallying (no longer as an active participant, but as an administrator), and his interest in, and use of, the Irish language. Given the wide range of his commitments, one of his earliest and most necessary innovations at St Peter's was the appointment of a part-time secretary, Mrs Anne Cromie, to assist with administration.

Within months of Mr McCollum's appointment, there was further stark evidence

The Institution Service of Rev Charles J McCollum, held at St Peter's on 29th March 1996.
(Left to right): Shiela Chillingworth (People's Churchwarden); Canon Jim Moore (Rural Dean); Canon R.E. Turner (Diocesan Registrar); Rev Brian Stewart (Chaplain to Bishop); Rt Rev James E. Moore, Bishop of Connor; Rev Charles J. McCollum (incoming Rector); The Venerable Alan Harper, Archdeacon of Connor, preacher; Daphne McClements (Rector's Churchwarden)

of how, in the words of Rev Tom McAlister (who had been a curate in the Parish), 'social changes and population movement' were continuing to impact on the life of the Church within the area. On 7th November 1996, the Diocesan Council decided to group together the parishes of St James's and St Peter's under the Rector of St Peter's. St James's was the older church; its foundation stone was laid in 1869, it was consecrated in 1871, and a rectory and a school had been added by 1875. It had been severely damaged by enemy action during Easter Tuesday night, 15–16th April 1941, though its tower, steeple and belfry all survived. It was subsequently rebuilt, the new building being consecrated on 11th September 1954. Like St Peter's, it too was well known for its strong tradition of liturgy, and of church music.

The conjoining of the two churches was a direct consequence of the continuing decline in the number of Church of Ireland parishioners in North Belfast. The congregation attending St James's had already begun to fall during the 1950s, and this trend was exacerbated further by the impact of the 'Troubles'. By mid 1991 (according to the Select Vestry Minutes of St Peter's) the congregation of St James's had fallen to a little over thirty families. Thus, it was as part of its programme of rationalising church resources, that the Diocesan Council favoured its amalgamation with St Peter's when its incumbent, the Venerable Archdeacon J.O. Rolston retired, and also the closure of St Silas's (which had been grouped with St James's since 1979). This approach was later confirmed by the Church of Ireland Synod. Archdeacon Rolston retired in 1996, and subsequently the Select Vestries of St James's and St Peter's collaborated in the practical details of the merger scheme. In 2007, the Diocesan Council finally decided to turn the grouping arrangement of the two parishes into a union, and St James's formally closed.

The closure of St James's – in mid 2008 – was perhaps inevitable, but nonetheless painful (an arrangement was made with the Antiochian Orthodox Church of St Ignatius permitting it to use the church and hall for liturgical and pastoral use, and outreach under licence). The Rt Rev Alan Abernethy, Bishop of Connor, referred to this in his address at the closing service held in the Church, on Sunday, 29th June. 'There is much pain and sadness. For some there is still anger and confusion,' he said. He continued:

> I cannot fix that pain but I have to help us all find ways of celebrating a wonderful proud history of a parish church that has brought much blessing to so many. The focus needs to lift us above the moment and find ways of thanking God and celebrating or we will fail those who have served in this parish faithfully and lovingly.

In the autumn 2008 issue of *Connor Connections* several of its most ardent parishioners recorded their memories. Terry Pateman had joined the Boys' Brigade in St James's when he was just nine, eventually becoming Captain before the company closed down in 1975 – it was the second oldest in Ireland. Reflecting on how numbers in the Parish had dwindled rapidly because of the impact of the 'Troubles', he said: 'it was a pretty grim period. People in the thirty-five to fifty age bracket disappeared almost overnight, and we were left with an ageing parish.' This he contrasted with the heyday of the Church when, he wrote, we had organisations going every night of the week – BB, Guides, Scouts, GFS, badminton, an operatic society, woman's guild, youth club and one of the oldest Mothers' Union branches in Ireland.' He added: 'I was very sad to see [St James's] … close. It was a lovely church to worship in. There was a great sense of feeling in it. There was so much history in it too. It was the last sandstone church built in the United Kingdom, and the first ever, live, colour BBC television morning service was broadcast from St James's in the late fifties.

At the time of the Church's closure Margaret Macbeth, aged seventy-six and a retired school headmistress, was rector's churchwarden and her sister, Hazel, two years younger and a retired accountant, was people's churchwarden. Both had been members of St James's all of their lives; Margaret's earliest recollection was of falling down the chancel steps on Gift Sunday just before her third birthday. One of the many fond memories of the Church, which they both shared, revolved around their brother, Billy, who had been born with cerebral palsy, and had defied their doctors' prognosis by living into his seventies. Margaret recalled that

> Billy couldn't talk or sit up until he was about five, but Dad taught him to whistle. Once my mother took him to evening service and, leaving home, Dad said: "Now Billy, no whistling in church." As soon as the sermon started, Billy began whistling!

During the air raid which destroyed the Church their own home was also damaged;

Fund raising sponsored walk, held on 23rd May1998. Included are:
(back row): Ian McManus; Mrs Anne Cromie; Miss Wendy Cross; Roy Entwistle; John Cross
(middle row): Rosemary Johnston; Anne Noblett; the Rector, Rev Charles McCollum; Thelma Cross
(front row): Samuel and Rebecca Cromie

Margaret, then aged nine, recalled: 'we were hiding under the dining table, and thankfully no one was hurt. Mother said that if we had been in our beds we would have been killed.' In due course, their house was also rebuilt, and so the two sisters remained faithful members of the Parish. Margaret records that 'St James's was blessed with very talented and dedicated clergy in the thirties and forties, and the Sunday School teachers were magnificent.'

Meanwhile, for the congregation of St Peter's, as the year 2000 approached real cause for celebration, hope and renewal was beckoning; the hearts of parishioners must have been gladdened by the prospect of the centenary of their church. This major chronological milestone was reached in the millennial year and, fittingly, the occasion was marked by a series of special events. Their combined purpose was not only to mark the achievements of the one hundred years just past, but also to reinvigorate the spiritual life of the Parish, and to serve as an opportunity and stimulus to make preparations for the century which lay ahead. Already, in May 1998, the Select Vestry had initiated its preparations, under the direction of Rev C.J. McCollum. Its members had begun then to consider issues such as: 'worship and music', 'hall reconstruction', 'the enhancement of the building and property', the publication of a history of St Peter's updating that produced by Dr Breene in 1950, and the re-naming of the side chapel in the south transept.

St Peter's Centenary Lunch, held at the Church after a Sung Eucharist on Sunday 25th June 2000. (Left to right): Most Rev Dr Richard Clarke, Bishop of Meath and Kildare (the preacher on that occasion); Anne Cromie (Rector's Secretary); Right Rev Samuel Poyntz, former Bishop of Connor; Rev Dr Alan McCormick, Chaplain of Trinity College, Dublin, and one time chorister in St Peter's

The celebrations organised during the course of the year took a variety of forms. A beautiful, cut glass representation of St Peter's was issued, copies being made available for parishioners to purchase (it had been produced by Tyrone Crystal). The earliest 'special event' to be held in the church took place on 9th January 2000 – the broadcasting of divine service on *Radio Telefís Éireann*; by common consent, the choir excelled (St Peter's had a long tradition of such engagements – the earliest broadcast from it had been aired on 19th April 1938, and had taken the form of a programme of hymns).

But the undoubted climax of the year's activities was reached at St Peterstide, 2000. The central act of

One of the exquisitely modelled figures of four Archangels which surmounted the Reredos in the Chapel of the Resurrection, and is now found in the south side of the nave of St Peter's.

One of two statues which originally occupied panels on either side of the Reredos in the Chapel of the Resurrection, and is now in St Peter's.

The four manual organ in St Peter's Church, which was rebuilt in 2005.

The Kinahan windows in the south wall of the Chancel. The window on the left side is dedicated to the memory of Marian Elizabeth Kinahan, and the other to her husband, Frederick.

The great East Window, erected by Frederick Kinahan in memory of two of his children.

The World War One Memorial Window, or 'Victory Window', in the south transept which was dedicated two years after the Armistice, on 21 November 1920.

The Pearson Memorial Window in the west wall (south of the porch), dedicated on 13 May 1934.

The Berwick Memorial Window in the north wall of the baptistry, which was dedicated on
St Peter's Day, 29 June 1934.

HOPE

FORTITUDE

The Brett Memorial Window in the west wall of the south porch, which was dedicated on
St Peter's Day, 29 June 1935.

The Handforth Window in the west wall north of the porch is in memory of Lieutenant Claude Lowry Handforth, who was reported missing in Burma on 17 February 1943.

The Megaw Memorial Window on the north side of the west door, dedicated on 19 October 1944.

The Taylor Memorial Window in the west wall of the baptistry, which was dedicated on 17 December 1944.

The World War Two Memorial Window in the north transept, which was dedicated on 5 November 1955.

The Durnan Memorial Window in the west wall (south of the porch),
dedicated on 22 October 1961.

A study of the north-east corner of the Sanctuary showing the delicately worked mosaic panels, recessed behind richly detailed stone carving.

The High Altar and, behind it, the Reredos – 'The Empty Tomb' – designed by George Tinworth.

Lectern, carved in linden wood, which originally stood in the Chapel of the Resurrection, and is now in the side chapel in the south transept of St Peter's.

BELOW: The Side Chapel in the south transept, which was re-dedicated as 'The Chapel of the Resurrection' on 7 May 2000.

Lectern of finely carved oak and, behind it, the Bishop's chair and Reredos of the Side Chapel.

The Reredos in the Side Chapel, which was carved in alabaster by Maurice Harding, RHA, OBE, on the theme of 'The Ascension into Heaven'.

The magnificently carved Reredos from the Chapel of the Resurrection, which is now in the south transept of St Peter's.

worship, thanksgiving and celebration organised then was the Centenary Service – a Sung Eucharist, held on Sunday, 25th June, at 11.00am. It was attended by members of the clergy who had previously served in St Peter's, by ministers of other denominations representing the major neighbouring churches, and also by local political figures, and by past members of the congregation (some of whom had travelled over from England and elsewhere).

The church was filled to capacity, and many of those present afterwards commented on the meticulous planning and preparation which had helped make the occasion so memorable. Its solemnity and significance is evident from the Procession Plan. The Crucifer, Choir and Churchwardens, were followed by Rev Stephen McBride, carrying the gospel, two Acolytes (Ashley Lloyd and Debbie Lloyd), and ten clergy (amongst them were: Rev N. Bayly, a former Curate at St Peter's; Canon Ernest Shepherd, the Assistant Priest in St Peter's and St James's; Rev Margaret Johnston, Presbyterian Minister, Fortwilliam; Rev Dr A. McCormick, Church of Ireland Dean of Residents in Trinity College, Dublin, and former choir boy at St Peter's; Rev D. Clendon, Church of England, attached to the neighbouring Columbanus Community; Rev Fr Sean Emerson, Parish Priest, Holy Family, and Rev Fr Paul Symonds, St Malachy's College). The verger, Jenny Stark, entered next, then Rev C. McCollum, and finally the two bishops present – Most Rev Dr Richard Clarke, Bishop of Meath and Kildare, and Rt Rev Samuel G. Poyntz, who was Bishop of the diocese. The clergy occupied reserved seats on the northern and southern sides of the sanctuary, and pews near the prayer desk, and in the nave.

The Service had throughout the warm, intimate atmosphere of a family gathering. The choir sang the anthem 'O Thou, the Central Orb' by Charles Wood (as referred to earlier, the composer's brother, Henry Evelyn Wood, had been killed in an accident outside the church after evensong in mid 1962). The first reading was by Peter Breene, grandson of the Church's longest serving rector, and the second by Patrick Harris, son of the third rector. The gospel reading was by Rev S.R. McBride, the fourth rector who had preceded Rev C.J. McCollum. The prayers of the people were read by Anne Stewart, as a representative of the Parish's organisations, James Moyna from St Peter's Church on the Falls Road, Geoffrey Gray of Rosemary Street Presbyterian Church, and Rosemary Hinds, a member of St Peter's choir. The sermon was preached by Bishop Clarke; Rt Rev S. Poyntz, Bishop of Connor until 1995, delivered 'The Blessing'. The historic nature of the occasion was well captured by the words of one of the hymns – 'O Christ the same through all our story's pages'. Complimentary lunch was served in the parish halls, following the service.

At 6.30pm that Sunday evening, 25th June, St Peter's hosted the ordination of priests for the Diocese of Connor. It was a unique honour and privilege for the church, and a major element in its centenary celebrations. The Bishop of Connor, Rt Rev E. James Moore, assisted by the Rt Rev Martin Lind, Bishop of Linkoping, Sweden, ordained four deacons to the priesthood (the Diocese of Linkoping is twinned with the Diocese of Connor). The 'candidate Priests' (they sat along with their families in the front rows on the north side of the nave) were: Ronald Elsdon, for the Curacy of Kilconriola and Ballyclug, Ballymena; Terence Philip Kerr, for the Curacy of Antrim; Paul Jack, for the Curacy of Jordanstown; and Elizabeth

Rev Charles McCollum with Laura Simpson, about to cut the Centenary cake, decorated by Carolyn Hinds. Laura celebrated her 100th birthday on 24th November 2001.

Henderson, in the Auxiliary Ministry for the Curacy of Belfast and as Assistant Chaplain in the Royal Victoria Hospital. After the Presentation, the Declarations, the Ordination, and the laying on of hands, Bishop Lind delivered the sermon. Once again the members of the choir performed the anthem, 'O thou, the central orb' (they had first sung it – during the centenary year – at the RTÉ broadcast in January). Bishop Moore was the celebrant at the communion which followed. The elements were administered first to the Bishop of Linkoping, then to the newly ordained priests and their spouses, followed by the administering clergy, the choir, the visiting clergy and readers, and the members of the congregation. In anticipation of the very large numbers attending, those receiving the sacraments could communicate at the sanctuary, or the side chapel in the south transept or the baptistry. Once again, following the service, supper was available in the Parochial Hall.

For the Patronal, held on Thursday 29th June 2000, the St Peter's choir sang Festival Choral Evensong in the church at 7.30pm. It was an apt choice – many consider this to be the most beautiful and spiritually uplifting service within the Church of Ireland liturgy (as Mr McCollum has stated, the choir prepares for and leads this service twice monthly throughout the year in a manner that would be the envy of many cathedral churches). Bishop E.J. Moore presided over the proceedings, and the family atmosphere, which had characterised the Centenary Service held four days earlier, was retained. The preacher was Rev J.R.B. McDonald, who had been ordained for the Junior Curacy in St Peter's almost exactly sixty years earlier. All of the four rectors who had preceded Rev C.J. McCollum, and had served the Parish over the previous one hundred years, were at least indirectly represented in the scrip-

Della Burrowes with Right Rev E. James Moore, Bishop of Connor, and Rev Charles McCollum. The photograph was taken in March 1998, when Della was celebrating her 105th birthday; Della was associated with St Peter's for over sixty years.

ture readings and prayers. The first lesson was read by Derek Noblett who had been baptised by the Rev H.R. Brett, and the second by John Wright who had been baptised by Dr Breene. The occasional prayers were read by Jessica Thompson who had been baptised by Canon Harris, and the offertory presentation was by Rory Saville who had been baptised by Rev S. McBride. The responses were led by Neil Moore, the Canticles were by Herbert Sumsion, and the choir performed the anthem, 'Evening Hymn', by H. Balfour Gardiner.

As well as being a time of celebration and thanksgiving, the year 2000 was also seized upon by Rev C. McCollum and the Select Vestry as an opportunity to prepare and plan for the future. In a booklet produced to mark the Church's Centenary, Bishop J.E. Moore stated emphatically:

> St Peter's … is one of the most attractive churches in Connor Diocese … [It] continues to provide a sanctuary and a house of prayer and worship for all who will enter its doors.

'Furthermore', he continued, 'you, today's parishioners, are looking to the future with courage and faith in your Centenary project to provide a new Parish Centre.' Elsewhere in this publication, the Rector elaborated on what was being planned. He observed:

> it is fitting that we should mark the Centenary in some very special way, and we are doing so by embarking on a major building adventure. We are in the final planning stages of replacing the existing parochial halls with new premises.

The old Parochial Hall – just before its demolition began on 13th March 2006, and the construction of The McCollum Hall was begun.

He pointed out that the Parochial Hall had originally been erected as a temporary structure (in 1927), and stated that though 'it has been improved several times over the years … we believe now is the time to act decisively'. In fact the Parish had little choice but to proceed with this new construction, as quite apart from its age and temporary nature, the Hall no longer met official health and safety requirements owing to the use of asbestos in its construction. In appealing for funds, the Rector reminded the congregation that 'at the early years of the century … the founders took onto themselves the motto: "I will not offer unto the Lord that which costs me nothing"'. He suggested that this 'motto, if relived, will serve us well today as we embark upon this major project … the biggest effort of the past fifty years'. And indeed, the last 'major project' undertaken by the Parish had been at the time of its Jubilee celebrations in 1950, when preparations were made for the construction of the Norritt Hall.

A 'Service of Thanksgiving for St Peter's Parochial Hall' was held there at 7.30pm on Wednesday, 8th March 2006. During these proceedings, Rev C. McCollum reviewed its history, and echoing Dr Breene's memorable comments at its opening (in October 1927), he said:

> We should thank God for all the blessings brought to so many through the use of this hall. It has served the parish well despite it always being a temporary building … It is time to let it go … For now let us leave this old building behind us with glad hearts.

Demolition work was due to begin five days later (on 13th March). By this time, the construction of the new premises – 'The McCollum Hall' – and improvements to the grounds of St Peter's had been virtually completed. Writing for this publication,

Rev Charles McCollum conducting the closing service in the old Parochial Hall at 7.30pm on Wednesday, 8th March 2006.

Rev C. McCollum explains in detail the context for and rationale behind this work, and how the project developed:

'The parish halls attached to St Peter's Parish were never typical in any definite way of parish halls in other parishes. They were spread out in appearance reflecting the ready availability of land at the time in this area. Another probable factor was that when they were first built their purpose was to be in use only in a temporary capacity until this young parish could afford better accommodation. The old hall was opened in 1927 and replaced in the parish Skegoneill School which was being handed over to the Education Authority. The hall was added to and improved several times in subsequent years. In 1954 the Scout Hall was constructed as a result of the munificence of J.H. Norritt – and was home to a very active scout movement until the late 1990s. The main hall itself suffered come car bomb damage in July 1987, though it was not as grievously affected as was the church. It was repaired and the damage, mostly to windows and roof slates, was made good.

Despite their shanty-like external appearance, the parish halls served the parish well, particularly until the '90s when community expectation and needs had changed so much. Generations of young people have very fond memories of the vibrant, active and well-patronised youth guild that made the place famous for many. Many people, some without any parish connections or association, claim that it was within this context that they met their future partners. These halls also staged many a fine theatrical production and play.

With the stringent demands of health and safety legislation pressing in on the parish the debate that had periodically surfaced every few years since the 1950s, in the 1990s became so pertinent that action was called for. The choice centred, as it so often did over the years, on two options. Does the parish undertake substantial and fundamental repairs or does it attempt to build a new hall?

The first mention of hall replacement as a serious option was at the Select Vestry meeting of 5th June 1999. The idea was encouraged by one member in particular, Ernest Stewart. At its meeting on 7th August 1999, the Select Vestry unanimously decided to seek outline planning permission for a development. An architect was commissioned to prepare plans and to investigate outline planning approval. To finance the project six apartments would be built on the surplus land after the new hall was accommodated. At its meeting on 8th December 1999, the Select Vestry then gave approval for full planning permission to be sought. Six months passed as planning made its way through the system. In June 2000, Rodney Hughes, an employee of Gardiner & Theobalt, was appointed as quantity surveyor.

At the Centenary Service all plans and drawings were on display. The thorny question of making the finance figures match up to the projected budgetary costs continued to occupy the thinking of the parish. By early July notable opposition was surfacing from local residents against the idea of apartments, coming to a head at a meeting in the City Hall with local residents and attended by the Rector, Ernest Stewart and the architect on behalf of the parish.

By December 2000 the Select Vestry decided in the face of this opposition to opt for two detached houses on the land as well as a scaled down hall; the houses to be built by the parish and sold on to finance the building of the

The McCollum Hall during the early stages of construction.

project. On 21st February 2001, full planning approval was sought for the project. Planning permission was granted in June 2001, but by then it was a concern that the project was not going to be financially achievable and that the parish would be forced into considerable fundraising. The project was dropped and lay dormant until July 2004, when the debate started up again. A different firm of architects, Alan Cook, Crawfordsburn, was appointed in February 2005. The Select Vestry appointed a sub-committee to promote a new project, consisting of the Rector, Derek Noblett, Stanley McDowell, Victor Davis together with the architect and the quantity surveyor. They were mandated to make all administrative decisions.

This time the proposal centred on the idea of selling a piece of the unneeded land to a developer and building a scaled down hall with the residue. Plans for this hall which were only slightly modified from the earlier one, were drawn up and an agent appointed to sell the remaining land. The services of quantity surveyor, Rodney Hughes, now with his own company, Intra Consulting, were retained. Planning approval for this project was submitted in June 2005.Its passage through approval was again subjected to much scrutiny because of the new building's proximity to a listed building. To slow down matters the parish sought an amendment to its own plans to allow for a dual-pitched roof to the main hall. Eventually, final approval was received in September 2006.

The sale price of the surplus land, handled by agents Morton & Co., Cavehill Road, was agreed in June 2005. The purchaser was NMC Developments, at a figure of £490,000. The Bill of Quantities was prepared by the quantity surveyor and a building contractor was duly appointed. The contract was granted to Canavan Construction Ltd., Magherafelt, Co.

The McCollum Hall nearing completion, 2008.

The McCollum Hall – construction almost finished, 2008.

Londonderry. Work started on the site on 6th November 2006. The key of the completed hall was handed over on 10th August 2007, with some external

Some of the key figures involved in the construction of The McCollum Hall
(left to right): Raphael Bleeks (foreman; director, Irwin Electrics, Armagh); Brian Moyes (Beattie, Flanaghan,
Consulting Engineers); Alan Cook (architect); Dennis Canavan (chief contractor); Rev Charles J. McCollum;
Mark Foster (director, Alan Cook, Architects); Victor Davis (Select Vestry); Stanley McDowell (Select Vestry,
Parish Treasurer); Derek Noblett (Select Vestry)

work outstanding. Meanwhile NMC Developments, the purchaser of the adjoining and surplus church land, proceeded to demolish the old hall and construct four large detached dwellings of approximately 187 square metres each.

The new parish premises consist of a main sports hall 17.2 m by 8.77 m, finished in height to accommodate most sports and with a Junker sports floor, a minor hall 6.2 m by 7.1 m, kitchen and toilets all on one level, and with direct access to the church from an attractively designed entrance foyer. A doorway from the north transept of the church was itself created to provide access to the new hall. At a lower level is a large basement area equivalent in size to the main hall for future development by the parish, as well as a spacious office for parish administration. An attractive feature of the new building was the construction of the road-facing gable wall which was finished in coursed stonework to match the existing church. The stone was salvaged from a building of the same period. The stonemason for this module was from Ardbo, Co. Tyrone.

All this development work rendered the need for major landscaping of the church grounds and the surrounds of the hall. The church grounds had remained unaltered since the early years of the last century. Some old scrub trees were removed and many new specimen trees and a variety of shrubs were planted, together with re-designed car parking facilities, new boundary railings and gates. The total cost to the parish in undertaking this project and all associated works to final completion in 2008 was £502,000. The total expenditure had been provided for in the immediate period before the work started and involved the parish in minimal fundraising. The overall appearance is one of pleasing public acceptance and much commendation.

In a note written specifically for this publication, the Rector described the

The interior of The McCollum Hall, 2008

The exterior of The McCollum Hall, 2008

building of the new parish centre and revamping of the entire surrounds of
the church and its landscape [as] ... by far the biggest and most demanding
achievement of his work in St Peter's.

The only note of sadness was the fact that Tommy Young, who died in April 2006,
did not live to see the new hall completed; he had occupied the position of sexton
under three of the Church's five rectors to that date, and been the last to hold this
post. But its construction provides tangible evidence that despite the numerous difficulties and tribulations of recent decades – including twenty-five years of the
'Troubles', severe bomb damage to church property, and persistently unfavourable
population movements – St Peter's has survived. Indeed, it has done more than that;
it has flourished, and has now prepared itself to meet the challenges of the twenty-
first century by successfully completing the largest building project in its history –
apart from the construction and extension of the church itself. In addition, it has
done so without being encumbered by debt. For over one hundred years it has provided a tranquil, dependable, spiritual oasis, in a changing, unpredictable and
increasingly materialistic age. It was with ample justification therefore that Rev C.
McCollum had adopted a highly optimistic tone in the booklet produced to mark
St Peter's Centenary. He had then stated:

> our church is thriving. Membership is basically constant. The Parish is recog-
> nised as a centre of excellence for choral church music; the choir has for the
> past eighteen months been augmented by the new junior choir. The Sunday
> School has over the same period experienced modest growth.

And those clergy who had attended the Centenary celebrations at St Peter's in June
2000 would have fully echoed these sentiments; they had been deeply impressed by

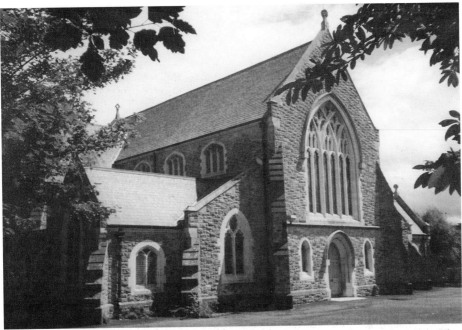

St Peter's in the late 1990s, just before the extensive landscaping of church property was carried out whilst 'The McCollum Hall' was being built.

the experience. In their correspondence with Rev C. McCollum afterwards, they commented on how 'beautifully ordered' the services had been, and on their detailed preparation. The church itself was described as 'flourishing'; this was suggested by the fact that it had been 'full ... twice in the one day', and by the congregation's ambitious building programme. One correspondent wrote: 'you seem to have a band of keen people around you'. The visiting clergymen were also struck by the quality of the music. One described it as 'first rate', adding that 'the parish is fortunate to have such a good organist and choir-master who is obviously able to attract and hold younger members ... Congratulations'. Another alluded to the great 'musical tradition of the choir', and its capacity 'to inspire worship.'

Such views evoke memories of those expressed in the years immediately after St Peter's had been built. Writing just over one hundred years ago, on 30th June 1906 – as noted – William E. Livingstone had described it as 'a slice of a cathedral', and had said of the choir that 'under such guidance as they have [from their organist] there is no doubt of their ultimate perfection'. The congregation might justifiably take pride in the fact that this earlier promise had now been amply fulfilled, and indeed exceeded. But so also might their Rector, Rev Charles J. McCollum, who could reflect on a highly successful and productive ministry at St Peter's; he conducted his last service there on Sunday, 23rd November 2008 and, in early December, took up his appointment as incumbent of the Dunleckney group of parishes in the Diocese of Cashel and Ossory. The church in its physical appearance and facilities now far excels anything achieved in its earlier history – both would undoubtedly have delighted its original founders – whilst its musical tradition has been nurtured and continues to blossom.

Rev. Adrian T.W. Dorrian

Shortly after the departure of Rev C.J. McCollum, Rev Adrian Terence Warren Dorrian was instituted as incumbent of the parish of St Peter and St James – on 22 June 2009. Exactly three years earlier, in June 2006, he had been ordained Deacon by the Bishop of Down and Dromore in Shankill Parish, Lurgan, to serve as Curate Assistant in the Parish of Newtownards; twelve months after this, he was elevated to the priesthood in Down Cathedral.

Adrian grew up in the parish of Groomsport in the Diocese of Down, and was educated for seven years at Groomsport Primary School, before attending Bangor Grammar School for a further seven years, during which time he was appointed Deputy Head Boy. In his final year he was also a winner of the Northern Ireland Schools Debating Competition. He pursued his academic career at the Queen's University, Belfast, where he became the first ever student to graduate with a BA (Honours) in Drama and Theology. In 2004 he entered the Church of Ireland Theological College, where he was awarded a BTh from Trinity College, Dublin. Before he entered the Church of Ireland Theological College, Adrian was a Youth Drama Worker with Youth Initiatives, a West Belfast Christian outreach organisation. He has maintained throughout a keen interest in the theatre, having been a member of a number of drama groups, and with these he has performed in the Group and Lyric theatres in Belfast, and in the National Theatre in London. He serves as Vice Chair of the Ulster Association of Youth Drama, and has been Chair of the Down and Dromore Youth Council. He has a particular interest in liturgy and in the different expressions of Christian spirituality. It is thought that upon taking up post at St Peter's at the age of twenty seven, he became the youngest serving Rector in the Church of Ireland. In this, he was following in the footsteps of Rev Stephen McBride, one of his predecessors at St Peter's, who could have made the same claim at the time of his appointment to the incumbency on the Antrim Road in 1990; he was then 29 years of age.

It is entirely appropriate to conclude this history of St Peter's with a brief consideration of its musical tradition. When considering this on the eve of his retirement, Rev C.J. McCollum writes:

The north wall of the Chancel of St Peter's in *c*. 1904, with the newly installed three-keyboard organ, but before the choir stalls had been constructed.

the building that is St Peter's with its sandstone and oak furniture boasts a very pleasing acoustic environment for singing. It is remarkable that in 1900 when the church was built no scientific equipment existed to decide and plan out the acoustic dimensions of the building; yet the planners, architects and builders of the time were able to get it right without such aids.

However, one facility which the new church did lack at the time of its consecration was choir stalls (see photograph above). But it was an omission which was to be quickly rectified. The front stalls in the chancel bear an inscription which reads: 'Erected in Memory of James, William and Catherine Spiller by their sister Susan A.D. 1910. Susan Spiller erected these seats. Died A.D. 1914.' The centre stalls on both sides were added shortly after the church was extended in 1933; they were 'The Gift of Annie and Clara Taylor, 1935.' The stalls reward close inspection; they are made from oak, and carved with minstrels bearing a variety of instruments, and with grapes and wheat sheaves – both emblematic of the elements used in Holy

The choir of St Peter's Church in 1954 with the Rev Dr R.S. Breene. The Choirmaster, Lister Wood, is seated beside the Rector in the front row.

Communion. The lights which illuminate them enhance the beauty of the chancel, and provide abundant lighting for the choir. They were dedicated on 20th June 1982, and are inscribed: 'To the Glory of God and in loving memory of Roberta Evelyn Mitchell the lights in the choir were given by her family.' Mrs Mitchell was a long-serving member of the St Peter's choir (she was the grandmother of Mrs Anne Cromie, the Rev C.J. McCollum's secretary).

As noted, from its foundation, St Peter's has had an enviable reputation for choral music; the singing of the choir energises the liturgy, and exemplifies and preserves the strong musical tradition within the Church of Ireland. The photograph of its members taken in 1954 (see photograph above), gives a clear impression of its numerical strength then; but for over a century it has constantly been in attendance at church services, and has consistently made a priceless contribution to them. In the Parish Notes in early 1985, Canon W.E. Harris reflected on the 'high level of dedication from our organist and choir', and stated that:

> music plays an important part in our worship. Choral evensong … is one of the glories of Anglican worship. We in St Peter's are fortunate in having a long tradition of musical excellence.

Such comments have been the often-repeated refrain of successive incumbents at the church. Writing for this history, Rev C.J. McCollum comments: 'It is notable how frequently people who may have lived in the Parish at one time will gladly proclaim that they sang in the choir of St Peter's'. He proceeded to comment on the range of choirs at St Peter's of which they had been members, writing:

St Peter's Youth Guild Choir in c.1950 [1950 Booklet, p. 14] (Seated, left to right): Miss S. Perry; Miss J.M. Rogers; Rev T.G. McAlister; Rev Dr R.S. Breene; S.R. Roberts (Choirmaster); Miss S.E. Young; Miss M.L. Donaldson (Middle Row, left to right): Miss O. Young; Miss D.L. Walker; H.T. Jackson; Mrs L.H. Roberts (Robes Mistress); N. Jackson; Miss F.I. Nelson; Miss S.A. Jackson (Back Row, left to right): E.C. Caughey; H.F. Robinson; J.A. Rogers; A. Donaldson; E.T. Ward; S.D. Roberts

another smaller choir, usually looked after by the Curate, was the Youth Guild Choir. The photograph above shows its members in their robes. As well as performing in the Guild's own stage productions in the famous old hall (such as the pantomimes written by Sydney and Stanley Roberts), it also sang at the 8am Holy Communion, and afterwards retreated to the kitchen for a cooked breakfast. Olive Wright and Marie Burrowes fondly recall the experience. The Junior Choir for most of the history of St Peter's was an integral part of the music of the Parish and was at its greatest strength in the 1960s and '70s, but with the changes in the population of the area became smaller in the 1980s and '90s. The Rector also stressed how 'the choir has, since the 1940s, benefited in a remarkable way from the continuous support of many stalwart families – most notably the Mitchells, and the Hinds family which has given sterling and continuous service to the singing life of the Parish. The late Harry Hinds was himself the gifted possessor of a distinguished bass voice which he used to the enrichment of worship in St Peter's.

The electronic bell system was installed and dedicated in his memory in 2006. This system brought to fulfilment an ambition that the Parish held for most of its history – that the absence of bell ringing might eventually be supplied. A plaque on the west wall bears the inscription: 'The Church Bell was dedicated to the Glory of God and in loving Remembrance of Samuel Henry Hinds 1925–2004.'

From its establishment, St Peter's has boasted a fine organ; it was built by Messrs Norman and Beard, of Norwich and London and, with its splendid chamber and casing, was set against the north wall of the sanctuary. It bears the inscription:

> To the glory of God and in Loving Memory of his Daughter Mary Edith, who died 25th August 1887, and of his Wife Martha Elizabeth, who died 9th June 1992, this Organ was erected by Edward Platt-Higgins, Rathcoole, Fortwilliam Park, in this Parish, March, 1903.

The organ in St Peter's Church, in 2008, after recent restoration

The original instrument had a pneumatic action and three keyboards, each controlling a set of stops, each in turn controlling a set of pipes – one for each key on the keyboard. It was in constant use for the next seventy years, during which time it received, and perhaps required, little attention beyond occasional tuning and minor repairs.

However, by 1972, the organ was in urgent need of restoration – not just cleaning and re-voicing, but comprehensive repair and modernisation. In the Select Vestry it was suggested that there was otherwise a real risk of the instrument breaking down completely, and the console was described then as being 'so old fashioned it would be hard to find a more dilapidated one in Belfast'. For a time, consideration was given to the purchase of a new electronic organ of comparable type and tone, for a cost of £5,000. But after a period of trials at church services, it was decided not to adopt this course. Given the strength of the musical traditions of St Peter's, and the integral role which music had always played in its worship, it was felt that the necessary repairs and improvements to the organ should be carried out – despite the Parish's straitened financial circumstances at the time and the estimated cost of £14,000. It was an immensely courageous decision. A Vestry sub-committee was established, and an Organ Fund launched and, after tenders from various specialist firms had been sought and considered, it was decided to have the work conducted by the firm which had originally built it (then called Messrs Hall, Norman and Baird).

When their specialists had successfully completed their work, the organ was re-dedicated in June 1975. Unfortunately, it suffered severe damage as a result of the 1987 explosion at the Lansdowne Court Hotel, as a consequence of which it was impregnated by rain and dust. It was subsequently dismantled, its wall and ceiling rebuilt, and the instrument fully restored at a cost of £15,000. Rev C.J. McCollum records that again,

> in 2005, it underwent another major rebuild, had some electronic additions included, and was further extended to be a four manual instrument ... under the direction of Stephen Hamill, [the organist].

Mr McCollum continues:

> Since 1900, as is to be expected, the list of names who have held the post of organist and choirmaster in St Peter's is extensive; some for just a few years and others for a long time such as Lister Wood, the longest serving, from 1944 to 1963. The full list (see Chapter VIII) includes many distinguished musicians.

He adds that, under their leadership,

> St Peter's over the years has played host to concerts and productions of different levels facilitated not least by the acoustic environment of the building. In more recent times the co-ordinator of these has been Noel Beattie. [In addition], the importance of choir music and its part in the life, worship and liturgy of the Parish has been widely recognised. At different stages in its century plus of history, the choir undertook various external engagements ... In the 1990s, it was invited to sing the services in several Cathedral situations, including St Patrick's Cathedral in Dublin.

From the Parish's archives, the earliest reference to a broadcast from St Peter's was a programme of hymns recorded on 19th April 1938. That the high quality of the choir's singing was sustained is suggested by the fact that on at least three occasions its musical renditions were aired by the BBC between 1956–1962, and a further ten times between 1966–1983. Undoubted highlights in this period included: the recording of the 'St John Passion' by Charles Wood in April 1957; and of 'Songs of Praise' at the church on 6th June 1966, with Henry Hinds as soloist (broadcast on 7th August 1966). These prestigious engagements continued – for example, the BBC again recorded 'Songs of Praise' from St Peter's in April 1992 and, during the Centenary year, divine worship was recorded for RTÉ on 9th January 2000. The extent of the reputation established by the choir is also evident in other ways. It was perhaps most notably illustrated when the *Alternative Prayer Book* – in modern English – was produced in late 1984, after twenty years of drafting. This volume was intended to provide an 'alternative' to the first prayer book in English (it had been first published in 1549, and then with revisions to 1662). Many churches in the West of Ireland rely on recorded music at services – either because of lack of numbers or of facilities – and when a new set of recordings was being prepared with Canticles and Psalms from the *Alternative Prayer Book*, St Peter's was honoured that its choir was selected to provide them. It was a considerable accolade – both timely and impressive recognition by the broader Anglican community of the excellence of their music.

Meanwhile, the church's Christian responsibilities beyond the parish have certainly not been neglected; it has also maintained its strong tradition of charitable giving. In this regard, a significant recent initiative was the establishment of the Charities Action Group roughly two years ago (it currently has four members – Sandra Hutchman, Peter Grey, Wes Holmes and David Cromie). It was formed with the express purpose of enabling members of the congregation to be more directly involved with charity work, and to provide them with an active focus for some of their giving – rather than allowing it to be merely an annual allocation from church funds. After much research in the charitable sector, Child Aid was selected as the preferred vehicle for action because of the immediacy and high impact nature of its work with abandoned children in the Siberian city of Chita, and also its tight control of administration and finance (it is involved in charitable work in 'Russia and the Republics', and produces a magazine, Child Aid Matters, which provides information regarding its progress, its goals and its needs).

In conjunction with Child Aid, St Peter's has actively supported a number of practical projects, such as providing shoes and winter coats, buying food for a mobile kitchen, and supporting the cost of employing a child psychologist to work with mentally and spiritually damaged children. The Select Vestry has actively supported this project with finance, and many individual parishioners have responded with generosity, and encouraged the group with their money and their prayers, as well as providing other means of support.

VI
The Chapel of the Resurrection

Dr Breene, in his *Jubilee* history of St Peter's, suggests that the origins of the Chapel of the Resurrection can be traced back to events, late on Sunday 25th April 1708. That night the old castle in the centre of the town was gutted by fire and, as George Benn notes in his famous history of Belfast (first published in 1823), in consequence its citizens lost their only building with any long historical roots and associations. For over one hundred and fifty years there was no Belfast Castle – until George Hamilton, the 3rd Marquis of Donegall, decided to have a new one erected. Dismissing any thoughts of rebuilding Ormeau House (itself burned down in August 1861), he had plans drawn up for his proposed structure to be erected in his

The Chapel of the Resurrection and Belfast Castle in *c.* 1870 shortly after their completion; they were then the only buildings in the entire area.

deerpark, along with a chapel, on the bare southern slopes of Ben Madigan (Cave Hill), overlooking Belfast Lough.

But there was a further 'reason' for the 3rd Marquis's decision – the response of the people of Belfast to the death of his son, Frederick Richard, Earl of Belfast. Frederick Richard was born on 25th November 1827 and died in Italy on 11th February 1853, aged 25. He had succumbed to scarlet fever in Naples and, because of the stringent sanitary laws which applied there, had to be buried almost immediately. Consequently, he was duly interred next day in the Protestant cemetery, the *Campo Santo Inglese*, which overlooked the Bay. A year later, in October 1854, the 3rd Marquis had his remains exhumed, brought back to Ireland and re-buried in the Chichester vault at St Nicholas's Church, Carrickfergus, the ancient burial ground of the Donegall family.

Frederick Richard's death occasioned much sadness amongst the citizens of Belfast. They loved a lord – all the more so when he was no longer their landlord, the Donegalls having long since been obliged to sell off their estates owing to the indebtedness of the family. But they also held him in high esteem because of himself – his personality, interests and talents. The Earl had been a young man of great promise. He had taken a keen interest in literature and in social questions. A small book of lectures, entitled *Poets and Poetry of the 19th Century* and published in 1852, is all that remains of his considerable literary output. Typically, they were delivered in the Music Hall, Belfast (in the March of that year) for the benefit of the library fund of the local Working Classes Association.

During the days of grief following his death, a group of influential men in Belfast discussed how he might best be remembered and honoured. It was agreed that a bronze statue should be erected in College Square, adjacent to the Royal Belfast Academical Institution, with funds raised by public subscription. Patrick MacDowell, a Belfast born sculptor then living in London, was commissioned to execute the work; it reached Belfast in October 1855. Shortly afterwards George William Frederick Howard, 7th Earl of Carlisle, the Lord Lieutenant of Ireland spoke at the inauguration ceremony; in his address he commented on 'this touching and remarkable commemoration of sorrow and of love …' He referred to Frederick Richard's 'published compositions in walks of literature', and to his 'strong, fervent wish to apply the faculties which the Creator had given him to the service of his fellow countrymen.' He also highlighted – as a consequence – the 'affection of his friends and the idolatry of his family' towards him.

The statue became a Belfast landmark and rendezvous point, universally and fondly known by it citizens as the 'Black Man' – though it is still unclear precisely why it should have acquired this name – was it so-called because of its original dark bronze colour? Or was it at one time painted black? Or was it on account of the patination which formed on the work as a result of 'weathering'? Whatever the reason, it may be that the initial interest and pride which the people of Belfast had shown in Frederick Richard (as evidenced by the erection of the memorial) awakened in his father, the 3rd Marquis, a desire to return from England and take up residence once again in the City. His new home, the proposed Belfast Castle, was begun in 1868 and completed by 1870. On 21st December 1869, the *Belfast News Letter* reported that its construction was 'being carried on with energy and effect by the builder, Mr McMaster, the walls having already reached a considerable height.' It also recorded that the principal avenue had been laid out 'and the cutting and filling nearly completed.' Planting had been going on vigorously, it said, for three or four years, and was still in hand. The writer suggested that in a very short while the new demesne and Castle should present a fine and striking appearance. The same issue of the newspaper carried a description of the consecration of a mortuary chapel – the Chapel of the Resurrection – close to where the Castle was being built (it is currently accessible from Innisfayle Park). At the time of the report its construction had already been completed.

The 3rd Marquis and his wife, Harriet Anne, daughter of the 1st Earl of Glengall, had had the Chapel built not only as a memorial to their son, but also as a burial place for members of the Donegall family. As noted, their ancient burying ground was at St Nicolas's, Carrickfergus. This church had been built in 1180 and, in 1614, Sir Arthur Chichester had commanded that the 'Donegall Aisle' (the north transept) be constructed to house the vault; the floor was raised to permit the remains to be interred below, and a magnificent memorial was erected along the north wall of the transept; it shows Sir Arthur, his wife, Lettice, and between them their only child, Arthur, who had died in infancy. It also bears a Latin inscription, which reads in translation: 'Behold me Triumphing.' However, by the late nineteenth century, the family had come to regard the vaults there, as 'inconvenient and unsuitable.' Consequently, the 3rd Marquis 'determined to change the place of interment, and to have it in connection with the new chapel.' Accordingly he had vaults constructed, gouged out of the rock on which the Chapel of the Resurrection stands.

The 3rd Marquis succeeded in acquiring the requisite authority from the Church of Ireland Bishop of Down, Connor and Dromore to use the vaults for this purpose. Amongst the archives now held by St Peter's Church is the indenture drawn up between the 3rd Marquis, Rt Hon George Hamilton, and the Rt Rev Robert Knox, DD, Lord Bishop of Down, Connor and Dromore and later Primate of All Ireland, on 13th May 1869. It relates to a 'parcel of land … part of his [the Donegall] family's estate and … demesne lands in the … Townland of Lowwood … Parish of Shankill.' It states that

> the said Marquis has expended a large sum of money in building a mortuary chapel on the said parcel of ground … containing about one rood and twenty perches … and in constructing thereunder vaults as a burial place in substitution of the ancient family burial place at Carrickfergus which has become unsuitable … The said Marquis … is desirous that … the chapel and the vaults … should be consecrated … in order that burials may lawfully be performed there according to the liturgy of the United Church of England and Ireland [for] … the exclusive use of the said Marquis and his family and successors … and for no other use, intent or purpose whatsoever … The said … Bishop … has … consented to consecrate … the said chapel for the purposes aforesaid … The said Marquis … and his heirs … shall forever hereafter keep the said burial place in decent order and condition and fenced off from the rest of the demesne.

The Chapel was to be 'under the jurisdiction or control of the Bishop.'

On the morning of Monday, 20th December 1869, the whole building, including the vaults, were opened and consecrated by the Rt Rev Robert Knox (during his long episcopate, 1849–1893, he ordained 586 clergy). It was described by one member of the congregation as having been 'a magnificent occasion.' The Bishop, accompanied by his Vicar General, Mr C.H.K. Knox, and by Mr J.M. Higginson, Diocesan Registrar, was received at the gate by the Marquis's agent, Mr James Torrens, and was conducted through the Chapel and vaults. After this inspection, he proceeded to the south door, where the Petition for Consecration was read by the Registrar. A procession was then formed, which included several neighbouring clergy, and while the 39th Psalm was being read, the Bishop took up his place at the North end of the Holy Table, with the Vicar General at the south end. Next, prayers were read by the Rev G.A. Chadwick, then Senior Curate of St Anne's (afterwards Bishop of Derry), after which the Bishop and clergy descended again to the vaults, where a lesson from Thessalonians was read by the Rev G.C. Smythe, the Vicar of Carnmoney. The Bishop read the prayers of Consecration, after which all present returned to the east end of the Chapel. There the Sentence of Consecration was read by the Vicar General, signed by the Bishop and laid on the Holy Table. Having ordered that the building be duly registered in the records of the Church of Ireland, the Bishop gave the Blessing.

The Donegalls had spared no expense on the little Chapel. It is in the decorated Gothic style, four bays in length, with apsidal ends and an octagonal turret. Paul Larmour, a renowned local architectural historian, described it as 'very craggy with many rough-hewn uncarved blocks.' It was built by Messrs John Lowry, to the designs of Sir Charles Lanyon (of Messrs Lanyon, Lynn & Lanyon) and, in the words of one enthusiast, stood 'immediately on the edge of a precipice [actually, a quarry] overlooking the Antrim Road and the Lough.' The beauty of its interior was much remarked on. Few, if any, of those present at the consecration service, held in December, had failed to notice and admire the two effigies inside the church – both the work of Patrick MacDowell, RA. One was the plaster model from which the sculptor had worked when creating the statue (of Frederick Richard, the Earl of Belfast) which had been erected in College Square, and said by some to be even finer than the bronze. It remained for many years in the Chapel of the Resurrection and at its foot was a wooden scroll which bore the words:

> He was permitted in a career thus brief and in a private station to exhibit rare accomplishments and virtues. In sorrowful commemoration of the bright promise and early close, all classes of his fellow citizens have raised this statue.

The other piece, carved from 'the purest white marble', had been commissioned by Harriet Anne and filled a niche in the north-west corner, facing the south door. It was a life-size representation of her only son, Frederick Richard, Lord Belfast, on his deathbed, being mourned by herself – his sorrowing mother, who is seated on the bed holding his hand. A brass plate beside it bore the inscription: 'Sacred to the Memory of Harriet Anne, wife of George Hamilton, 3rd Marquis of Donegall, and

Daughter of Richard, 1st Earl of Glengall. Born 3rd January, 1799, Died 14th September, 1860, and Frederick Richard, Earl of Belfast, their Son. Born November 25th, 1827. Died 15th February, 1853'. For later visitors to the church, the poignancy of this image must have been heightened by the knowledge that in the vaults below, carved out of the rocks on which the building stood, lay the copper coffins of both of the figures depicted – 'the young Earl' and his mother, Harriet Anne (she had died in Paris in 1860, aged sixty-one). These, along with those of four of their immediate family, had been transferred from the Chichester burial place at St Nicholas's, Carrickfergus, and laid to rest in the vaults under the south side of the floor of the mortuary chapel (they were George Augustus, 2nd Marquis of Donegall, his wife, Anna, and two of their sons – Spencer Augustus and Hamilton Francis). When the 3rd Marquis died, in 1883, his remains too were deposited in the Chapel's vaults.

Thus, in the 1860s Belfast could boast of having two magnificent, and apparently permanent, memorials – both in memory of a young nobleman, Lord Belfast, whom everyone, especially in Belfast, had loved – the Chapel and MacDowell's statue cast in bronze. It might have been assumed that the Chapel would be used by the Donegall family in perpetuity as a private burial place, and that the statue in College Square would remain as an outdoor testimonial to the affection of all classes for the Earl who bore the city's name. Both, it seemed, would preserve his memory for generations yet unborn; however this expectation was not to be realised. As Dr W.A. Maguire writes:

> pride and respect for the statue, and later for the Chapel, declined. But even in the early years of disinterest in both – and in the man they had sought to honour, no one could have foretold the fate that awaited them.

The statue did not in fact remain for long at its College Square location; all too soon, the memory of Lord Belfast receded. And in 1875 his effigy, the original 'Black Man', was dismantled, removed, and replaced at the original site by another, 15 feet high, of Rev Henry Cooke, DD, LLD, a Presbyterian clergyman. It was inaugurated at a huge Orange rally held on 11th May 1876. Almost immediately it too was referred to as the 'Black Man'. Meanwhile, Frederick Richard's statue was restored and re-erected at various locations in the city: the Town Hall in Victoria Street, the Free Library (now known as the Central Library), the City's Museum. At last, in response to a request made by the 9th Earl of Shaftesbury to Belfast Corporation, it was moved to the City Hall in 1906, where it can still be seen today at the head of the main staircase.

The Chapel of the Resurrection survived for longer, but had an equally unfortunate and ill-deserved fate. Following the 3rd Marquis of Donegall's death in 1883, the family's connection with the Antrim Road ended. Most of his estate, including Belfast Castle and the Chapel, passed from the direct line to his daughter, Harriet Chichester, then Countess of Shaftesbury. In 1857, she had married Anthony Ashley-Cooper, better known as the 8th Earl of Shaftesbury, eldest son of the eminent crusading social reformer of Factory Act fame. As owners and occupiers of the Castle, both clearly revered the little Chapel and regularly worshipped there. Indeed, in December 1891, five years after the 8th Earl's death, it was opened for worship, as the private chapel of Belfast Castle. During the preceding months, the interior of the building had been entirely redecorated and made complete. This work of refurbishment was of the highest quality; it was designed and executed by the firm of Cox & Sons, Buckley & Co., of London and Youghal, Co. Cork.

The altar was perhaps the Chapel's most remarkable and distinguished feature. Designed in a rich fifteenth century style, it was carved in Irish woods (oak, walnut, yew) which had grown on the banks of the River Blackwater – a similar example can be found in the chancel of Holy Cross Abbey, Tipperary. The centre of the reredos was filled with a magnificently carved, almost life-sized, group of the Crucifixion, in oak. It depicted the figures of Mary Magdalene, Mary, the Mother of Jesus, St John and the Centurion, standing at the foot of the Cross. Christ was attached to the Cross by four nails, his feet resting on a footstool (or scabellum), and His arms widely extended – His right hand in a gesture of blessing to the world. On the board above His head was engraved the full title of our Lord in the three languages,

Hebrew, Greek and Latin – rather than the usual abbreviation, 'INRI'. At the time the piece was regarded as being one of the finest examples of woodcarving to be found anywhere in Ireland; it had taken over a year to execute. All of the work is in high relief; the expressions of the personages are full of dignity, grace, and devotional feeling. In panels on either side, there were two statues – one of St Patrick and the other of St Columbkille – the patrons of the area around Belfast; both are carved in low relief in linden wood on a walnut background. Surmounting the reredos, was a richly carved arch containing buttresses standing on which were exquisitely modelled figures of the four Archangels – St Michael, St Gabriel, St Raphael, and St Uriel, each

The Chapel of the Resurrection in its prime, showing its magnificent altar and reredos.

bearing his emblem or attribute. All six of these figures had been carved in Bruges.

In addition, the interior of the Chapel was adorned with finely carved candle-sticks, graceful vases in walnut wood, and a number of brasses on the walls commemorating various members of the Donegall family, and also Anthony Ashley-Cooper, 8th Earl of Shaftesbury. The credence table rested on the figure of an angel in linden wood, issuing from a cloud, with wings extended and hands joined in an attitude of prayer and praise. It too had been executed in Bruges. So also was the lectern, which was thought to be amongst the most beautiful bookstands in Ireland; it represented an angel, delicately crafted in linden wood, bearing the book of the Gospels across the world. The reading desk and minister's seat (or sedile) were both fine specimens of ornamental carving in oak. The organ consisted of two manuals, fifteen stops and radiating pedals, and was built by Wordsworth & Co., Leeds. Its elaborate case was made of Irish woods at Youghal, and is capped by the figures of four angels, bearing musical instruments, in allusion to the words of one of the Psalms. According to a contemporary description of the Church, the three resplendently etched windows in the chancel, with their rich and harmonious tones, 'formed a jewelled crown' above the magnificent altar and reredos. They showed respectively: the 'Resurrection of our Lord', the 'Raising of the Widow's Son' and the 'Morning of Easter day' (the other windows of the Chapel were filled with toned glass). Most of these several works were erected by Harriet, Countess of Shaftesbury. She dedicated the windows to the memory of her father, George Hamilton, 3rd Marquis of Donegall and Harriet Anne, her mother, and the organ to the memory of her brother, Frederick Richard, Earl of Belfast. She had the reredos and altar built in memory of her late husband, Anthony, 8th Earl of Shaftesbury.

The service of re-dedication of the Chapel was held on Wednesday, 30th December 1891. Harriet had arranged it for that day so that it would coincide almost exactly with the date on which the building had first been opened and consecrated in her brother's memory, twenty-two years earlier (on 20th December 1869). For those present, the refurbished building with the MacDowell effigies of the young Earl still *in situ*, must have brought back powerful memories of Lord Belfast. The service was described as 'semi-private'; only a few seats were made available to the general public. Harriet herself (then a widow of five years) attended, as did a large number of local clergy. Rev H.D. Murphy, the Rector of St George's (1880–1926), and the Rev R.C. Oulton, Vicar of Glynn (1878–1910), intoned the service. Rt Rev William Reeves, Bishop of Down, Connor and Dromore (1886–1892), was the officiant (Dr Breene described him as 'one of the outstanding figures in the nineteenth century Irish Church – a theologian, scholar, antiquarian, archaeologist … [with an] international reputation … On 12th January 1892, he died of severe chill and flu'). He dedicated the three memorial windows, the altar with its magnificent reredos, and the organ, lectern, credence, prayer desk, and minister's seat (it was later to be used by the Dean in Belfast Cathedral). Mr G.W. Price of St Georges's Church was in charge of the music, which was led by St George's choir. Sullivan's *Te Deum* was sung before the Benediction was pronounced.

After her death, on 14th April 1898, Harriet was succeeded by her son, Anthony, the 9th Earl of Shaftesbury, who inherited the demesne, the Castle and the Chapel (he was then aged 29, had succeeded to the Shaftesbury estates in 1886, and married the daughter of Earl Grosvenor in 1899). Aware of the great love his mother had borne for her brother (Frederick Richard), he sought to ensure that everything possible was done to keep his memory alive. The Chapel remained untouched, its beauty intact. The Shaftesbury family continued to use it for private and semi-private services even though they had no need of it, as they could worship in an Oratory located inside the Castle itself. From the early 1890s, it had also been open to the public on Mondays and Thursdays – on payment of one shilling for admission, the proceeds being given to the Society for Providing Nurses for the Sick Poor. For a period, services were also held there every Sunday afternoon. St George's assisted with the music (as did St Peter's after the church was opened in 1900), and Belfast's most renowned vocalists at the time often joined the choir, or performed as soloists there. The 9th Earl, who had a fine tenor voice, frequently assisted too; he was, a contemporary said, 'renowned for his musical and dramatic powers'. Worshippers were drawn from all parts of the City. In 1906 the Rev Richard Brome de Bary, who had originally been ordained to the Catholic priesthood, became private chaplain to Lord Shaftesbury (he lived in a cottage on the demesne). Thereafter, he served both in the Oratory at the Castle, when the family was in residence, and in the Chapel, where he conducted the Sunday services in Latin. However, in 1915, he was appointed to a living in England. It was about this time – shortly after the outbreak of the First World War – that the services in the Chapel were discontinued, except very occasionally. It was not used with any regularity again until 1938 and then in circumstances which had profoundly changed.

In the aftermath of the First World War and the great depression, the 9th Earl of Shaftesbury reluctantly determined that he had no option but to relinquish Belfast Castle and his estate on the Cave Hill – however much he may have wished it otherwise (his family's seat was St Gile's, Dorset, with additional property in Somerset). In 1934 he generously presented both to the City. Four years later the Chapel of the Resurrection was itself transferred to the Church of Ireland, along with the freehold of the grounds on which it stands – a plot of about two acres. Amongst St Peter's archives is an indenture (dated 1st April 1943) signed by Anthony, 9th Earl of Shaftesbury and his son, Lord Ashley (who became 10th Earl in 1961), along with 'The Representative Body of the Church of Ireland'. It stated that Lord Shaftesbury and Lord Ashley

> are desirous of vesting the said parcel of land with the Chapel and burial vaults … in the Representative Body … In pursuance of this said desire … [they] irrevocably direct limit and appoint … that all that piece or parcel of land [3 roods and 5 perches] … shall henceforth go and remain to the use of the Representative Body … In witness where the Corporate Seal of the Representative Church Body hath been hereunto affixed and the other parties hereto have set their hands and affixed their seals …

Though this deed vested the Chapel in the 'Representative Body', in effect it had become the responsibility of St Peter's. It was the nearest parish church, and had had long associations with Belfast Castle; consequently, if the Chapel were to be sold, the 'allocation of the proceeds from the sale of the property would be held in trust for

UNIQUE Opportunity to Visit

BELFAST CASTLE AND GROUNDS

By kind permission of the EARL OF SHAFTESBURY, K.P.

Grand Summer Garden FÊTE

JUNE 20, 21 & 22, 1929, from 3 to 10 p.m. each day.

OPENING CEREMONY:

THURSDAY, 20th JUNE, at 3 p.m. by

THE LADY MAYORESS (Lady Coates).

Chairman—Rt. Hon. J. MILNE-BARBOUR, D.L., M.P.

Pageant of Ulster History each evening by the 11th Girl Guides Troop (Captain, Miss Magill).
Exhibition Dancing (under the direction of Mr. and Mrs. Alec. Gardiner) each afternoon.
Half-hour Dances in the Castle—7 to 10 p.m. each evening.
MONGREL DOG SHOW · Friday Afternoon (See Special Bills).
Cake, Sweet and Fancy Stalls, and Many Other Attractions.
Amusement Park—All the Fun of the Fair!

Grand Gymkhana and Horse-jumping on Saturday at 2-30 o'c. p.m.
(SEE SPECIAL BILLS)

TEAS AND REFRESHMENTS. Catering by the ULSTER MENU CO.

BELFAST CITY TRAMWAYS MILITARY BAND will Perform Daily.

ADMISSION TO GROUNDS - - 1/-

MOTOR CARS — PARKING FEE - 2/6
GYMKHANA PARKING GROUND - 2/6 EXTRA

Proceeds in aid of ST. PETER'S CHURCH (Antrim Road) PAROCHIAL HALL BUILDING FUND.

Hon. Secretaries, { Mrs E. R. WADE, Craigowen, Somerton Road.
{ Mr. J. D. CAMPBELL, Coolgreany, Somerton Road.

Advertisement for a Grand Summer Garden Fete to be held on 30th June 1929 at Belfast Castle and Grounds;
the 11th Girl Guides Troop referred to, was attached to St Peter's.

the Parish of St Peter's' by the Church of Ireland.

Prior to the Chapel's transferral to the Church of Ireland in 1938 a great deal of decoration and renovation work was carried out – thanks to the generosity of Lord Shaftesbury himself, of the Rt Rev Dr MacNeice, Bishop of Down, Dromore and Connor, and of other benefactors. Damaged stained glass windows were mended. The fish-tail gas burners which had been located around the walls were removed and electric lighting installed. The record of the accounts for the Chapel in the fourth quarter of 1938 (which is held by St Peter's) also shows expenditure on organ repairs, fencing, pathway improvement and painting. In addition, there were some changes to the interior furnishings of the church. Two olive wood desks from Jerusalem, which had formerly been used in the Oratory at the Castle, were brought to the Chapel, and a massive, simple, pottery font, originally used at St Peter's, was also transferred there.

On the afternoon of Sunday, 18th September 1938, Dr MacNeice officiated at the first service held in the Chapel 'under the new conditions'. The services, re-commenced in 1938, continued throughout the Second World War. A new boiler was installed in 1942 and provision made to blackout the building. Military Chaplains were amongst those then using its facilities to celebrate Holy Communion. Sunday worship continued without interruption despite the fact that the Chapel suffered some superficial structural damage during the Luftwaffe air raids on Belfast in April–May 1941 (windows were broken, and the roof subsequently needed to be repaired). During the Chapel's extensive pre war renovation, its bell had not been cleaned of rust or re-erected. But it had been re-hung by the end of the conflict and, appropriately, after a silence of many years, it was rung in celebration of Allied victory.

On Sunday, 18th September 1948, a crowded congregation celebrated the tenth anniversary of the reopening of the Chapel of the Resurrection. In his address the Rector, Dr Breene, gave a brief account of its history and, on this occasion, the full choir of St Peter's Church led the singing. At first, after its reopening, Mr Crossley Clitheroe, the Organist and Choirmaster at St Peter's (1933–1944), and the Church Choir had made themselves exclusively responsible for the music at the Chapel each Sunday. But progressively, owing to the disruption caused by war, it had proved impossible to continue in this way, and numerous other parishes began to provide support, each taking their turn. By the late forties, these included: St Matthew's; St Katharine's; St George's; St James's; St Stephen's; St Silas's; Carnmoney; Upper Falls; Dunmurry; St Bartholomew's; St Paul's; St Ninian's; Jordanstown; Trinity College Dublin and Southern Missions; St Brendan's; St Mary's; St Luke's; St Michael's; St Nicholas's; St Bride's; Ardoyne; St Barnabas's; St Thomas's, and St Martin's. In addition, the clergy of these and other parishes likewise voluntarily took their turn in conducting services and in preaching at the Chapel.

In his *Jubilee* history of St Peter's, Dr Breene gave a relatively optimistic review of the position regarding the Chapel of the Resurrection in 1950. He stated that its 'congregations have been well maintained and indeed in 1948 were better than at almost any time since the reopening'. He also noted that the building was being

The Chapel of the Resurrection

ANTRIM ROAD

Service

Every Sunday Afternoon

AT 3-30 P.M.

Music by Chapel Choir and String Orchestra

ENTRANCE FROM INNISFAYLE PARK

VISITORS WELCOME   BOOKS PROVIDED

Undated notice relating to the Sunday afternoon service at 3.30 pm to be held in the Chapel of the Resurrection. From the end of the Second World War until the early 1960s, this service was held regularly throughout the year.

used for many occasional services on weekdays and is available for services in connection with Church organizations other than those of St Peter's. Mothers' Union, Scouts, Youth Guilds, etc, have taken advantage of its facilities.

Moreover, he recorded that

> it was licensed for marriages by the Lord Bishop, with the approval of His Grace the Governor of Northern Ireland, on 18th March 1941. Marriages and baptisms in it are becoming more frequent. Confirmation has also been administered twice to groups of adults … The annual Chapel Choir Party in St Peter's Parochial Hall has become a crowded, happy and helpful reunion.

But, Dr Breene did conclude his account with words of caution and concern. He highlighted the fact that in relation to the upkeep of the Chapel 'there is no endowment of any kind and all outgoings like costs of cleaning, lighting, heating, etc, have to be met from the collections' during the nine months of the year in which Sunday services were held. 'So far', he added:

> it has been possible to cover ordinary running expenses, but there must always be a measure of anxiety about the situation which would arise should major structural repairs – say to the roof – at any time be needed. Ordinary repairs have so far been met out of income.

Shortly before he wrote these words, sufficient funds had been available to make it possible for a new boiler to be installed for its heating apparatus. But there was clearly genuine cause for concern; freewill offerings at the Chapel appear never to have been sufficient to cover necessary expenditure. The refurbishment costs during the fourth quarter of 1938, prior to it being reopened, had totalled roughly £300; the offertory for the same period had been £27. In 1942, the offertory was £21 – again, not enough to cover outgoings which included £45 on a boiler; £5 on war damage insurance and blackout material; £2/12/4 on roof repairs; and £9/5/0 for the sexton.

Throughout the post war years, up until 1965, congregations continued to meet at the Chapel for divine worship each Sabbath, as well as occasionally on weekdays. An undated advertisement from this period reads:

> The Chapel of the Resurrection, Antrim Road, Service, every Sunday afternoon, at 3.30pm, music by Chapel Choir and String Orchestra, entrance from Innisfayle Park, visitors welcome, books provided.

From time to time weddings were also held there and, from 1962, it was used for the depositing of ashes after cremation (St Peter's had no such facilities). On 20th December 1969, a centenary service was held in the little church. However, the problems which increasingly afflicted St Peter's Parish during this period inevitably impacted also on the Chapel of the Resurrection. It too was affected by the movement of Church of Ireland members out of the city, the general long-term decline in levels of church attendance, and the onset of the 'Troubles' in Northern Ireland from the late 1960s. But it was beset by one further difficulty – arguably more insidious than any of the others – the scale of the vandalism directed against the fabric of the building. This was despite it being surrounded by private suburban housing;

indeed its only entrance was through a fifteen feet wide right of way. Already, in September 1957, the problem of trespassers unto the property over recent years had prompted the Select Vestry of St Peter's to consider means of making the grounds more secure (especially the crypt), and the removal of the bodies of the Donegall family buried there back to St Nicholas's, Carrickfergus.

The frequency with which worship was conducted in the Chapel diminished in the1960s. The St Peter's Annual Report for 1962 indicates that the weekly Sunday afternoon services were then being held there 'over the greater part of the year' – rather than all year round. During 1965, they were terminated altogether but, over the next eight years, the congregation of St Peter's sought to sustain the Chapel's function and tradition by holding Evensong there during the summer months (July and August) rather than in its own church. The 1973 Annual Report for St Peter's Parish makes depressing reading. It stated:

> a matter that has given us great concern is the future of the Chapel of the Resurrection. Because of the rising tide of vandalism it becomes increasingly difficult for us to keep the building in adequate repair. Indeed so poor is its condition that last summer we were unable to use it for the customary services. In the light of this the future use of the Chapel becomes a matter of urgent concern.

In fact what proved to be the last service ever to be held there had already taken place – on 27th August 1972; the preacher was the Rev S.N.M. Bayly, Curate of St Peter's (1969–74).

Throughout the 1970s and 1980s vandalism at the little church was a recurrent theme of St Peter's Notes and Annual Reports. The Notes for late 1974 dolefully recorded that

> the Select Vestry has been much exercised in thinking about the future of the Chapel site. Particularly is this so because of the very extensive vandalism which has occurred recently. No one wants to see the Chapel disappear, and yet we must take into account hard facts. We have had to remove all furnishings from the building. The organ has been sold to a country parish. The heating system has been dismantled ...

(The Select Vestry had been reluctant to do this – in November 1972, for example, it decided to 'make one more effort to preserve [the Chapel] and its contents'). In similar vein, the 1976 Annual Report recorded 'sadly ... that the Chapel ... has suffered very badly from vandalism ... Apart from removal of furnishings and bricking-up, there is little that we can do at the moment.' In 1977, its electricity supply was disconnected, and progressively during these years its exquisite carvings, altar, reredos, and remaining stained glass were removed. Various pieces of this beautifully crafted furniture were donated to other Belfast churches; some are in St Peter's. McDowell's magnificent white marble memorial of the Earl of Belfast being lamented over by his mother, Harriet Anne, was transferred to the Ulster Museum in April 1979; eventually it was placed in the foyer of the City Hall, Belfast.

But despite St Peter's never ending and heroic efforts to make the building secure through the erection of fencing and barbed wire, sealing of doors, placing of protective sheeting and wire guards on windows, and removal of the heating system, organ and all movable furniture, this provided no deterrent against the constant scourge of vandalism and theft. In July 1980 the Chapel's lower roof was stripped of lead and slates, so accelerating the pace of the building's deterioration. By then, graffiti covered the walls, and much of the floor tiling and almost all of the stained glass windows had been smashed. The carved wood panelling – formerly a part of the altar and the organ – had been torn down, and empty beer cans been strewn everywhere.

The worst ignominy which the Chapel of the Resurrection ever suffered came on 21st February 1982, when grave robbers made their way down into its vaults. There, they desecrated the tombs, stripping the lead off some; not one was left intact. The thieves had apparently hoped to retrieve jewellery or family heirlooms (some reports suggest that jewellery was indeed stolen, but later recovered). The human remains of the seven members of the Chichester family buried there, including those of the Earl of Belfast, were removed from their graves, which had been emptied out. Some of those held responsible were later brought to court (11th November 1982), and sentenced to periods of community service. The whole episode attracted much publicity – in the local press, and on television and radio.

Afterwards, the truly awful task of collecting the human remains had to be undertaken; these were then brought to Belfast Crematorium, where a cremation ceremony took place on 26th March 1982. It was subsequently arranged with St Nicholas's Church, Carrickfergus that the ashes would be brought there on 29th March, where they were to be placed in the Chichester vaults. Rev Raymond McKnight, the Curate (1980–82), along with several parishioners, prepared their reception and awaited their arrival; Charles McConnell, a member of

The Chapel of the Resurrection as it was in the early 1980s – a building which seemed to have been discarded and abandoned.

the congregation and local historian, vividly remembers that day. The seven little caskets were conveyed to the church by car; each was smaller than anticipated (measuring approximately 15cm by 15cm by 35cm) and, to enable identification, had a Christian name marked on its side. One bore the inscription: 'Frederick Richard'; this was the fourth occasion on which the Earl had been buried, and the second time on which he had been interred in the Chichester vaults at St Nicholas's'. At the same time, the seven names were entered in a special flyleaf of the Parish's burial register.

Meanwhile, on 20th November 1974, the Department of the Environment had declared the Chapel of the Resurrection to be a listed building – class 'Grade B +' – owing to its being of special historical or architectural interest (in effect, this meant that for as long as it remained out of ecclesiastical use it could not be demolished, or substantially altered, without permission from the Department). At the time, a member of the St Peter's Select Vestry observed that the decision had been taken at a time when the church was 'empty, vandalised and no longer in use.' In fact, during these years it had developed an almost frightening appearance – both its interior and exterior. In the space of twenty years it had degenerated, in effect, into a ruin. For those who knew and loved it, it seemed as though the Chapel had been 'grievously hurt'; it appeared to have been 'abandoned and discarded.' And yet, in the words of one St Peter's parishioner, it continued to 'possess a richness and blessedness.'

However, this appearance of neglect was deceptive; the Notes for St Peter's Church for November–December 1974 had commented that the Select Vestry had been 'much exercised in thinking about the future of the Chapel site ... Let us hope that we shall find a solution to the problem which is acceptable to all'. And it is true to say that no issue 'exercised' the minds of the minister and of the congregation more over the decades that followed. The 1975 January–February Notes stated that all 'practical suggestions for the future of the site ... would [be] welcome'. The Parish's Annual Reports frequently repeated such phrases as '[we are] exploring ways of dealing with' (1980), or '[are] still looking for a solution to' (1981). But, unfortunately, there was no obvious 'solution'.

The repeated attempts made by St Peter's to secure the Chapel were constantly frustrated by wanton vandalism. In truth, the responsibility for maintaining it and of providing for its future had reached crisis point at a time when St Peter's could least afford it. It was, as Canon Harris stated in June 1981, an 'ever-decreasing parish' with just 300 families then. Its congregation had no urgent purpose for the building other than somewhat contrived ones – such as the holding of Evensong there during the summer months. Its acute problem of lack of funds was accentuated by the fact that no endowment was available for the Chapel's upkeep. In June 1983, after the Parish entered a £6,000 Criminal Damage Claim for building repairs to it, the Northern Ireland office offered the risible sum of £750 'for burial of bodies and structural repairs'; the Church's solicitors advised the Rector that it was 'probably reasonable given the state of the church prior to the actual damage'. Any proposal regarding its future use would, of necessity, have to take into consideration the views of local residents who regarded the site as an amenity. But the grounds were hazardous to trespassers – in particular the quarry, located just beside the

Chapel. It was, in the words of Canon Harris, 'a very real danger to the unsuspecting public ... a precipice of some 70–100 feet.' Moreover, the fact that it dominated the small site – which in any case had poor access – greatly restricted its development potential.

However, despite the apparent intractability of these difficulties, genuine efforts were made to find a solution to them; the growing concern felt by many Belfast citizens about the Chapel's future during these years provided an additional spur for the members of St Peter's Parish to seize the initiative. But these circumstances also meant that when they did attempt to do so, their actions attracted the full glare of publicity. Thus when, in October 1974, the Church made a formal planning application in relation to the property, local residents – Protestant, Catholic, and Jewish – immediately mounted a petition as part of a preservation campaign. In response, the Rector, Canon Harris, was quoted in the local press as saying that:

> No decision has been made to demolish the chapel. The church body only applied to see if they could get outline planning permission. It was only the most tentative enquiry.

But, at the same time, he did concede publicly that whilst there were 'no plans to get rid of the building', if the application proved to be successful, the Select Vestry would have to consider the possibility of selling the land for development.

In fact the Department of the Environment was contacted several times during the 1970s and '80s by St Peter's Parish, with the support of the Representative Church Body of the Church of Ireland. Their objective was to arrange grant-aid for an agreed restoration scheme; as a listed building the Chapel was eligible for aid. Though DoE officials acknowledged that they regarded any such proposal as 'a low priority', they were 'sympathetic' in their response, and gave every encouragement to the attempt to find 'alternative uses' for the property. In June 1982, the Department offered a grant of roughly 33% of the approved costs of restoration,

> provided [the Chapel] ... would no longer be used for worship, or indeed would revert to being a place of worship in the future'. It specifically stipulated that 'de-consecration would be needed.

A wide range of ways in which the Chapel might be utilised was considered. At the outset – in 1968 – a pipe organ had been installed and an electric heating system during the following year, together with a programme of interior renovation. Peter Cavan, a member of the Select Vestry in St Peter's, and Douglas Lee, the Assistant Organist, been the driving force behind these initiatives; their intention was that regular musical performances might be held on the premises, and that it might become a cultural centre. The apparent success of this approach prompted Canon Harris to inform the Vestry (in April 1969) that at last a 'wider use had been found' for the Chapel. But, as Mr Cavan later recalled: 'sadly the events of 1969 and later [i.e. the outbreak of the 'Troubles'] put an end to what might have been a new use for the building.'

As the violence intensified, other possible usages for the Chapel were considered. These included suggestions that it might be converted into a conference centre, or

a Franciscan retreat, or be used by the Witness for Peace Movement as an inter-communal meeting place for local youth. It was also mooted that the Corporation might
wish to take it over – as it had done Belfast Castle and Castle grounds, or that the
building might be re-located to the Ulster Folk Museum, Cultra, or that the
Education and Library Board might find a purpose for it. Charles Kinahan (a member of the Historic Buildings Council of the Department of the Environment) proposed that it might be utilised as a private dwelling, or a home for the mentally
handicapped. Early on in these deliberations, in July 1966, a member of the St
Peter's Vestry had suggested that the advice and assistance of the National Trust
might be sought. It is not clear whether this potentially fruitful line of approach was
ever acted upon and, if so, what the Trust's response was.

From 1974 much of the Select Vestry's energy was directed towards obtaining
planning permission for building development on the land surrounding the Chapel.
This would have provided St Peter's with 'much needed income', whilst also perhaps
helping to eradicate the problems of vandalism in the building itself. Initially it was
unclear whether the land-locked quarry which lay close to the south, or Belfast
Lough, side of the Chapel had been included in the deed of 1st April 1943 (referred
to earlier), and was therefore the Church's property. Its acquisition was regarded as
an essential 'first step in any development of the area'. To remove any uncertainty,
on 18th June 1981, Lord Shaftesbury was asked if he 'would be prepared to transfer the quarry to St Peter's'. This he immediately agreed to do, and he indicated that
'no [financial] consideration would be required' (29th June '81). The Select Vestry
then applied to the Belfast Corporation's Planning Authority for permission to in-
fill the quarry, stressing that 'in its present state' it was 'a danger to the public.'

However the Corporation received a number of objections to this proposal from
the public. In due course, a report produced by Oliver Hetherington, Belfast City
Council's Principal Public Health Inspector (Noise Control), dated 27th November
1982, came out strongly against granting permission. His objection was rooted in
the anticipated noise levels that would be generated both by the resulting activities
within the site, and by the additional traffic (i.e. heavy vehicles continuously using
Innisfayle Park, slowly climbing its steep incline in low gear to gain access to the site,
etc). This, he stated, would be 'detrimental to [local] residents … interfere with
speech or radio listening … [and] be unacceptable and constitute a nuisance.' He
concluded that the Council would therefore have to

> require that steps be taken to have the [noise] nuisance abated. However, in
> this case I consider that, short of requiring that the tipping activities cease, no
> practical steps could be taken to reduce noise to a reasonable level.

The Church's efforts to develop the site therefore foundered. Also, in the end, the
Department of the Environment's offer of grant-aid for the Chapel's restoration was,
in its own words, 'never taken up.' The DoE was itself fully aware of the root cause.
In a letter to the Church of Ireland Diocesan Council (dated 21st November 1985;
the Diocesan Council had set up a sub-committee with regard to the Chapel in May
1978) it acknowledged that

any such scheme would of course involve considerable expenditure ... [We] understand from the Rector of St Peter's [Rev Harris] that he and his parish would face extreme difficulty in this respect.

In their reply (dated 11th December 1985), the Representative Church Body commented sadly that

> in conjunction with the Select Vestry of St Peter's Parish, various alternative uses for the Chapel ... have been considered over the years but, on investigation, none of these have proved to have potential viability ... Your Department can be assured that both the Select Vestry and Diocesan Council are sensitive to the environmental difficulties caused by this building in its dilapidated state and will continue to seek some acceptable solution to the problem.

It also indicated that 'arrangements are in place to have the building de-consecrated as it no longer serves any useful purpose in the work and witness of the Church.'

In March 1988, the Select Vestry considered the options open to it with regard to the Chapel. One, which was readily dismissed, was to do nothing; in this case the property would deteriorate even further – to the point where it would have to be demolished. A second was to develop it; but St Peter's lacked the funds to do the work necessary, and this avenue had been fully explored. The third was to sell it for development; this was the choice that was made. The Chapel had already been deconsecrated – without any publicity – on Remembrance Day, Tuesday 11th November 1986. In May 1989, the Church of Ireland sold it, by public auction, to non-ecclesiastical interests – Glenbrook Homes – for £56,000. The new owners duly submitted a planning application for permission to use the 1.5 acres surrounding the Chapel for housing development. But, in mid October 1990, this was unanimously rejected by Belfast City Council Planning Committee, on a recommendation by the Department of the Environment (on the now familiar grounds that the work entailed would result in local traffic congestion, etc). Fearing a renewed application, one week later, Tom Campbell, a Belfast City Councillor, launched a campaign

> to save one of the city's most historic landmarks ... [which was] under threat from developers ... [and] ensure that this important part of our historical heritage remains intact.

The objective was to coerce the DoE into restoring the Chapel; at the time Glenbrook Homes denied any intention to 'tear' it down, or turn it into flats.

Subsequently, those with a deep affection for the Chapel (and those living in close proximity to it) were apprehensive as to what would become of it – concerned, in particular, that it might face demolition. In his study of the Donegall family, Dr W.A. Maguire asked:

> what of the fate of Belfast's second memorial to the young Earl, the Chapel of the Resurrection? Are the relevant authorities going to allow to stand derelict and vandalised the place where the mortal remains of the Earl of Belfast once reposed? Is no one prepared to honour the memory of the young nobleman by restoring the Chapel to its former beauty?

Similar questions were frequently raised in the correspondence sections of the local press. In an anonymous letter, published in the 15th November 2004 issue of the *Belfast Telegraph*, the church was described as an 'architectural treasure ... tragically ... now a vandalised skeleton'. The correspondent appealed for 'the restoration and preservation of this beautiful chapel ... with such close connections to our city', and concluded:

> many city churches have closed in recent years but they all appear to have been turned to good use after de-consecration. Why was the Chapel of the Resurrection never given back to the safe custody of our City Fathers?

At present private developers are sealing the building (the roof and windows) with a view to ultimately converting it for use as a private dwelling, and they intend to construct apartments on the adjacent property.

The Chapel of the Resurrection does, however, live on at least vicariously, and not just in the memories and hearts of those who knew it in better times. On 7th May 2000, Rt Rev E.J. Moore, Bishop of the Diocese, renamed the side chapel in St Peter's Parish Church as the Chapel of the Resurrection. And it has been adorned with a number of its original exquisitely crafted artefacts. Amongst these are: the reredos (the crucifixion scene, with the figures of Mary Magdalene, Mary, the Mother of Jesus, St John, the Centurion, and Christ on the Cross); the altar; the statues of St Patrick and St Columbkille, and of the four Archangels; the Credence table; and the Lectern.

VII
A Guide to the
Building and Ornament of St Peter's

The Church:

The oldest section of St Peter's Parish Church (the chancel, transepts, and east section of the nave – erected between 1898–1900) was built of Scrabo sandstone with Giffnock dressings (from Dumfries) to the designs of Samuel P. Close; it was constructed by Henry Laverty & Sons. The western extension – the west front, the two most western bays of the nave, the porches, and baptistry – was completed by Richard M. Close, son of the original architect, during 1932–3 (a small notch, carved into the wooden flooring of the central aisle of the nave, marks the full extent of St Peter's prior to its extension). The contractors then, Messrs J. & R. Thompson Ltd, used Ballycullen stone from their own Scrabo quarries for the interior of the new portion and for the flags on the floor of the porch in the extension; Portland stone was used for dressings and for the tracery of the windows. The entire nave – both in the original section and the extension – and the transepts were laid with wood blocks.

The architectural style of the Church is Gothic; this flowered in Western Europe

The gates of St Peter's Church in 2008

between the twelfth and the sixteenth centuries, and is distinguished most by its use of pointed arches; these displaced the traditional rounded arches which are associated with the Greco-Roman period. St Peter's is therefore a late Victorian Gothic Revival Church; it is a 'happy and effective' blend of both decorated and perpendicular Gothic styles (the tracery in its windows is regarded as providing excellent, modern examples of decorated Gothic architecture). According to the original plans there had been an intention to erect a tall tower in the northwest corner; this was never built, but proper regard was paid to the correct east–west orientation of the building. Viewed from the Antrim Road, its rough, green, Westmoreland slates give it a highly satisfying and durable appearance (now repaired after bomb damage in 1987). On the porch and baptistery roofs the courses become narrower as they ascend, giving a receding and very pleasing effect.

The church's property is entered via either the double gates on Fortwilliam Drive or the single gate on the Antrim Road – both of which were erected in *c.* 1933, after the completion of the extension to the nave. They originally bore plates with the inscription: 'Made by the Hughes Bolokow Shipbreaking Co. Ltd Blyth Northumberland from teak taken from HMS "POWERFUL".' The *HMS Powerful*, and her sister ship *HMS Terrible*, were the largest cruisers in the world in the 1890s. *HMS Powerful* was built by the Naval Construction and Armaments Company in Barrow-in-Furness, and launched in July 1895. After three years service in China, it subsequently became famous for landing a naval brigade (consisting of seamen and Royal Marines) at Durban in October 1899. It was equipped with a battery of heavy guns, which was unloaded from the ship, transported a distance of 190 miles over land by train, and then hauled across rocky terrain so that it could be placed in position at Ladysmith. There, the men and their arms performed a vital role in relieving the 118-day siege of the town during the Boer War (the Field Gun Run, which was initiated at the Royal Tournament in 1907, is a tribute to and a commemoration of this incident). The crew of the *HMS Powerful* was greeted as heroes when they returned to Portsmouth in April 1900. The ship was later used in harbour service and for training purposes, before eventually being broken up in 1929 by the Hughes Bolokow Company. This firm proceeded to make the gates for St Peter's from the teak from the vessel.

The present Church is entered by the west porch, the beauty of which is enhanced by its leaded lights, impressive panelled ceiling, and by the extensive use of carved Austrian oak (in 1933, when newly completed, it also had double swing doors of oak). This carving is most notably exemplified in the Ewart Screen, located on the east side of the porch. It remains a worthy memorial to G. Herbert Ewart, the first treasurer of St Peter's. Its panels contain the inscription: 'To the glory of God and that there may be had in perpetual remembrance the name of George Herbert Ewart, this screen has been placed here by his wife and children. A founder of St Peter's Parish and a generous benefactor, he at all times gave of his best for its spiritual life and for the erection and adornment of this church. He fell asleep in Christ on the 26th day of March, 1924'. It was dedicated on 'St Peter's Day, 1933'.

In one of his sermons, which was inspired by the interior of St Peter's, Canon Harris referred to the 'Three Ps'. He was referring to the fact that it has no pews, no plaster and no paint. On entering the church, both before and after its completion in 1933, the congregation was seated on chairs rather than on the customary pews (a feature shared with St Anne's Cathedral). Viewed from the interior, the roofing of St Peter's is of open timberwork, using stained, but unvarnished oak; in its construction it shows much variation in the different portions of the building. It is simple and in harmony with the general design – a pleasant and refreshing feature of which is the entire absence of plasterwork. Nor has pitch pine been used anywhere; there is nothing but wrought stonework. The Church's entire furnishings are of oak (with the exception of the artefacts which were transferred from the Chapel of the Resurrection). Close study of these, and of the windows and stonework, reveals their immense richness and variety, and never fails to uncover interesting detail; the source of its inspiration varies, but there is throughout a strong influence of medieval ecclesiastical buildings found elsewhere in Ireland.

This feature of St Peter's has constantly impressed visitors. When it was being consecrated, in June 1933, the *Belfast News Letter* reporter commented:

> throughout the building there are very few repeated features. While it could not be said that no two windows in the church are alike, no two windows together are alike, unless where they form a pair and similarity is essential. This applies to the older portion of the church as well as the new. The tracery of the windows is different, even in the very large transept windows, and the pillars in the interior also show differences – some are circular and some are octagonal. It need hardly be said that this imposed a difficult task on the architects, but it has added considerably to the interest of the building. The carved stone finials above the west gable, the south porch and baptistery similarly show difference of treatment [in design and workmanship].

Likewise, in 1950, Dr Breene in his erudite and concise description emphasised the meticulous care taken when designing the church's interior. He described how

> 'the transepts are divided from the nave by two arches, worked in plain chamfered orders, and supported by columns which rise to a much greater height than the arches of the nave and aisles. In this latter case, the column on the north side is circular, and the corresponding one octagonal, an old idea of variety now happily revived, and carried on in smaller columns in the nave. Where the arches abut on piers they terminate in moulded corbels of some length, another old idea, and a good one. One broad arch spans the nave in a bold and dignified manner and the chancel floor is somewhat higher than that of the nave' (there is a crypt beneath the chancel with a three-light window).

Overall, Dr Breene concluded, '[St Peter's] has an appearance and dignity such as is rarely met with in our local ecclesiastical structures'. One recent structural change to the church is the construction of a door in the north-east corner of the north transept; its main purpose is to provide access to and from 'The McCollum Hall'.

The Chancel

As already noted, an inscription on one of the brasses to be found on the south wall of the chancel in St Peter's reads: 'To the Glory of God and in Memory of the Family of Frederick Kinahan of Lowwood who erected this Chancel and who died 17th March, 1902.' This dedication gives some indication of the extent of the Parish's debt to the benefaction of the Kinahan family during these early years; its members also provided three of the stained glass windows to be found in this portion of the church.

The exquisitely carved communion table in the sanctuary bears a small brass plate which reads: 'Richard Vaughan Macaulay, 28th March 1899. Anna Georgina Macaulay, 16th February 1924'. It is covered by fine linen cloths, rich in religious imagery, many emblazoned with the 'cross and keys' – the symbols of St Peter's; since the creation of the Parish, these have been gifted to the church by parishioners. Behind the High Altar, on the east wall of the chancel, are delicately worked mosaic panels, recessed behind stone carving which is exceptionally rich in detail. To the left of the altar is an aumbry – a recessed cupboard in the wall (normally on the north side of the High Altar) in which the Blessed Sacrament is reserved. There are only three of this type to be found in Ireland (the others are at St George's Parish Church, Belfast, and at Christ Church Cathedral, Dublin). The Holy Table and aumbry door were dedicated on 2nd November 1924. Set into the wall, south of the High Altar, is the piscina – a basin with a drain, used for washing the sacred vessels. It is in the form of a 'pelican in her piety'; the pelican is piercing its breast to feed

"HE IS NOT HERE . . . . HE IS RISEN!"

By George Tinworth.

The Reredos, 'The Women at the Sepulchre', designed by George Tinworth for the private chapel of Lord Northampton in Castle Ashby

The Reredos in St Peter's, 'The Empty Tomb', designed by George Tinworth for St Peter's; it is very similar to the Reredos which the same artist produced for Castle Ashby. The photograph also shows the delicate mosaic work and intricate stonework along the east wall of the Chancel

its young with its own blood – it is a traditional Christian image, symbolising Christ's sacrifice on the cross. It is inscribed: 'Joseph Bigger *in Christo Quievit* XIII February MDCCCXC.'

The reredos behind the High Altar is the work of George Tinworth, the celebrated Victorian ceramic sculptor. He began his career as a wood-carver but soon turned to modelling in clay. He was trained at Lambeth School of Art, and exhibited at the Royal Exhibition in 1866 when just twenty-three years of age. He entered the highly acclaimed pottery firm of Doulton's of Lambeth during the following year, and became one of its most notable and celebrated craftsmen. A description of him, written by a well-informed contemporary in 1898, and quoted by Dr Breene in his *Jubilee* history, stated that he was much influenced by the 'early training of his mother'. Elaborating on this, it explained how

> her thorough knowledge of the Bible and devoted life … left their impress upon the character of the young modeller … This acquaintance with the Scriptures influenced his life, and made his career, for his panels of the Life of Joseph, and his treatment in clay and terra cotta of the Life of Christ, are full of feeling … [and] frequently the result of thought extending over years.

The spiritual quality and profundity of his compositions, and the skill with which they were executed, attracted the praises of contemporaries such as John Ruskin, the most renowned and influential art critic of his generation.

The Reredos in the Side Chapel on the theme of 'the Ascension into Heaven' by Morris Harding

As his reputation grew, Tinworth received requests to produce secular work, including busts of leading celebrities; amongst these were Rev Charles H. Spurgeon, the well-known evangelical preacher, and Charles Bradlaugh, the controversial politician and confirmed atheist. But he was still best known for his work on religious themes. Thus he was commissioned to produce a reredos at York Minster, and he modelled a series of twenty-eight panels in terra cotta for the Royal Military Chapel in London. One of the most acclaimed of his conceptions was the reredos which he executed for Lord Northampton's private chapel in Castle Ashby; it illustrated: 'The Women at the Sepulchre'. This piece was seen, during a visit there in the late 1890s, by Herbert Ewart (a member of both the founding committee of St Peter's formed in 1896, and of its first Select Vestry established four years later). He was so deeply impressed by it that he at once approached the artist and asked him if he would reproduce it for the new Church then under construction in Belfast's northern suburbs. Tinworth accepted, and the commission was duly completed.

The reredos in St Peter's sanctuary is in unglazed terracotta; it shows some minor differences in detail from the Ashby panel, and is somewhat smaller in scale. The theme of the original was 'The Women at the Sepulchre', but in St Peter's it has always been taken to illustrate 'The Empty Tomb', and Christ's resurrection. Its outline is distinctive, firm and emphatic; it depicts the scene clearly without being overburdened by detail. In his description of it, Dr Breene noted that some parishioners had captioned it: 'He is not here'. The Rector responded by suggesting that this

was true of the tomb in the garden outside Jerusalem long ago. But, in St Peter's, we would wish rather to think that the Master is amongst us always, even where no more than two or three of us are gathered together in His name.

The chancel rails were provided by the Breene family (relatives of the second Rector of St Peter's), and dedicated in March 1980. A brass plaque on the east wall of the south transept reads: 'To the glory of God and in grateful memory of Richard Simmons Breene, Dean of Connor, Rector of this Parish, 1926–1963, and of his wife, Louisa Denison, who supported him with devotion in his ministry'. A frequently used lectern often stands in the chancel, and was provided by the congregation as a memorial to Dr Breene's successor, Canon Harris, in 1996. Its inscription reads: 'In Memory of the Rev Canon William Ernest Harris, Rector of this Parish, 1963–1990'.

The Side Chapel:

A plaque located on the east wall of the south transept bears the inscription:

> To the Glory of God and to preserve the History of the earlier Chapel this area was dedicated as "The Chapel of the Resurrection" by Rt Rev James E. Moore, Bishop of Connor, 7th May 2000.

The Reredos from the Chapel of the Resurrection showing the crucifixion of Christ; it was carved from Irish oak and, when produced, was regarded as one of the finest examples of wood carving in Ireland.

The communion table in the side chapel is inscribed around the base as follows: 'This Table and Rail were placed here in Memory of Henry Robert Brett, First Rector of this Parish, by Parishioners and Friends. St Peter's Day, 1937.' The image on the reredos in the sanctuary is complimented by the two other reredos to be seen in St Peter's. The reredos in the side chapel in the south transept is a very striking, unusual and effective conception on the theme of 'The Ascension into Heaven'. The figures were carved with immense skill in alabaster by Morris Harding, RHA, OBE, who had previously completed a number of commissions for St Anne's Cathedral. The surrounding frame is in warm-tinted, Derbyshire marble, and it adds greatly to the profound visual impact of the overall design. It also bears an inscription along its northern and southern edges: 'In Memory of Ellen Ferguson, died November 3, 1931, and of her Sister

St Peter's Side Chapel in the south transept of the church as it was shortly after it was dedicated on 29th June 1935. It shows the distinct patterns of the McNeill window in the east wall of the south transept, which were inspired by fifteenth century Irish designs.

St Peter's Side Chapel after it had been re-dedicated as 'The Chapel of the Resurrection' as part of the Centenary celebrations, on 7th May 2000.

Mary, died January 15, 1914'. Nearby – along the south wall of the south transept – is the reredos which had originally been erected in the Chapel of the Resurrection; it depicts Christ's crucifixion. In combination, therefore, the three reredos in the Church illustrate the defining moments in the life of Christ, which together provide the very foundations of the Christian faith – Christ's Death, Christ's Resurrection, Christ's Ascension.

The other splendidly crafted artefacts transferred from the Chapel of the Resurrection to St Peter's are to be found along the south side of the Church. As

noted, the reredos is in the south transept, and so also are the credence table (affixed to its east wall) and the lectern (in the side chapel). The statues of St Patrick and St Columbkille are to be found along the south wall of the south transept, and those of each of the four archangels along the south wall of the nave. The altar from the Chapel, which was carved in Irish woods, has been placed at the mid way point of the west wall, close to the entrance from the west door. (See Chapter VI for a description of the interior of the Chapel of the Resurrection).

The Windows
Gothic architecture is characterised by the pointed arch (which, as noted, succeeded the classical, rounded arch), and when two or more windows (or lights) were placed together, the spaces between their heads were pierced with small windows. This was known as tracery and, in the later decorative Gothic period, it became increasingly intricate and elaborate. The windows of St Peter's Church, largely inspired by old Irish examples (such as Devenish, Holy Cross, and Culfeightrin), are widely regarded as fine modern examples of this decorated Gothic style. (The stained glass windows in St Peter's are by Messrs Heaton, Butler and Bayne, London; Messrs James Powell and Sons, London; and Messrs W.F. Clokey, Belfast).

One of the four archangels carved by craftsmen in Bruges, and transferred from the Chapel of the Resurrection to St Peter's, where it is to be found along the south wall of the nave.

The Chancel Windows
On entering St Peter's today through the west door, and looking towards the High Altar, one's eyes are immediately drawn towards the great east window behind it. When the church was licensed on St Peter's Day, 1900, its centre light was the only stained glass in the entire building (it sustained bomb damage in 1987, and has subsequently been restored). It depicts Our Lord rescuing St Peter from drowning (its tracery is based on the east window in Devenish Abbey, now

in Monea, Co. Fermanagh). The window was later completed by the addition of the two studies in the lights on either side of it – on the left Christ is shown in St Peter's boat instructing the people; the other, on the right, represents His appearance to St Peter and others after His Resurrection. Below these vertical sections, the scenes depicted are referred to in a series of Biblical texts – 'He sat down and taught the people out of the ship'; 'Jesus stretched forth His hands and taught him and said unto him, O thou of little faith'; 'Bring of the fish which ye have now caught.'; 'Blessed are the pure in heart for they shall see God. St Matthew V, 8'. The entire window was erected by Mr Frederick Kinahan, of Lowwood, in memory of two of his children. A daughter, Beatrice Kinahan, was born on 28th May, and a son, James G. Kinahan, a Lieutenant in the Royal Irish Regiment, died at Nowshira, India, on 28th May, 1889. The window bears the inscription: 'In loving memory of James Kinahan who died 28th May, 1889, and of Beatrice Kinahan who died 4th January, 1902'.

Close by are two companion, stained glass windows erected in the south wall of the chancel, and both of them are fine examples of decorative Gothic tracery; their strik-ing differences from English models suggest that the Irish medieval originals, on which they are based, were inspired by sources and designs brought direct from the continent. Both are also intimately associat-ed with the Kinahan family. Frederick Kinahan died before the east window had been placed in position. Fittingly a window a short distance from it was dedi-cated to his memory by the

The great East Window, erected by Frederick Kinahan in memory of two of his children, Beatrice and James. The centre light was the only stained glass in the church when it was licensed on St Peter's Day 1900.

Rector before the service on Sunday 2nd August 1903. It was the gift of his family, and illustrates the story of St Peter's deliverance from prison by an angel. The inscription reads:

> To the Glory of God and in Loving Memory of Frederick Kinahan of Lowwood who died 17th March, 1902, this Window was erected by his sorrowing Wife and Children. "Arise up quickly, and his chains fell off from his hands. Acts XII".

The second window was erected to the memory of his widow, Marion Elizabeth Kinahan; she had laid the foundation stone of St Peter's Church on 28th May 1898. It was donated by her children. Its theme is 'Motherhood', and it was the work of the highly reputable firm of Messrs James Powell & Sons, Whitefriars Glass Works, London, who had completed a number of commissions for stained glass in St Anne's Cathedral (both in the great west window, and in the aisles). It shows the Virgin Mary with the Child Jesus, and St Elizabeth with John the Baptist. And below these, Hannah is portrayed presenting Samuel to the Lord and King Lemuel who, according to the Biblical passage, remembered 'the prophesy that his mother taught Him' (Proverbs, Chapter XXXI, Verse I). It was dedicated on a date which was clearly redolent with memories for the Kinahan family –

The World War One Memorial Window or Victory Window, in the south transept

28th May 1915. It is inscribed:

> In Loving Memory of Marion Elizabeth Kinahan, wife of Frederick Kinahan of Lowwood, who died 21st February, 1914, This Window was erected by her Children'; "Of His Kingdom there shall be no end"; "To guide our feet into the way of peace."

Windows in the South Transept

Perhaps the most distinctive or unique window in St Peter's is to be found nearby – in the east wall of the south transept. Its design was suggested by Francis Joseph Bigger, himself an expert on Irish artefacts and decoration, and it too was produced by the firm of James Powell & Sons. It has been described as being 'of a grisaille pattern in gold, and silver, painted on antique glass, surrounded by a richly coloured border painted on similar material. The effect produced is that of fifteenth century glass'. This was in fact the date of the original design for the stonework in the window; it is copied from tracery found in Culfeightrin Old Church (now in ruins), which was erected between 1450 and 1500 AD. It was dedicated on 22nd September 1907, and bears an inscription which reads: 'This Window is Dedicated to the Memory of Henry Hugh McNeill of Parkmount. Born November 29, 1829. Died July 6, 1904.' St Peter's Church is built on land which had belonged to the McNeill family of Parkmount.

Victory Window – First World War, South Transept

In the aftermath of the First World War, a further great window was added to the Church. Known as the Victory Window, it is located in the south transept, and was dedicated two years after the Armistice, on Sunday 21st November 1920 (thankfully it escaped bomb damage in 1987). It was erected by St Peter's parishioners not only as a memorial to all those connected with the congregation who died in the Great War, but also to those who fought in the conflict and to those who performed war services of any kind, either at home or abroad. It also was manufactured by the firm of Messrs Powell & Sons. It is in the late perpendicular Gothic style, and is on a considerable scale, covering two hundred square feet. The six main lights are fourteen feet six inches high and twenty-one inches wide – a size rarely encountered in a parish church. The design is complex, but the whole window conveys one central and fitting idea – the transformation of Struggle and Sacrifice into Victory. As it uses Christian imagery throughout, this theme is expressed as a spiritual struggle and sacrifice, and as a spiritual victory. The first three lights on the left represent the Struggle and the Sacrifice, and the three on the right the Victory. On the upper level, the central figure in the left-hand group is the Angel of the Cup, 'richly dight in royal robe', looking down on the world to which she is bringing the cup. Around her shoulders, and hanging over her arm, is a rich stole, and over the rich purple under-robe is a royal garment – suggested by its rich embroidery of white and gold. She is flanked on the left by St Michael, the warrior Angel, a strong, proud figure in red and gold armour, firmly placing his foot on the green dragon. On the right is The Angel of Death holding a scythe – a traditional motif. She is dressed in a hooded black robe, but there is also a richness, and a significance perhaps, in the green undergarment. Still on the upper level, in the right-hand group of three, representing Victory, the central figure is the Angel beating the sword into a sickle. The soft grey of the anvil highlights the strong purple robe, and here again there is a suggestion of an embroidered outer garment. She is flanked on the left by the Angel of Mercy, dressed in a red robe and green cloak, and carrying a scroll from the Beatitudes. On the right is the Angel of the Resurrection, in red and gold, who points the observer towards Heaven. The central figure in each group is slightly raised.

On the lower level there is also a row of six, slightly smaller, figures. From left to right they are: Gideon (below St Michael), the victorious warrior of God, carrying a vessel and torch, and about to blow his horn; Christ, the Good Shepherd (below the Angel of the Cup), slightly raised, with a 'Lamb of God' symbol below; then The Virgin Mary, at the foot of the Cross – the quintessential Christian image of sorrow. Just right of centre, below the Angel of Mercy, Dorcas is depicted with a basket. Dr Breene recalls that she was described by a Canon at St Paul's Cathedral (in a sermon to women workers during the Second World War) as 'the woman who worked'. Then, again slightly raised and to balance the figure of Christ the Good Shepherd on the left, is the figure of Christ 'Come unto me', with the 'IHS' symbol below. On the far right is Elijah, set appropriately beneath the Angel of the Resurrection, ascending to Heaven in a chariot of fire.

In the tracery above these twelve figures are eight narrow, smaller lights, each containing a figure representing the cardinal virtues highlighted in the New Testament,

THE HOLY DOVE
The love of God brooding over all

FAITH				HOPE
The				The
Crown of Thorns				Crown of Victory

Fortitude–Truth–Justice–Purity–Temperance–Wisdom–Patience–Humility

St MICHAEL	ANGEL of the CHALICE	ANGEL of DEATH	ANGEL of MERCY	ANGEL of the SWORD and SICKLE	ANGEL of RESURRECTION
GIDEON	The GOOD SHEPHERD	St MARY	DORCAS	'COME UNTO ME'	ELIJAH

The Scheme of the Memorial Window in the South Transept

and fashioned with the same care and exquisite attention to detail as the main panels of the window below: Fortitude, has a shield and lance; Truth, a shimmering glass; Justice, has scales; Purity a lily; Temperance quenches the flames; Wisdom grips a serpent; Patience has a yoke, and Humility has a lowly offering. These provide a link with the grand theme of the design – the transformation of Sacrifice and Struggle into Victory. This is further emphasised in the two quatrefoils above each group of four: the left one contains the Crown of Thorns, and the right one the Crown of Victory. At the apex of the window, is 'the holy Dove' – emblematic of 'the love of God brooding over all', flanked by two angels below: Faith, with a cross and shield, and Hope, with a spray of tender almond blossom.

The whole window is treated softly; though the figures are rich, the tracery is delicate, and, thus, its general effect is not to darken the Church to any significant extent. Dr Breene states (in his *Jubilee* history) that the scheme of the window

> brings out the full purpose of life and the full purpose of all the self-sacrifice which has gone to secure for us those things, in and beyond Life, which are precious to us. It is a memorial which will always be a memory, speaking its story and its lesson in unmistakable language. There will never be a sorrowing soul who looks on this window but will be led to think of the ultimate things – the Conquest, the Consolation.

The images in the window inspired Rev H.R. Brett, the then Rector, to write a series of seven sermons for Lent, 1921.

Below the Victory Window a tablet (also the work of Messrs Powell & Sons), framed in Derbyshire stone, contains the names of those members of the Parish who died in the Great War and the dates of their deaths. The inscription panel, which is surrounded by a line of gold mosaic, is composed of glass tiles; during its manufacture, glass was mixed into the paint which was used when forming the letters and when fired it came to the surface of the paint and formed a flux; this technique was applied in order to ensure that the names will remain there in perpetuity; it has the inscription: 'Our Glorious Dead 1914–1918. Their name liveth for evermore'. On the east side of the window is a memorial tablet of oak, designed and executed by Messrs Harry Hems &, Sons, Sculptors, of Exeter. The upper portion is rich in carving and pierced tracery, the central panel contains a shield bearing the Cross Keys (the arms of St Peter's), and in side panels are minor shields containing the dates 1914–1918. On another, below this, is a list of names – in raised characters and gilded – and also a dedicatory inscription: 'To the Glory of God Who gave us Victory and in Remembrance of the War Services of Men and Women of this Parish of whom those named Served Overseas this Window is Dedicated' (see Appendix I).

Windows in the West Wall and Baptistry

The completion of the extension to the nave of St Peter's, and of the west front, porches and baptistry in 1933, stimulated the further adornment of the Church. The west window has six lights filled with leaded glass, measures approximately fifteen by twenty-five feet, and is itself a beautiful feature which bathes the whole interior with light. Like the reredos in the side chapel, the 'Angel Font' in the baptistry (which is located in the north west corner of the Church) is the work of Maurice Harding. The resplendent figure of an angel, seated and holding the stoup, was carved from French Portland stone, and the large, imposing base supporting them from Connemara marble. In 1933, the *Belfast News Letter* said of it that it was

> a feature found in no other Belfast church and very rarely found in England. [It] … is a simple piece of sculpture full of symbolism. There are doves typifying the Holy Spirit, the vine representing mother earth, and around the stoup is a decoration of shamrocks …

In his *Jubilee* history, Dr Breene suggested that: 'the Baptistry and Font, though so serenely simple, are most impressive and beautiful as seen from the South Porch across the whole West End of the Church', from which vantage point they are some sixty feet distant.

This position also affords excellent views of the stained glass windows which were erected after the extension had been completed; eight windows were added between 1934 and 1961 – three during 1934–35, two in the course of the Second World War, two more in the 1950s, and another in 1961. Considering these chronologically, the first was placed in the west wall south of the Ewart Screen and porch, and dedicated at the Sunday morning service, on 13th May 1934. It was erected in memory of Hugh Pearson by his family; the subject is St Peter. It bears the inscription: 'To the Glory of God and in Loving Memory of Hugh Pearson. This Window was erected by his Widow and Daughters. AD 1934. "A good man leaveth an inheritance."' In close proximity to it (in the north wall of the baptistry), a window was dedicated to the memory of Walter Berwick and his wife, Lucy, during the Patronal celebrations of that year, on the evening of Friday, 29th June 1934. It is composed of four studies: the Presentation of Samuel; the Presentation of Jesus in the Temple; Our Lord speaking with Nicademus; and the Confirmation by Saint Peter and Saint John. It bears the inscription: 'To the Glory of God and in Loving Memory of Walter Berwick, died 28th November 1921, and of Cornelia Lucy, his Wife, died 22nd March, 1899. This Window was erected by his Daughters and Dedicated on St Peter's Day, 1934.'

Its four themes are brilliantly illustrated, each combined with an appropriate text – 'As long as he liveth he shall be lent to the Lord'; 'Lord, now lettest Thou Thy servant depart in peace'; Ye must be born again of water and the spirit'; and 'Then laid they their hands on them'. Twelve months later, on 29th June 1935 (St Peter's Day), a window in the west wall of the south porch, illustrating Hope and Fortitude, was dedicated to the memory of Rev H.R. Brett; it was the gift of his widow and sons, and is inscribed: 'In Memory of Henry Robert Brett, Rector of this Parish, 1900–1926. Dean of Belfast, 1926–1932'. Recently the attraction of this section of the church has been enhanced further by the addition of two oak units, which were donated by the family of Mervyn and Greta Patterson and dedicated in their memory, on 8th September 2002.

The embellishment of the Church continued during the Second World War. A window to match the Pearson Window, placed on the north side of the Ewart Screen and porch, was dedicated by Rt Rev Charles King Irwin, Bishop of Connor, on Sunday, 19th October 1944; it was a memorial to D.C.S. Megaw, and was the gift of his parents. The subject is St Patrick on Slemish. It is inscribed: 'To the Glory of God and in Memory of Denis Cyril Stanley Megaw, 1916–1941'. Two months later, on the Sunday morning of 17th December 1944, the Taylor Memorial Window in the west wall of the baptistry was dedicated, also by the Bishop. The south light represents the baptism of Our Lord in the River Jordan, and it is inscribed with the text: 'This is My beloved Son, in whom I am well pleased.' The north light shows the baptism of the house of Cornelius, and is illustrated with the text: 'Can any man forbid water, that these should not be Baptised?' The dedicatory inscription reads: 'In Loving Memory of Annie Taylor, who fell asleep on the 11th of January, 1942. This Window was erected by her Sister, Clara, and her Brother, Victor Alexander, 1944'.

Memorial Windows – Second World War

The stained glass in the Church also bears eloquent testimony to the casualties suffered and sacrifices made by members of the congregation during the Second World War. In 1950 a beautiful window, placed between the Megaw and Taylor windows in the west wall north of the porch, was erected to the memory of Second Lieutenant Claude Lowry Handforth, of the 15th Punjabi Regiment, Indian Army. He was a talented young man (attended Royal Belfast Academical Institution), with a particular aptitude for languages; he was captured while broadcasting to the Japanese in their own tongue. Below two figures depicting 'Truth' and 'Valour', the window bears the inscriptions: 'To the Glory of God and in memory of Claude Lowry Handforth Lieutenant 1/15 Punjab Regiment, missing at Rathedaung, Burma, 17th February 1943, aged twenty years', 'Faithful and True, His name the word of God', and 'A good soldier of Jesus Christ'. Lieutenant Handforth is one of 26,000 members of allied forces who lie in the Burmese jungle with no known grave; his name appears on the War Memorial in Rangoon. The window was the gift of his father, Claude Handforth, a church warden, and his mother.

One of the comparatively recent windows to be unveiled in St Peter's was erected by the congregation to commemorate the sacrifices of fellow parishioners during the Second World War. The 'War Memorial Window' in the north transept was dedicated by the Rt Rev Charles King Irwin, Bishop of Connor, on Saturday 5th November 1955 (unfortunately, it was severely damaged in the explosion of 1987, and had to be replaced – but this was done in its original form). Its design, from the studios of W.M. Morris, London, is less complex than that for the memorial window in the south transept relating to the Great War, which it counterbalances. The main central section is dominated by two great pictures. On one side Christ is shown, descending from the cross; Joseph of Arimathea is depicted in the act of lowering His body, while St John and the Virgin Mary kneel at his feet. The other side illustrates Christ's triumphant ascent from the tomb, while two watchmen can be seen cowering to the ground in terror. Hovering over both representations, are the figures of the four Archangels – St Raphael, St Uriel, St Gabriel and St Michael. The essential theme of the window is one of triumph – expressed through the medium of New Testament symbolism. It is a 'Victory Window' because its images link the agony of Christ's death and the glory of His resurrection. Death is defeated utterly, and Christ's sacrifice is seen as the great and effectual door to newness of life for all mankind.

The central message of this Memorial Window is brought out clearly in these two dominant groups. Everything else in the design is subsidiary but, nonetheless, still has its place and function, in the articulation and integration of the whole. On both sides of the lower sections of the window are two groups of figures. It is evident from their uniforms, arms and equipment, that they are representative of those who served King and Country in the Second World War. Between them, the Four Horsemen of the Apocalypse trample down ruined buildings in a scene of devastation. A brilliant rainbow rises behind them; it is the token of God's promise that all flesh shall never be totally destroyed on earth. Collectively these images suggest to the observer a period of conflict, the Second World War, and a particular moment in time: 1939–45. Others identify a specific place. Two shields are depicted in the window; one of them bears the Arms of the City of Belfast and, the other, those of the state of Northern Ireland. The precise location is defined further by the inclusion of a number of ecclesiastical symbols, relating to the religious side of our community life. Two shields, similar to those mentioned, and held in angelic hands, appear at the apexes of the long lights; these bear the arms of the Diocese of Connor, and of the Ecclesiastical Province of Armagh. Furthermore, as the eye ascends, four small lights can be seen. These depict: St Anne (the mother parish of St Peter's) and St Katharine (our daughter

The Handforth Window in the west wall, north of the porch, dedicated in 1943

parish), with St Peter (our parochial Patron Saint) and St Patrick (our national Patron Saint) between them.

Finally, approaching the highest levels of the window, there are four still smaller lights. These contain: two sacrificial symbols of Christ – the Paschal Lamb, and the Pelican in her piety; and also two symbols emblematic of triumph – the Phoenix, and the Lion of the Tribe of Judah. Above these, are three golden crowns, the two lower ones supported by angelic figures; they are representative of our three armed services – the Navy, the Army and the Royal Air Force. They prompt the observer to reflect with admiration and with gratitude on those of our parishioners, now beyond the veil, who volunteered to join the fighting forces – the principal temporal instruments of victory in the struggle against Fascism which the window commemorates. However, in addition, the combination of all of these symbols points to a loftier plane. It is a reminder of Christ's victory – His death and His resurrection, His sacrifice and His triumph, and that God's love overrules all our designs and destinies. In St John's words, 'God is Love'. '*Amor vincit omnia*'. 'Love conquers all'.

Just below the window, a plaque bears the names of those from the congregation who died during the fighting in the Second World War. It bears the inscription: 'The Supreme Sacrifice, 1939–1945. These have put off the mortal clothing and put on the immortal'. A second plaque, placed in memory of those who served and survived, is located in the north wall beside the window, bears the inscription:

> The Memorial Window in this Transept is dedicated to the Glory of God in grateful acknowledgement of the War Services of Parishioners during the years 1939–1945. The names of those who, in the Divine Providence, were spared to return are recorded on this Tablet.' (See Appendix I).

The last stained glass window to be erected in St Peter's is the Durnan Memorial Window; it is located in the west wall, south of

The World War Two Memorial Window, in the north transept

the porch, beside the Pearson Window (which had been the first to be placed in the newly extended church in 1934). It was dedicated by Rt Rev R.C.H.G. Elliot, Bishop of Connor, before a packed congregation at the morning service, on Sunday 22nd October 1961; it depicts scenes from the life of Christ, was designed by Messrs W.F. Clokey, Belfast, and bears the inscription:

> To the glory of God, and in loving memory of John William Durnan obiit August 1948 and his wife, Emma Rebecca Durnan, obiit October 1961, also their son, James Norman Durnan, obiit August 1958.

The Interior Furnishings

The woodcarving in St Peter's is by Messrs Harry Hems and Sons, Exeter; and Messrs Purdy and Millard, Belfast, and all of the stone-carving in the earlier section was by John Baker, an 'artist in stone', who flourished in the early 1900s (his work is to be seen in several English churches, notably Selby Abbey). Both, along with the rest of the interior – the stained glass, etc – are exceptionally rich in detail and in religious symbolism; the inspiration for this work has been drawn from a wide range of different sources and traditions. Writing in 1913, thirteen years after the Church's opening, Rev H.R. Brett observed:

> perhaps the first impression which … [St Peter's] creates in the mind of a careless visitor is that of newness. To us who have taken pains to study it and learn its lessons, its windows and walls tell in outline the story of nineteen centuries of Christianity … In writing that story in an infinite variety of design we have much original work, but we have also borrowed from models which can be traced back to the Catacombs; from Canterbury Cathedral, Westminster Abbey and Beverley Minster; from Melrose and Linlithgow; and from our own Irish foundations of Culfeightrin and Devenish, Glendalough, Kilconnell, and Drumahaire.

Numerous examples can be cited to lend support to the Rector's foregoing description. There is a double equilateral triangle in the south transept; amongst other designs, this motif is widely recognised within the Christian artistic tradition as being emblematic of the Trinity (which has three elements and is yet a unity, 'three in one'). The Trinity is represented in the chancel as well – by a circle enclosing a trefoil within which there are three crowns. This particular pattern was copied from the Chapter House in Canterbury Cathedral. In the east window and inscribed in the stonework in the north transept, are the words: 'DEXTER DEI', or 'Right Hand of God', the first person in the Trinity. Likewise, clearly visible in the four upper corbels of both transepts, are the four letters 'DEUS' – 'God'; they are carved in a design made up of interlacing Celtic beasts derived, or borrowed, from the panels of one of the ancient Irish crosses, the Clogher Cross. At a lower level the corbels below each of these letterings bear the inscription, 'AMEN', or 'so be it'. In the south transept, and in the east window, there are representations of a dove – the symbol of the third person in the Holy Trinity, the Holy Spirit.

It is, however, the representations of Christ in St Peter's which, in Rev H.R. Brett's words, 'speak to us most persistently from window, from wood, and from stone'. Christ is depicted in the east window, and in those commemorating the First and Second World Wars, and in the three reredos in the Church (located behind the high alter, in the side chapel, and in the south transept). The carving on the piscina of a pelican feeding her young with her own blood is intended to illustrate the religious symbolism of the liturgy of the communion – that it is with His own body and His own blood that Christ feeds His church. Likewise, in the north transept, the lamb is a reference to the New Testament and the Gospels – to the 'Lamb of God' who 'taketh away the sins of the world.' Similarly, the paten and the chalice, and the sacred initials which occur again and again in the chancel, are a constant visual reminder of the absolute centrality of the life of Christ to the teachings of the Christian Church.

The foregoing description does not come close to exhausting the richness of the symbolism to be found in the Church. The Four Evangelists are represented in its ornamentation by their traditional emblems, derived from the content of the Gospels which each wrote –

> the first had the face of a lion [i.e. St Mark, who begins with 'the voice of one crying in the wilderness, Prepare ye the way of the Lord' – like a lion roaring, according to St Jerome], the second had the face of a calf [i.e. St Luke, whose first chapter describes the piety of Zacharias, who as a priest would have sacrificed calves], the third had the face of a man [i.e. St Matthew, whose account starts with the genealogy of Christ], and the fourth was like a flying eagle [i.e. St John, because in his Gospel he is said to have taken on the wings of an eagle and soared to the heights in presenting the word of God].

Flowers and foliage, and the cereals and fruits of life, also form an important element in the decoration of St Peter's – rose, passion flower, *fleur-de-lis*, vine, oak, thorn, fig, grape, pomegranate, wheat. They appear repeatedly in the mosaics, in the stonework around the top of the chancel, and in the woodcarving. Apart from their individual symbolism, they serve to remind the faithful of God's bounty and to illustrate God's love. Around the top of the arches in the main aisle are carvings of sparrows and swallows; their inspiration is drawn from Psalm 84, verse 3: 'Yea, the sparrow hath found an house, and the swallow a nest for herself, where she may lay her young, even thine altars, O Lord of hosts, my King and my God'. These, along with the birds whispering into the ears of St Francis in one of the windows in the west wall, remind us of God's tender care for the smallest and weakest of His creatures. Along the west wall of the church is also to be found an illustrated memorial litany book – the work of Mr Mark Garrett, whose gift it was to St Peter's church; Mr Garrett had illustrated Gospel themes on several pages. His carving on the oak memorial case was Celtic in character to harmonise with the book which it contained. An inscription indicates that the 'case was the work and gift of the Men's Working Party', and that it was dedicated by the Lord Bishop of Down and Dromore, on St Peter's Day 1956.

But no account of the religious symbolism to be found in St Peter's would be com-

plete, however, without reference to its architectural style. Rev H.R. Brett concluded his description of the Church by stating that all of its disparate elements were:

> united ... in a building whose very framework points to the Heaven where
> Christ dwells. For the essential note of Gothic architecture is aspiration ... To
> rise higher and higher, nearer and nearer to heaven, was the passionate desire
> of the Gothic builder. The pointing of the arch, the vaulting and pitch of the
> roof ... the pinnacle, the spire or lofty tower, all tell of a determination to soar
> above the limitations of earth.

VIII
Bishops, Clergy, Parochial Officers, Organists and Choirmasters associated with St Peter's

BISHOPS
(from 1st January 1945, the United Diocese of Down, Connor and Dromore was divided into two separate Dioceses – the Diocese of Down and Dromore, and the Diocese of Connor):

Thomas James Welland	1892–1907
John Baptist Crozier	1907–1911
Charles Frederick D'Arcy	1911–1919
Charles Thornton Primrose Grierson	1919–1934
John Frederick McNeice	1934–1942
Charles King Irwin	1942–1956
Robert Cyril Hamilton Elliot	1956–1969
Arthur Hamilton Butler	1969–1981
William John McCappin	1981–1987
Samuel Greenfield Poyntz	1987–1995
Edward James Moore	1995–2001
Alan Harper	2002–2007
Alan Abernethy	2007–

(Bishop A.H. Butler was the first in recent times not to live in the Bishop's House, or 'See House', on the Antrim Road).

THE 'FOUNDER' OF ST PETER'S:
Rev Henry Stewart O'Hara

Henry Stewart O'Hara was the eldest son of the Rev James O'Hara, Rector of Coleraine. He was born on 6th September 1843, and educated at the Collegiate School, Leicester, and at TCD. He graduated with honours in ethics and logic in 1865, obtained a BD in 1868, and a DD in 1900. He was ordained Deacon in 1867, and Priest in the following year. He was Curate in Ballyrashane, 1867–68, and Kildollagh, 1868–9. He succeeded his father as Rector of Coleraine (1869–94). In July 1894 he became Vicar of Belfast, following the death of Rev Dr Robert Hannay, and served until 1900. He was also Chancellor of Connor, 1884–97, and Canon of St Patrick's Cathedral, Dublin, 1897–9. In 1899 he was appointed the first

Dean of St Anne's Cathedral and, in the following year, Bishop of Cashel, Emly, Waterford and Lismore. According to Dr Breene, it is recorded that 'he was the first clergyman appointed by the Bishops in the exercise of their sole patronage. The Diocesan Synods of Cashel and Waterford had failed to elect, and the election had by lapse been referred to the Bench.' He was instrumental in the rebuilding of St Patrick's Church, Coleraine, one of the most beautiful in Ireland (consecrated 28th April 1885). He initiated the replacement of old St Anne's, Belfast, by the present Cathedral, and he is regarded as having been the 'founder' of St Peter's. The first Rector of the Parish, the Rev H.R. Brett, came with him to Belfast from Coleraine, where he had been his Curate. Bishop O'Hara was an enthusiastic pioneer of the movement to give women a fuller share in the councils and government of the Church. He resigned his See in 1919. On the occasion of his elevation to the Episcopate the parishioners of St Peter's presented him with his Episcopal Seal, and former parishioners and friends in Coleraine with a handsome Pastoral Staff. He died on 11th December 1923, aged 80, in Coleraine.

RECTORS OF ST PETER'S CHURCH:

Rev Henry Robert Brett

On 1st November 1898, Rev H.R. Brett was placed in charge of St Peter's Parochial District (in succession to the Rev A.G. Stuart who had set the process of forming the new district in motion). He was born on 18th October 1868, educated at Kilkenny College, and graduated from TCD with a BA in 1892, and an MA in 1896. He was ordained Deacon in 1893, and Priest in 1894. He served as Curate in Coleraine, 1893–4 (Rev H.S. O'Hara was then Rector). He came to St Anne's, Belfast, with Rev O'Hara when the latter was appointed Vicar of Belfast in 1894, and served there as Curate until 1900. He was formally instituted as the first Rector of the Parish on 30th March 1900; he served until 1926. He was appointed Prebendary of Tassagard in St Patrick's National Cathedral, 1919–20, and a member of the Representative Church Body in 1921. He was Diocesan Registrar of Down, Connor and Dromore, 1920–26, and Archdeacon of Connor, 1920–26. He was appointed Vicar of Belfast and Dean of St Anne's Cathedral, 1926–32. He was one of the Chaplains to the Northern Ireland Parliament, established in 1921. He resigned in September 1932, and died later that year in Belfast on 2nd November.

Dr Breene records that during his twenty-eight years at St Peter's, Rev Brett built up a strong parochial life with fine traditions, and he also secured the Parish's finances. At St Anne's he saw the baptistry, the west front and the Chapel of the Holy Spirit completed. Many other improvements (carvings, mosaics, etc) were also carried out during his short period there. On his resignation, the Cathedral Board placed on record its appreciation of his unceasing labour and devotion; during his all too short tenure at the office of Dean, he had enlarged and beautified the building, and added lustre to its services and prestige to the Church within the whole city.

Rev Dr Richard Simmons Breene

On 14th May 1926, Dr R.S. Breene was instituted as second Rector of St Peter's. He was born on 25th June 1886 (shortly before St Peter's Day). He graduated in arts and law at Queen's University in 1910, took an MA in modern history in 1914 and an LLD in 1919. He became a Deacon in 1911, and was ordained Priest in 1912. After serving the Curacies of Ballynure, 1911–13, and Glenavy, 1913–15, he became a Chaplain to the forces until the beginning of 1920. He was Rector of Killinchy and Kilmood until 1926, when he was appointed to St Peter's (1926–63). He was Rural Dean of North Belfast, 1931–47; Domestic Chaplain to the Bishop of Down, 1935–45; Diocesan Registrar of Connor, 1941–63, and of Down and Dromore, 1941–60; Chancellor of Connor Cathedral, 1941–56; Dean of Connor and Precentor of St Anne's Cathedral, 1956–63. He was a Member of the Faculty of Theology of Queen's University from 1944, and was Examining Chaplain to the Bishop of Down and Dromore, 1938–57, and Domestic and Examining Chaplain to the Bishop of Connor, 1942–63. He was a distinguished scholar. He edited the *Irish Churchman* from 1920 to 1934; was Church of Ireland correspondent to the *Belfast News Letter*, contributing the weekly *Viator* column; and was author of *St Peter's Jubilee Book, 1950*. He also wrote the carol 'O Bethlehem is a small Place' (Carol 13, *Irish Church Hymnal*), which he had included in his *Songs of the Nativity*. In the year 2000, his daughter, Molly, indicated that this 'collection of carols … [was] written for various occasions over the years between 1946–58, [and] he had the book put together in memory of his wife who died in 1957 … He used to write a carol most Christmases, and found an artist in the parish who would design a card to go with it'. He died on 4th February 1974.

Rev William Ernest Harris

On 18th December 1963, Rev W.E. Harris was instituted as third Rector of St Peter's. He was born in Cahir, Co. Tipperary, 28th May 1921. He was educated at the Church National School, Bishop's Palace, Cashel and, aged six, became a boarder at Bishop Foy's School, Waterford; for a time, he was head choirboy at Waterford Cathedral. He went to TCD in 1938, but his studies were disrupted when he enlisted in the RAF in 1941. He served in North Africa, Malta and Gibraltar. After being demobilised in 1946, he resumed his studies, graduating with a BA in 1948, and MA in 1957. He also won a Silver Medal in the College Theological Society competition. He was made Deacon in 1948, and ordained Priest in 1949. He had a varied ministerial career. He was Curate in the Parishes of St Matthew, Belfast, 1948–51, and of St Thomas, Belfast, 1951–53. He was Head of the Southern Church Mission (Ballymacarrett, Belfast), 1953–59, and Registrar of the Dioceses of Down and Dromore, 1959–63. On 2nd July 1954, he married Margaret Jephson of Waterford. He was the Incumbent of Annahilt, Co. Down, 1959–63, before being instituted as Rector of the Parish of St Peter's, 1963–90.

Canon Harris's love of music fitted well with the musical tradition of St Peter's; he was a talented pianist and organist (he enjoyed improvisation, and liked both classical and jazz music), was a great enthusiast for the scout movement, and a gifted hockey player and capable swimmer. Partly because of his military service, he was able to illustrate his sermons with a rich vein of anecdotes, many of them gleaned from this phase of his life. He was also a competent and unpretentious poet; his poems revealed his keen sense of humour. He was a fervent supporter of ecumenism;

he was a founder member of an inter-denominational clergy group in North Belfast. This was a progressive and courageous initiative, taken at a time when the 'Troubles' were at their height within the area. He felt gratified to be elected by his fellow clergy to the Prebendary of St Audeon, 1983–90 – delighted particularly by the connection which this involved with the National Cathedral of St Patrick, Dublin. He retired in 1990, and was predeceased by his wife, Margaret, in March 1993; they had shared a very strong partnership. He maintained his love of music and reading into his retirement, until his death in 1996. He was survived by his children, to each of whom he was devoted (Brian, Patric, Michael, Clodagh and Sheila).

Rev Stephen Richard McBride

On 9th November 1990, Rev S.R. McBride was instituted as fourth Rector of St Peter's. He was born on 28th September 1961, and grew up in the neighbouring parish of Holy Trinity, Joanmount. He was educated at the Royal Belfast Academical Institution, and then progressed to QUB, where he graduated with a BSc (Hons) in architecture in 1984. At TCD he gained a BTh in 1989, and later an MA, and won the Downes Divinity Premiums and the Ebrington Prize (1989). In 1996, he was awarded a PhD, by thesis, at QUB. He was a keen athlete, gaining colours for QUB (where he was captain of the Athletics Club) and for TCD; he also represented Northern Ireland at both junior and senior levels. In June 1987, he was made Deacon in St Anne's Cathedral, Belfast, and Curate Assistant in Antrim Parish, 1987–90. He was ordained Priest in June 1988 in St Patrick's Church, Ballymena. In1990, he was appointed Rector of St Peter's Parish, and served there until early 1996, when he returned to Antrim, as Vicar. He married Helen Clyde, BSc, MA, in September 1987, and they had two children – Rachael Sara and Alexander Richard John (who was baptised in St Peter's).

Rev Charles James McCollum

On 29th March 1996, the Rev Charles J. McCollum, the fifth incumbent of St Peter's, was instituted as Rector of the Parish. He was born into a farming family near Cavan town on 1st September 1941, and attended Cavan Royal School for five years. He then trained for the teaching profession at the Church of Ireland Teacher Training College in Dublin. His first teaching post was in Monaghan Model Schools (1963–1975), where he became principal teacher in 1970. In 1975, he was appointed head of the Practising School in the Church of Ireland Teacher Training College (1975–1985). In 1985, he entered the Church of Ireland Theological College, and was awarded the Downes and Ebrington prizes. On completion of his third year he undertook further theological study – at Trinity College, Dublin – and was awarded a BTh (Hons). He was made Deacon in 1989, and ordained Priest in 1990. In 1989, he was ordained to serve a curacy in Larne and Inver (1989–91), and was then appointed to the Parish of Whiterock, West Belfast (1991–96). After becoming Rector of St Peter's in 1996 he undertook various commitments to the wider diocese and community; he served for five years as Chairman of the Church of Ireland Youth Department, undertook tutorial and teaching work with candidates for the

Auxiliary Ministry, and also with those in training as diocesan readers, served on the boards of several local schools (including St Therese of Lisieux), and was Chaplain to the Mater Hospital in Belfast. In December 2008 he was appointed incumbent of the Dunleckney group of parishes in the Diocese of Cashel and Ossory.

Rev Adrian Terence Warren Dorrian

On 22 June 2009, Rev Adrian Terence Warren Dorrian was instituted as incumbent of the parish of St Peter and St James. It is thought that upon taking up this post at the age of twenty-seven, he became the youngest serving Rector in the Church of Ireland. In June 2006, he had been ordained Deacon by the Bishop of Down and Dromore in Shankill Parish, Lurgan, to serve as Curate Assistant in the Parish of Newtownards and, in 2007, was elevated to the priesthood in Down Cathedral. He grew up in the parish of Groomsport in the Diocese of Down, and attended the local primary school. He continued his education at Bangor Grammar School, where he was appointed Deputy Head Boy and, in his final year, was a winner of the Northern Ireland Schools Debating Competition. He then proceeded to Queen's University, Belfast, where he was the first ever student to graduate with a BA (honours) in Drama and Theology. In 2004 he entered the Church of Ireland Theological College, where he was awarded a BTh from Trinity College, Dublin. Before entering the Church of Ireland Theological College, he was a Youth Drama Worker with Youth Initiatives, a West Belfast Christian outreach organisation. He has a keen interest in the theatre, having been a member of a number of drama groups, and performed with these in the Group and Lyric theatres in Belfast, and the National Theatre, London. He also serves as Vice Chair of the Ulster Association of Youth Drama, and has been Chair of the Down and Dromore Youth Council.

CURATES:

Rev Vivian Fielding Smith was licensed as Curate of St Peter's on 3rd October 1920, where he remained until the end of September 1926. He was born in 1894, and attended TCD, graduating with an MA in 1919. He became a Deacon in 1920, and was ordained as Priest in 1921. After leaving St Peter's, he went to India as a missionary under the auspices of the Society for the Propagation of the Gospel. He became Head of the Moradabad Mission, Lucknow, North West Provinces, 1926–56, and for a time worked as Chaplain and in various other posts in India, until his death in 1963, at Moradabad.

He was the first Curate-assistant at St Peter's. In 1950, Dr Breene wrote that: 'during his [Mr Smith's] time in the Parish he laid the foundation of most of our junior organisations – Cubs, Scouts, Rovers, Brownie's, Guides, etc, all of which have gone from strength to strength in the years since he left us'.

Rev G. G. Hammond was licensed as Curate of St Peter's on 27th June 1927, and remained at the Parish until 30th June 1930. He attended TCD, where he graduated with a BA in 1917, and an MA in 1927. He became a Deacon in 1917, and was ordained Priest in 1918. He served as Curate of Holy Trinity, Belfast, and of St George's, Belfast, 1922–27, before coming to St Peter's. After leaving the Parish, he transferred to the Diocese of Chester, becoming Vicar of St John Baptist, Great Meols, Hoylake, 1937–62.

Rev W.J. Noel Mackey was ordained for the Curacy on Sunday, 28th June 1931, St Peter's Eve, and licensed as Curate of St Peter's on 29th June 1931. He was born in Dublin on 25th December 1907, educated at the High School, Dublin, and at TCD, where he graduated with a BA in 1929, and MA in 1951, and won a number of prestigious academic awards. He became a Deacon in 1931, and was ordained Priest in 1932. After leaving St Peter's in 1936, Mr Mackey became Rector of Billy, Co. Antrim, 1936–44, of Clonallon and Warrenpoint, Co. Down, 1944–61, of Kilbroney, 1952–61, and of Newry and Mourne, 1958–61. He held various ecclesiastical positions, including Examinations Chaplain to the Bishop of Down, 1957–71, before retiring in 1975.

Rev George Freeman was Curate at St Peter's between 1936–38. He was educated at Kilkenny College, was on the staff of the Ministry of Labour and a Lay Reader in Portadown, and then sat the General Ordination Examination. He became a Deacon in 1932, and Priest in 1933, and served as Curate at St Michael's, Belfast, 1932–36. After leaving St Peter's in 1938, he became Rector of Groomsport until 1944. In addition, Dr Breene indicates that he was the first clergyman to be put in charge of the emerging district of St Katharine's. He died suddenly on 18th April 1944.

Rev John Ernest George was licensed as Curate of St Peter's on 26th September 1938, and remained there until 1941. He was born on 24th April 1911 at Milford, Co. Armagh, educated at Armagh Royal School, and at TCD, from which he graduated with a BA in 1936, and MA in 1945. He won two academic prizes whilst completing his university training. He became a Deacon in 1937, Priest in 1938, and was Curate of St Paul's, Belfast, 1937–8. Subsequently, whilst at St Peter's, he was asked by the Bishop to take charge as Rector of the Parish of Upper Falls, Belfast, 1941–45, during the absence of the incumbent who was on duty as a Chaplain to the Forces; this appointment necessitated his resignation from the staff of St Peter's. After the war, he served as Curate of St Luke's, Belfast, 1946–47, and Rector of Craigs, Co. Antrim, 1947–63.

Rev Robert Preston McDermott was licensed as Curate of St Peter's on 22nd December 1938, and remained until 1940. He was born on 18th April 1911, and educated at Royal Belfast Academical Institution, and at TCD, from which he graduated with a BA in 1932, and where he won a number of academic awards. He became a Deacon in 1935, and Priest in 1936, and served as Curate in Ballymoney, 1935–38. After leaving St Peter's, he served briefly at St Katharine's – succeeding Rev Freeman – before retiring from this post due to a period of ill health (Reverend R.W.T.H. Kilpatrick then took up the work of the new district and, Dr Breene records, became its first actual Curate-in-charge). He was Curate-in-charge,

Ardclinis, 1940–44; then Sub Warden, St Deniol's Library, Hawarden, 1944–5; Rector at Borrisokane, 1945–48, and at Killenaule, 1948–9. Subsequently, he became Rector at St Mary le-Bow, Durham, 1949–55, Chaplain at Durham University – to women and to non-collegiate students in 1949, and held various other ecclesiastical and academic appointments in Durham until his retirement in 1976. He co-authored Irish Protestantism Today and Tomorrow: a Demographic Study.

Rev Robert William Thomas Howard Kilpatrick was licensed as Curate of St Peter's on 1st October 1940, and remained there until1944, acting as Curate-in-charge at St Katharine's. He was born on 19th September 1910, educated at Belfast Model School and Methodist College, Belfast, and graduated from TCD with a BA in 1937, and MA in 1948. He became a Deacon in 1937, and Priest in 1938. He was Curate at St Mary's, Belfast, 1937–40, before coming to St Peter's, and subsequently became Rector of Ardglass, 1944–48, and then of the Cathedral Parish of Dromore, Co. Down, 1948–60. He was Prebendary of Dromara, 1951–54; Treasurer of Dromore, 1954–57; Precentor, 1957–59; Incumbent at Ballymacarrett, 1954–68; Rector of Down with Hollymount, 1964–81; Precentor of Down, 1964–68, and Dean, 1968–81, when he retired. He died on 13th April 1988.

Rev John Richard Burleigh McDonald was licensed as Curate of St Peter's on 1st May 1941 (1941–45). He was born in Bangor, Co. Down, on 7th May 1917 and educated at Campbell College, and at TCD, from where he graduated with a BA in 1939, and BD in 1943. He became a Deacon in 1941, and Priest in 1942. He resigned as Curate at St Peter's in order to take up full-time work as a missionary in Uganda (1940–51). He was, Dr Breene wrote in 1950, 'our "own Missionary" under the Church Missionary Society in East Africa. We share him with Zion Church, Rathgar, Dublin. His wife, formerly Miss Dorothy Bill, a St Peter's parishioner, and their children are with him in Africa. He is Lecturer and Tutor at the Divinity school and Training College of the Church of Uganda'. Whilst in Africa he held various academic and ecclesiastical posts – tutor, college principal, examinations chaplain, etc. He returned to Ireland in 1961 to become Church of Ireland Education Officer, 1961–64, and then a lecturer, and later the Head of the Religious Studies Department at Stranmillis College, 1966–85. He also held various other posts – at QUB (1979–81), and within Connor Diocese, and in a range of bodies mainly concerned with marriage counselling. He was the author of numerous publications on religious education, and on health issues in Africa.

Rev Thomas George McAlister was licensed as Curate of St Peter's on 18th October 1945, and served until 1953. He was born on 29th May 1920 in Dungannon, and educated at the Royal School there, and at TCD where he graduated with a BA in 1942, and MA in 1947. He became a Deacon in 1943, and Priest in 1944. He served as Curate in Aghalee, 1943–45. After leaving St Peter's, he became Vicar of St Andrew's, Southport, England, 1953–59, and in London, 1959–69; Rector in Guildford, 1969–79; and Vicar in Blackburn, 1979–85, after which he retired.

Rev Maurice Edward Leeman was licensed as Curate of St Peter's on 23rd October 1953, and served until 1959. He was born on 20th May 1927, and educated at Friends' School Lisburn, and at TCD, graduating with a BA in 1949, and MA in 1954. He became a Deacon in 1950, and Priest in 1951. He served as Curate in Carnmoney, 1950–53. After leaving St Peter's, he became Rector in Ahoghill, 1959–89, and Rural Dean in Ballymena, 1966–74, and 1988–9. He died tragically in 1989.

Rev Edwin Adinya was licensed as Curate of St Peter's on 1st June 1960, and served until 1961. He completed his training at the Theological College, Limuru in 1954, became a Deacon in 1955, and Priest in 1957. He was a Priest in Mombasa Diocese, 1955–60. After leaving St Peter's, he became Archdeacon of Nairobi, 1963–66; Vicar of St Stephen's, Nairobi, 1961–64; Vicar of the Diocese of Nairobi, 1964–70; Priest of the Diocese of Maseno from 1970, and Honorary Canon of Maseno South from 1972.

Rev George Brian Moller was licensed as Curate of St Peter's on 2nd July 1961, and served until 1964. He was born on 4th July 1935, and was educated at Friends' School, Lisburn, and at TCD, from where he graduated with a BA in 1960, and an MA in 1964. He was awarded a BD from London University in 1984. He became a Deacon in 1961, and Priest in 1962. After leaving St Peter's, he was Curate at Larne and Inver, 1964–68, and Curate-in-charge at Rathcoole, 1968–69, and then incumbent there, 1969–86. Subsequently, he became Incumbent at St Bartholomew's, Belfast, from 1986. He was also Chaplain to Ordinands, 1970–81, Diocesan Director of Ordinands from 1986, and Prebendary of Cairncastle from 1990.

Rev Patrick Thomas Craig was licensed as Curate of St Peter's on 6th May 1965, and served there until 1968. He was educated at St David's College, Lampeter, from which he graduated with a BA in 1959, and at Bishop's College, Cheshunt. He became a Deacon in 1961, Priest in 1962, and was Curate at St Mary's, Belfast, 1961–65. After leaving St Peter's, he became RAF Chaplain, 1969–88, and then Rector at Hartfield and Coleman's Hatch, Chichester, from 1988.

Rev Samuel Niall Bayly was licensed as Curate of St Peter's on 16th March 1969, and served until 1974. He was educated at TCD, from where he graduated with a BA in 1964, and MA in 1970. He became a Deacon in 1965, and Priest in 1966. He was Curate of St Matthew's, Belfast, 1965–68, and then Temporary Chaplain at the Mission to Seamen, Belfast, 1968–69. After leaving St Peter's, he became Incumbent at Christ Church, Belfast, 1974–93, and Chaplain to the City Hospital, Belfast from 1974.

TEMPORARY ASSISTANT CURATES and ASSISTANT PRIESTS:

Two clergy helped as temporary assistant Curates in St Peter's during the interwar years:

Rev Thomas Parr, who graduated from TCD with a BA in 1915, and MA in 1923. He became a Deacon in 1915, and Priest in 1917. He served as a Curate in St Mary's Belfast, and in Holywood, 1920–29. He was Rector of Killyleagh, 1929–35; and of Seapatrick, Banbridge, 1935–61. He also became Rural Dean of Aghaderg, 1940–61, and a Canon of St Anne's Cathedral, 1945–65. For the seven years before his retirement he served as Rector of Killough, Co. Down (1961–68).

Rev Herbert Innes Law, who was educated at King's Hospital, Dublin, and graduated with a LTh from Emman College, Saskatoon in 1926. He became a Deacon in 1926, and Priest in 1927, and held various ecclesiastical posts in Canada, 1926–1935. In 1935–36, he worked as Northern Ireland Secretary of the Commonwealth and Continental Church Society, before holding a variety of ecclesiastical positions with the Church of Ireland, 1936–59. He became Curate-in-charge of Edenderry, Diocese of Derry, 1947–57; Chaplain for Tyrone and Fermanagh Mental Hospital, 1947–57, and then Rector of Tamlaght O'Crilly Upper, 1957–63.

During the First World War he was a Lance Corporal in the Royal Irish Rifles, 1915–18, and wounded on the first day of the Somme, 1st July 1916. He returned to military service and, as a Second Lieutenant, Royal Irish Regiment, again was wounded, on 2nd September 1918. He was active in the part-time force, the Militia of Canada, 1921–27.

Rev Ernest John Heatley Shepherd was born in Dublin on 21st March 1927, and educated at Mountjoy School, Dublin, and at TCD, where he graduated with a BA in 1948, and a BD in 1953. He became a Deacon in 1950, and Priest in 1951. He became Curate of St Mary Magdalene, Belfast, 1950–54, and of Whitehouse from April 1954. On 5th October 1954 he was instituted as Rector of Whitehouse (retiring in 1996). He was also Prebendary of Rasharkin, 1986–90; Treasurer from 1990, and Precentor from 1990. He became Assistant Priest at St Peter's in 1997, pending the grouping of St James's with St Peter's. He was awarded the M.B.E. in 2008.

AUXILIARY MINISTER:

Roger James Damian Kirkpatrick (religious name Brother Damian, Society of Saint Francis) was made Curate at St Peter's in 1986; his 'farewell' service was held on 26th October 1988. He was born on 8th May 1941, educated at Highgate School, and became a Fellow of the Institute of Chartered Accountants in England and Wales in 1963. He was made a Deacon in 1986. As well as being Curate at St Peter's, he was also Chaplain to the Royal Group of Hospitals from 1986, and Guardian of Belfast Friary Society of Saint Francis from 1970.

MISSIONARIES:

The following have gone from St Peter's Parish to serve as Missionaries overseas:

Rev Vivian Fielding Smith, MA, SPG, India, 1926

Right Rev Alexander Ogilvie Hardy, DD, SPG, India, 1917. (He became Bishop of Nagpur, and later Assistant Bishop of Bradford)

Rev Herbert Innes Law, LTh, Col and Con, Western Canada, 1926

Rev Percy Malcolm Stewart, SPG, Western Canada, 1924

Rev J.R.B. McDonald, BD, CMS, East Africa; 1946

Miss Aideen Wade, Col and C, Canada, 1934; East Africa, 1947. Miss Wade operated the 'Sunday School by Post' in Kenya, going there in 1947; she had previously carried out the same work for ten years in Western Canada.

PAROCHIAL OFFICERS

Churchwardens

1900 – G.W. Ferguson; F.P. Hughes
1901 – A.C. Capper; F. Robinson
1902 – F.J. Bigger; J. McDonald
1903 – W. Berwick; R. Nevin
1904 – W. Berwick; J.T. Keys
1905 – E.P. Higgins; J.T. Keys
1906-7 – E.P. Higgins; C. Nicholson
1908 – H. Ferguson; G. Higinbotham
1909 – H. Ferguson; A.S. Megaw
1910 –H. Kinahan; A.S. Megaw
1911 – H. Kinahan; C. Leathem
1912 – Col. Suddart; C. Leathem
1913 – Major Cunningham; J. Macoun
1914–15 – Major Cunningham; G. Raymond
1916–17/18 – R.H. Kinahan; J.W. Durnan
1919–20 – H.H. Stewart; J.D. McClure
1921–22 – H.C. Kennedy; A. Kelly
1923–24 – H. Magill; E.B. Waring
1925–26 – T.H. Johnston; Major Ewart
1927 – Sir A.S. Queckett; Major Ewart
1928–29 – Sir A.S. Queckett; R. Carruthers
1930–31 – T. Bill; H. Grubb
1932–33 –Professor F.T. Lloyd-Dodd; Major Ewart
1934–35 – Capt. Gill; E.E. Storey
1936 – Capt. Gill; R.R. Reid
1937 – J. Young; R.R. Reid
1938 – J.B. Armstrong; R.R. Reid
1939 – R.E. McClure; J.B. Armstrong
1940–41/42 –A.F. Hanna; G.W. Griffin
1943 – J.A. Noblett; G.W. Griffin
1944 – J.A. Noblett; W.H. Dunlop
1945 – J.H. Norritt; W.H. Dunlop
1946 – R.E. McClure; D. O'R. Haldane
1947–48 – H. Mitchell; R.L. Taylor
1949 – H.E. Campbell; H.R. Fry
1950 – H.E. Campbell; R.H.R. Fry [check initials]
1951 – J. Wright; G.C. Hall
1952–53 – T.M. McDonald; M.J. Regan
1954 – T.M. McDonald; J. Regan
1955 – E.B. McGuire; S.A. Hutchman
1956 – E.B. McGuire; S.A. Hutchman

1957 – H.E. Wood; W.G. Henderson
1958 – H.E. Wood; W.G. Henderson
1959–60 – W.G.H. McCarthy; T. Mayne
1961–62 – N. Deveria; H. Taylor
1963–64 – N. Deveria; J.M. Patterson
1965–66 – J. Regan; G.C. Wasson
1967 – P. Cavan; P. Worrell
1968 – J. Filor; W.A. Wright
1969 – D. Sloan; W.A. Wright
1970 – D. Sloan; J. Wright
1971 – R. Entwistle; J. Wright
1972 – J. Briggs; D.H. Dunlop
1973 – F. Wilson; W. Everett
1974 – D. Lowry; P. Rogers
1975 – Q. Mulligan; T. Swan
1976 – N.C. Beattie; Q. Mulligan
1977 – S. McDowell; B. Rogers
1978 – A. Jones; S.H. Hinds
1979 – B.I. Jeffers; H.T. Jackson
1980 – Mrs J. Sterling; Q. Mulligan
1981 – Mrs K.M. Dunlop; Q. Mulligan
1982 – H. Hutchman; V.G. Bridges
1983 – E. Murray; P.V.G. Worrall
1984 – T. Conville; P.V.G. Worrall
1985 – Miss D. Mc Clements; P.V.G. Worrall
1986 – Mrs D. Cochrane; P.V.G. Worrall
1987 – Mrs S. Hutchman; Miss D. McClements
1988 – Mrs J. Sterling; Miss D. McClements
1989 – J. McCreary; Miss D. McClements
1990 – Mrs J. Sterling; Miss D. McClements
1991 – R.D. Beattie; Miss D. McClements
1992 – S. McDowell; Miss D. McClements
1993 – D. McCausland; Miss D. McClements
1994 – E. Stewart; Miss D. McClements
1995 – Mrs S. Chillingworth; Miss D. McClements
1996 – Mrs S. Chillingworth; Miss D. McClements
1997 – Mrs M.S. O'Neill; I.H. McManus
1998 – S.C. Lowry; I.H. McManus
1999 – S.C. Lowry; I.H. McManus
2000 – I.H. McManus
2001–02 – Mrs S. Davison; J. Wright
2003–09 – Mrs S. Davison; Miss O. Haldane

Parochial Nominators

1900–01 – F.J. Bigger; G.H. Ewart; F. Kinahan
1902–05 – F.J. Bigger; G.H. Ewart; R.G. Campbell
1906–23 –E.P. Higgins; G.H. Ewart; R.G. Campbell
1924 – H. Kinahan; H.I. Johns; R.G. Campbell
1925–26 – H. Kinahan; H.H. Stewart; R.G. Campbell
1927–29 – H. Kinahan; Major Ewart; R.G. Campbell
1930–31 – A.S. Megaw; Major Ewart; R.G. Campbell
1932–36 – A.S. Megaw; Major Ewart; Sir A.S. Quekett
1937–38 – A.S. Megaw; Capt. L.P. Gill; Sir A.S. Quekett
1939–41 – A.S. Megaw; J.N. Robinson; Sir A.S. Quekett
1942–43 – A.S. Megaw; J.N. Robinson; R.R. Reid
1944–45 – A.S. Megaw; A.F. Hanna; R.R. Reid

Parochial Nominators

1946 – A.S. Megaw; A.F. Hanna; R.R. Reid
1947–50 – A.S. Megaw; Professor F.T. Lloyd-Dodd; R.R. Reid
1951–56 – H.E. Campbell; R.L. Taylor; R.R. Reid
1957–58 – R.R. Reid; Professor F.T. Lloyd-Dodd; G.H. Dunlop
1959 – G.H. Dunlop; Professor F.T. Lloyd-Dodd; R.R. Reid
1960 – H.E. Campbell; G.H. Dunlop; H.E. Wood
1961–62 – G.H. Dunlop; H.E. Wood
1963–71 – H.H. Mitchell; R.W. Montgomery; J.M. Patterson
1972–74 – C.H. Davis; H.H. Mitchell; G. Power; J.M. Patterson
1975 – C.H. Davis; J.M. Patterson; G. Power; K.J. Ivin
1976 – C.H. Davis; K.J. Ivin; J.M. Patterson; G. Power
1977 – C.H. Davis; K.J. Ivin; J.M. Patterson; G. Power
1978–83 – C.H. Davis; Mrs F. Greer; K.J. Ivin; J.M. Patterson
1984 – C.H. Davis; Mrs F. Greer; K.J. Ivin
1985–86 – V.G. Bridges; C.H. Davis; K.J. Ivin; P.V.G. Worrall
1987 – V.G. Bridges; C.H. Davis
1988 – V.G. Bridges; Mrs D. Cochrane; W.F. Ginn; P.V.G. Worrall
1989 – S.H. Hinds; Mrs D. Cochrane; W.F. Ginn; Mrs J. Sterling
1990–95 – S.H. Hinds; Mrs D. Cochrane; W.F. Ginn; Mrs H. Shields
1996 – S.H. Hinds; Mrs S. Chillingworth; W.F. Ginn; N.C. Beattie
1997–99 – S.H. Hinds; Mrs S. Chillingworth
2000–01 – S.H. Hinds; E. Stewart
2002–04 – S. McDowell; E. Stewart
2005–09 – N.C. Beattie; D.H.A. Cromie; Miss M.E. Macbeth; S. McDowell

Diocesan Synodsmen:

1900–20 – H.I. Johns; W. Berwick
1921 – H.I. Johns; W. Berwick; H.H. Stewart; H.C. Kennedy
1922–23 – H.I. Johns; A. Kelly; H.H. Stewart; H.C. Kennedy
1924–29 – J.A. Hind; A. Kelly; H.H. Stewart; H.C. Kennedy
1930–31 – J.A. Hind; Major G. Ewart; H.H. Stewart; H.C. Kennedy
1932–36 – Sir A.S. Queckett; Major G. Ewart; H.H. Stewart; H.C. Kennedy
1937–38 – Sir A.S. Queckett; Capt. L.P. Gill; H.H. Stewart; H.C. Kennedy
1939–40 – Sir A.S. Queckett; T. Bill; H.H. Stewart; H.C. Kennedy
1941 – Sir A.S. Queckett; T. Bill; G.W. Griffin; H.C. Kennedy
1942–44 – Professor F.T. Lloyd-Dodd; T. Bill; G.W. Griffin; T.S. Chambers
1945–46 – Professor F.T. Lloyd-Dodd; T. Bill; G.W. Griffin; R.R. Reid
1947–50 – Professor F.T. Lloyd-Dodd; J.H. Norritt; G.W. Griffin; R.R. Reid
1951–53 – H.E. Campbell; Professor F.T. Lloyd-Dodd; J.H. Norritt; R.R. Reid
1954–56 – Mrs E. Noble; H.E. Campbell; Professor F.T. Lloyd-Dodd; R.R. Reid
1957–58 – R.R. Reid; R.H.R. Fry; G.H. Dunlop; Professor F.T. Lloyd-Dodd
1959 – G.H. Dunlop; P.H.R. Fry; Professor F.T. Lloyd-Dodd; R.R. Reid
1960–62 – W.G. Henderson; T. Jackson; Mrs E. Noble; J.M. Patterson
1963–65 – R.J. Dixon; W.G. Henderson; Mrs E. Noble; H. Taylor
1966 – P.L. Cavan; R.J. Dixon; H. Taylor; G.C. Wasson
1969–71 – P.L. Cavan; Lt. Col. C.G.H. Filor; R.J. Dixon; H. Taylor
1972–74 – D.H. Dunlop; Lt. Col. C.G.H. Filor; K.J. Ivin; G.C. Wasson
1975 – D.H. Dunlop; Lt. Col. C.G.H. Filor
1976–77 – DH Dunlop; Lt Col CGH Filor; J Regan; PVG Worrall
1978–84 – Lt. Col. C.G.H. Filor; J.A. Morrison
1985–87 – Lt. Col. C.G.H. Filor; N.C. Beattie
1988–90 – Lt. Col. C.G.H. Filor; N.C. Beattie; Mrs D. Cochrane; R. Entwistle
1991–92 – Lt. Col. C.G.H. Filor; Mrs H. Shields; Mrs D. Cochrane; J. McCreary
1993–95 – Lt. Col. C.G.H. Filor; Mrs D. Cochrane
1996 – Lt. Col. C.G.H. Filor; N.C. Beattie
1997–2001 – Lt. Col. C.G.H. Filor
2002–04 – Mrs S. Chillingworth
2005–09 – T.V. Davis; Miss M.E. Macbeth

Honorary Auditors:

1900–31 – S. Smyth
1932–56 – J.D. McClure
1957–60 – N.G. Chantler; J.E. Rusk
1961 – T.F. McGhee; A.S. Treacy
1962–64 – R. Entwistle
1965–67 – A. Bell
1968 – L.F. Garland
1969–70 – L.F. Garland; G. Knox
1971–73 –K.E.D. Mackrell
1974–75 – V.G. Bridges
1976–77 – V.G. Bridges; D.H. Lowry
1978–81 – J.M. Patterson
1982 – D.J. McClure
1983–2004 – A.C. Hall
2005–08 – R.M.J. Ross

Honorary Treasurers:

1896–1923 – H.G. Ewart
1923–30 – H.H. Stewart
1930–35 – E.G. Oldham
1935–37 – J.A. Ross
1938 – J.H. Armstrong
1938–39 – J.H. Kerr
1939–40 – A.F. Hanna
1940 – G.H. Griffin
1941–43 – W.T. Scott
1943–47 – T.F. McGhee
1947–51 – R.W. Montgomery
1952–55 – J.M. Patterson
1956–58 – G.H. Dunlop
1959–63 – J.W. Monson
1964–68 – C.H. Davis
1969 – W.H. Taylor
1970–73 – Mrs E.S. Gordon
1974 – K.E.D. Mackrell
1975–81 – W.F. Ginn
1982–84 – D.J. McClure
1985–88 – H. Jacobs
1989–99 – G.V. Flynn
2000–09 – S. McDowell

Honorary Secretaries:

1896–1904 – F.J. Bigger
1904–05 – R.F. Ringwood
1905–10 – A.C. Capper
1910–18 – J.T. Keys
1918–30 – J. Hind
1930–38 – L.P. Gill
1939–59 – R.R. Reid
1959–60 – G.H. Dunlop
1960–61 – A.G. Treacy
1961–75 – G. Power
1976–90 – C.G.H. Filor
1991–93 – Mrs H. Shields
1994–97 – Mrs R. Johnston
1998 – Miss C. Harris
1999 – S.H. Hinds
2000–09 – R. Johnston

Organists and Choirmasters 1900–2009:

Herbert Hughes	1986–1903
A.M. Gifford	1903–1916
F.J. Neill	1916–1931
Roland Orton	1931–1933
J. Crossley Clitheroe	1933–1944
Lister Wood	1944–1963
Reginald Patterson	1964–1967
Peter Harris	1968–1973
Norman Finlay	1973–1980
Ronnie Lee	1980–1981
Michael McCracken	1981–1985
Brian Moore	1985–1988
Robert Thompson	1989–1991
Alfred Casement	1991–1993
Desmond Hunter	1993–1997
Robert Thompson	1998–2002
Stephen Hamill	2002–

Appendix I:
Lists of Members of St Peter's Congregation who served in the First and Second World Wars

FIRST WORLD WAR
The following served overseas during the First World War with the exception of those whose names are printed in italics; they served in some capacity, 1914–18 (e.g. were engaged in Home Defence or were in training for Military Service), but had not gone overseas at the date of the Armistice, 11th November 1918.

The Oak Memorial Tablet in St Peter's to survivors of the 1914–1918 War is inscribed as follows:

> **To the Glory of God Who gave us Victory and in Remembrance of the War Services of Men and Women of this Parish of whom those named Served Overseas this Window is Dedicated.**

Lieutenant J.S. ANDREWS, RNR
Apprentice G.J. ANDREWS, HM Transport (torpedoed twice)
Major WILLIAM BAIRD, Antrim Artillery
Corporal T. BELL, MMP
Lieutenant J.P. BRUCE, 8th Manchester Regiment, wounded
Corporal G.H. BRUCE, 4th Manchester Regiment, wounded
Captain R.H. CAIRNS, HM Transport (torpedoed)
Private G. CAMPBELL, 6th Manchester Regiment, wounded
Second Lieutenant J.D. CAMPBELL, RGA
Lieutenant R. CARRUTHERS, 2nd RIR, afterwards RE, wounded
Captain J.S.C. CHAMBERS, Army Cyclist's Corps, wounded
Lieutenant H.M. CHAMBERS, 6th Munster Fusiliers, now Captain, 117th Mahrattas,
    wounded
Lieutenant H.P. CONNAR, Tank Corps
Lieutenant R.L. CONNAR, 1st Royal Irish Fusiliers, wounded
Major F.A. CUNNINGHAM, 3rd (Cameronian) Scottish Rifles
Lieutenant W.A. CUNNINGHAM, 1st Royal Scots, wounded
Private R.L. CUNNINGHAM, 3rd Hussars
Private T. CUNNINGHAM, ASC, 36th Ulster Division
Private J.R. CUTHBERSTSON, MT, ASC
Captain E.S. DIXON, RAMC
Lieutenant E.T. DOBSON, 2/124th Baluchistan Infantry (accidentally killed at Port Said,
    8th June 1920)
Lieutenant J.N. DURNAN, 9th RIR, wounded
Second Lieutenant R.H. DURNAN, RAF
Lieutenant-Commander F. EYERS, DSO, RNR
Captain C.W. FAUSSETT, HM Transport
Captain G.C.S. FERGUSON, 6th Indian Cavalry

Private J. GLENN, 15th RIR, wounded
Sergeant W.H. KELLY, 14th RIR, wounded
Lieutenant G.H.B. KERR, 1/2nd Gurkha Rifles
Captain G. KIRKPATRICK, North Irish Horse
Captain D. KIRKPATRICK, 2nd RIR, wounded
Lieutenant K.C. KIRKPATRICK, DSC, RN
Second Lieutenant I. KIRKPATRICK, RAF
Sergeant-Instructor E.B. LAVELLE, MGC, wounded
Sergeant J.B. LEONARD, 14th RIR (awarded the Meritorious Service Medal)
Lieutenant W.K. LEONARD, 1st Gloucestershire Regiment
Nursing-Sister HILDA LEONARD, Royal Red Cross (Mons Star)
Lieutenant C.W. LEPPER, RN
Major E.F. LEPPER, MC, 14th RIR, now Captain, 93rd Burma Infantry
Company Sergeant Major J. MACOUN, RE, Mons Star and Meritorious Service Medal
Captain M.S. MAYNE, RE, wounded
Captain F.S. MAYNE, MGC, wounded
Second Lieutenant J.A. MAYNE, 3rd RIR
Signaller R.H. MANTLE, RN
Company Quartermaster Sergeant H. MORRIS, RE
Sapper R.J. MCDERMOTT, RE, wounded
Lieutenant F.T.V. MCDONALD, MGC
Bombardier H.T. OSBORNE, RGA
Midshipman E. PINKERTON, 5th Flotilla TBD
Major F.M. PLATT-HIGGINS, MC, 1st Cambridgeshire Regiment, mentioned in
  dispatches
Captain J.E. PITTAWAY, NIH, twice mentioned in dispatches
Lieutenant F.E. PITTAWAY, RFA, 86th Army Brigade
Corporal R. PROUDFORD, 15th RIR, certificate for gallantry and devotion to duty
Second Lieutenant G.A.K. ROBERTSON, RAF
Bombardier R.M. ROBINSON, RGA
Lieutenant H.F. ROBINSON, RFA
ANNIE ROBINSON, VAD
Quartermaster Sergeant E. ROGERS, Canadian RAMC
Corporal J. ROGERS, Canadian RAMC
Private G. ROGERS, Canadian Engineers
Private A. RUSH, 15th RIR
Private J. RUSH, ASC
Trooper W.H. SMYTH, North Irish Horse
Sapper A. SMYTH, RE
Sergeant P.M. STEWART, RAF
Corporal A. THURLEY, RE
Sergeant A.H. WEBB, RE
Sapper A.WEBB, RE
Private K. WEBB, MT, ASC
Midshipman L. WHEELER, RNVR

SECOND WORLD WAR

The roll of the names of those who joined Crown Forces from the Parish during the Second World War:

DORA ALICE ADAMS, RAF.
PHYLLIS ALLEN ALEXANDRA ADAMS, Navy
JOHN DOUGLAS ANDERSON, RAF.
RUTH MARY COTTON ANDERSON, Army.
ALEXANDER THORNTON ANNESLEY, Army
JOAN NORTH ARMSTRONG, RAF.
DENISE WESTON AUSTIN, Army

ANDREW MCMASTER BARNES, Army.
ARTHUR WELLESLEY BAXTER, Army.
DONALD BAXTER, Army
ANDREW THOMAS BELL, RAF
PATRICK BLACKER, Army
JOHN G. BLAIR, Army
ROBERT BRYAN BOYD, Army
ARHUR WILLIAM BOWYER, RAF
MARY ELMYRA SIMMONS BREENE, Navy
RICHARD ARNOLD SIMMONS BREENE, Army
CYRIL BROOK, Army
JAMES ALEXANDER BUSBY, Navy
JOYCE BROWN, Army

WILLIAM B. CARTER, RAF
WILLIAM GEORGE CAUGHEY, Navy
JAMES ALEXANDER CLARKE, RAF
LOOS JEAN CLARKE, RAF
THOMAS SINGLETON CLARKE, Army
AUDREY PARTICIA CONNELL, Army
ROBERT COSBY, Army
ALAN LANCELOT CROASDAILE, Army, awarded MBE
ALICE MARGARET ELIZABETH CUMMINGS, Navy

WINIFRED MAUDE DENISON, RAF
KATHLEEN PATRICIA DILLON, RAF
JOHN DIXON, Army
ELIZABETH LLOYD-DODD, Navy
JAMES DONALDSON, Army
IAN DOUGLAS, Army
HENRY WILSON DOWNEY, Army
CECIL ALEXANDER DUKE, Navy
PERCY MCLACHAN DUKE, Navy
WILIAM ARTHUR DUKE, Army, wounded
ROBERT HADDOCK DURNAN, RAF
JAMES NORMAN DURNAN, Army
JAMES ELDER, Army
JAMES STANLEY EWING, Army

MAURICE ESIER FERGUSON, RAF
CHARLES HENRY FLEMING, RAF

MARK BARNES GARRET, Army
FREDERICK GIBSON, Army
MAY GIBSON, Army
RONALD WARWICK GIBSON, Army
REGINALD GIBSON, Army, awarded MC

OSCAR STANLEY JACK GILES, Army
HELEN GILLESPIE, Navy
GEORGE GIRVAN, RAF

DESMOND O'REILLY FITZGERALD HALDANE, Army
GERALD REILLY HALDANE, Army
EVELYN FRANCIS HALL, Army
ISOBEL CALVERT HALL, Army
IVAN HALL, Navy
HAROLD HARPER, Army
SAMUEL JOHN HARRISON, RAF, awarded DFC
THOMAS EVANS CARLISLE HENDERSON, Army
JOHN CECIL HEWITT, Army
DOUGLAS ERIC HODGES, Army
VERA HOLT, Navy
MARIE HOLT, Navy
JOHN CYRIL HOLT, Army

WILLIAM JAMES IRVINE, Navy
WILLIAM JOHNSTONE IRVINE, Navy
CHARLES KING IRWIN, Army
EDWARD ALBERT JACKSON, Army
SUSAN ALBERTA JACKSON, Navy
ALAN N. JONES, RAF
ERNEST STANLEY JONES, Navy
W BRIAN S JONES, Army

C.H. KEMP, Army
GEORGE REGINALD KENNEDY, RAF
CHARLES GRIERSON KINAHAN, Army, prisoner-of-war.
ROBERT GEORGE CALDWELL KINAHAN, Army
CLARISSA KING, Army
EDWARD TOURNEY KING, Army

AGNES MARGARET LARMOUR, Army
EDWARD NOEL LARMOUR, Army
JAMES LEWIS, RAF
JOAN LOUW, RAF
MILLICENT LUKE, Navy
SARAH JOSEPHINE LUKE, Navy

WILLIAM MAGUIRE, Army
JOHN FREDERICK ROBB MARTIN, RAF
HUBERT OSBORNE MATEER, Army, prisoner-of-war, wounded.
MARY ELIZABETH MAYNE, Navy
PHYLLIS MAYNE, Navy
ROBERT ELLIS MCCLURE, Army, awarded MBE
ROBERT MCGARVEY, RAF, wounded
GEORGE EDWARD MCGARVEY, Army
HENRY DERMOTT MCKEE, Army
EDWARD HUGH MCMANUS, Army
EDMUND WILFRED MCMANUS, Army
LESLIE C. MCWILLIAM, Army
FRANCIS ALLINGHAM MOORE, Army
GEORGE MOORE, Army
JOAN MARY MORGAN, RAF
WILLIAM ALEXANDER MORISON, RAF
LINDSAY HUTCHINSON MORRISON, Army
DESMOND GEORGE MORRISON, Army

ERNEST HUTCHINSON MORRISON, RAF
GEORGINA MARY MUIR, RAF

ANNIE BURNS NOBLE, Army
DEREK HARRIS NOBLETT, Navy
NORMAN WILLIAMS NOBLETT, Army
DIANA NORRIS, RAF

ARTHUR OVER, Army

GEORGE MERVYN PATTERSON, Army
CHARLES HENRY PEARSON, Army
IVAN STANLEY POLLLIN, RAF
ARTHUR PATRICK POLLITT, Army

DAVID ARTHUR FRANCIS QUECKETT, Army
CHARLES EDWIN QUECKETT, Army

JOAN RAE, RAF
CECIL BERTIE REID, RAF
FREDERICK GEORGE REID, Army
ARTHUR JOHN REILLY, Army
ALAN REYNOLDS, RAF
ANDREW FREDERICK REYNOLDS, RAF
JAMES FORREST REYNOLDS, Army
SAMUES JOHN ROBNSON, RAF
WILLIAM SALMOND ROBINSON, Army
HILDRED RODGERS, Navy
HUGH HAGEN RODGERS, Navy
JOHN MOLYNEUX RODGERS, Navy
ROBERT GERRARD RODGERS, Navy

ERIC RIBTON SANDYS, RAF
MAURICE ARTHUR SANDYS, RAF
MARGARET REBECCA SAVAGE, RAF
OLIVER BERTRAND SHEPHERD, Army
MAUREEN SKINNER, Navy
CATHARINE SMYTHE, Army
ROBERT H STEWART, Navy
JAMES HAMILTON SWAIN, Navy, awarded DSO and Bar, DSC

EVELINE AUDREY TAYLOR, RAF
JAMES TAYOLR, RAF, awarded AFC
RICHARD WILLIAM TILBURY, RAF
LESLIE MARCUS TOZER, Army
BRIAN M TWEEDIE, Navy
IRENE FRANCES TWEEDIE, RAF
ROSEMARY JOYCE TWEEDIE, Army
SAMUEL TWEEDIE, RAF

EDWARD LANCELOT WADE, Army
JOHN WALLACE, RAF
ALFRED HENRY WALLER, Army
DERRICK BOYLE WHITE, Navy, awarded MBE
RAYMOND HAMILTON WHITE, Navy
ETHNA VICTORIA WHYMARK, Army
JOSEPH WILSON, Army
WALTER WILSON, Army
JOHN WRIGHT, Army

MERCHANT NAVY:

WILLIAM CAIRNS
ROBERT HYDE CAIRNS
GEORGE REA CAMPBELL
EVAN ARTHUR HENRY CHANTLER
CYRIL JOHN DUKE
JOHN CLIFFORD KINGSTON
GEORGE MORROW
CYRIL ERNEST PRINGLE
FRANK REA
ALAN GEORGE RODGERS
LESLIE THEODORE IRWIN

USA ARMY:

AGNES S. GLOVER

ST KATHARINE's DISTRICT:

The roll of the names of parishioners in St Katharine's District were included in St Peter's Roll of Honour up to the end of the year 1942, after which St Katharine's Roll was compiled independently.

Those who joined Crown Forces from St Katharine's District were:

JAMES MCATAMENY, RAF
ROBERT AULD, Army
WILLIAM BARR, Army
CECIL NOEL BRENNAN, Navy
ROBERT COBAIN, Army
BERTIE FOSTER, RAF
BENJAMIN FURNEY, Navy
ROBERT GLENN, Army
AMY HARRIS, Army
HUGH HARRISON, Navy
GEORGE HOPKINS, Army
JAMES JACKSON, RAF
ALBERT KINNON, Army
JOHN LEE, RAF
WILSON LEE, Army
ERNEST MARSHALL, Army
FRANCIS MAYNE, Army
ARCHIBALD MCMURTRY, Navy
WILLIAM PATEMAN, RAF
EDWARD PEARCE, Army
ALEXANDER POLLOCK, Army
HENRY RUSSELL, Army
ROBERT RUSSELL, Army
THOMAS SANDS, Army
WILLIAM JOHNSTON SAVAGE, RAF
WILLLIAM SMYTH, RAF
RICHARD STERRITT, RAF
JOHN STEWART, Navy
JAMES THOMPSON, RAF

Appendix II
Church of Ireland: Chronological List of Parishes created in Belfast, 1776–1914

1776 – St Anne's, Lower Donegall Street; from 1904, 'The Cathedral Church of St Anne'

1816 – St George's, High Street, or 'The Perpetual Curacy of Upper Falls, Belfast'

1827–28 Christ Church, Ballymacarrett

1833 – Christchurch, College Square North (deconsecrated 1993; now part of 'Inst')

1839 – Magdalene (old church)

1840 – Whitehouse (St John's)

1843 – Holy and Undivided Trinity, Trinity Street (destroyed 1941, and replaced by New Holy Trinity, Joanmount, in 1956)

1851 – St Paul's, York Street

1853 – St John's, Laganbank Road (demolished 1943)

1856 – St Mark's, Ballysillan (enlarged 1866, 1886)

1861 – St John the Baptist, Suffolk, Upper Falls (detached from St George's, 1868)

1863 – St Luke's, Northumberland Street

1868 – Mariners (closed 1922; later demolished)

1868 – St Mary's, Crumlin Road

1869 – St Stephen's, Millfield

1870 – St Andrew's, Hope Street (closed in 1970; demolished)

1870 – St Thomas's, Eglantine Avenue

1871 – St James's, Antrim Road (union with St Peter's, 2007; closed 2008)

1872 – St Philip's, Grosvenor Road (Drew Memorial – enlarged 1875, 1884)

1872 – St Matthew's, Woodvale Road

1872 – Willowfield

1873 – St Jude's (enlarged 1899)

1878 – St Mark's, Dundela

1892 – St Matthias's, Glen Road (joined with St Luke's, 1904)

1893 – St Patrick's, Ballymacarrett

1893 – St Barnabas's, Duncairn Gardens (former church destroyed, 1941)

1894 – St John the Evangelist, Malone (replacing earlier church)

1895 – St Aidan's, Blyth Street

1896 – St Columba's

1895 – All Saints'

1899 – St Michael's, Craven Street

1900 – St Peter's, Antrim Road

1900 – St Mary Magdalene, Donegall Pass (replacing earlier church built in 1839)

1901 – St Nicholas's, Lisburn Road

1903 – St Silas's, Cliftonville Road (former church destroyed, 1941)

1912 – St Donard's

1912 – Trinity College Mission, Riga Street

Select Bibliography

MANUSCRIPT SOURCES

ST PETER'S PARISH CHURCH, ANTRIM ROAD, BELFAST
The Church holds a wide range of archives, including the minutes of the Select Vestry, as well as Parish Notes and Annual Reports, etc.

THE REPRESENTATIVE CHURCH BODY LIBRARY, BRAEMAR PARK, DUBLIN
The Representative Church Body Library holds the Preachers Books, Account Books, Registers of Baptisms, Marriages and Confirmations, along with various miscellaneous papers, relating to St Peter's Parish Church. This book is based almost exclusively on the records deposited here, and those still held by St Peter's Church.

CENTRAL LIBRARY, BELFAST
Joseph Francis Bigger Papers.

PUBLIC RECORD OFFICE OF NORTHERN IRELAND, BALMORAL AVENUE, BELFAST
District Inspectors Reports, Roll Books, etc, relating to Skegoniell National School.

BOOKS AND PERIODICALS
Acheson, A.R., *A History of the Church of Ireland, 1691–1996* (Dublin, 1997).
Akinson, D.H., *Education and Enmity: the Control of Schooling in Northern Ireland, 1920–1950* (Newton Abbot, 1973); *The Irish Educational Experiment: the National System of Education in the Nineteenth Century* (London, 1970).
Beckett, J.C., et al, *Belfast; the Making of the City* (Belfast, 1983).
Belfast and Northern Ireland Directory (Belfast, 1890–2007).
Breene, Rev Richard, Simmons, *The Golden Jubilee Book of St Peter's Church, Belfast, 1900–1950* (Belfast, 1950).
Brett, C.E.B., *Housing a Divided Community* (Dublin, 1986).
Larmour, Paul, *Belfast: an Illustrated Architectural Guide* (Belfast, 1987).
Linder, Seth, *The Famous Faces of North Belfast* (Belfast, 2008).
Literary Belfast: A Guide to Belfast's Literary Landscape (Belfast, 2008).
McCourt, W.A., et al, *Forty Years On, Diocese of Down and Dromore, Diocese of Connor, 1945–1985* (Belfast, 1985).
McDowell, R.B., *The Church of Ireland, 1869–1969* (London, 1975).
McNiece, J.F., *The Church of Ireland in Belfast, 1778–1931* (Belfast, 1931).
Maguire, W.A., *The Donegalls: Living like a Lord, the Second Marquis of Donegall* (Belfast, 1984 and 2002).
Phoenix, Eamon., et al, *Feis na nGleann: A Century of Gaelic Culture in the Antrim Glens* (Belfast, 2005).
Rankin, J. Fred. (ed.), *Clergy of Connor from Patrician Times to the Present Day: based on the unpublished Succession Lists compiled by Canon J.B. Leslie* (Belfast, 1993).
Scott, V.E., *Churches of the Diocese of Connor: an Illustrated History* (undated).
Young, R.M., *Belfast and the Province of Ulster in the Twentieth Century*; edited by W.T. Pike (Brighton, 1909).

THESES (Queen's University, Belfast)

Cleary, P.G., 'Spatial Expansion and Urban Ecological Change in Belfast, 1861–1917, with Special Reference to the Role of Transportation' (PhD, 1980)

McConnell, S., 'Housing, Territory and Development Dilemmas; the Case of North Belfast' (MSc, 2005)

Shiels, D.M., 'Sectarianism in Housing in North Belfast' (MSc, 1990)

NEWSPAPERS AND PERIODICALS

Belfast News Letter
Belfast Telegraph
Connor Connections: the Magazine of the Diocese of Connor
Irish News
Northern Whig
North Belfast Historical Magazine, 1984, No. I

Also, newspaper cuttings, Central Library, Belfast

Index